Bella Coola

" ... a romantic history ... "

Bella Coola

" … a romantic history … "

Cliff Kopas

Heritage
House

National Library of Canada Cataloguing in Publication Data

Kopas, Cliff, 1911-1978.
Bella Coola

    Includes index
    ISBN 1-8943854-44-X

    1. Bella Coola Indians. 2. Indians of North America—British Columbia.
3. Bella Coola (B.C.)—History. I. Title.

FC3849.B4K6 2002   971.1'32   C2002-910173-5
F1089.2.B4K6 2002

First paperback edition, 1980; second printing, 1985; third printing, 1991; Heritage House edition, 2002.

Heritage House acknowledges the financial support for our publishing program from the Government of Canada through the Book Publishing Industry Development Program (BPIDP), Canada Council for the Arts, and the British Columbia Arts Council.

Cover design Darlene Nickull
Cover photographs by Michael Wigle
All uncredited photos are from the Kopas Collection

HERITAGE HOUSE PUBLISHING COMPANY LTD.
Unit #108 - 17665 66 A Ave., Surrey, B.C. V3S 2A7

Printed in Canada

Contents

Foreword

For my father, who wrote this book, the story of Bella Coola was one of drama, romance, adventure and intrigue. When he sat down to write, the characters and the clash of cultures became his world, all the more because he could step outside and see the mountains that had presided over the events, hear the river on which many of them had taken place, and breathe the air in which the echoes are still heard today. His tale is that of the early adventurers and the encounters between the Nuxalk people and the "whites."

When writing in the 1960s (the book was first published in 1971), it was appropriate that Cliff Kopas should end his narrative with the building of the road over the mountains. That project was, for him, the last and most recent dramatic deed by the people of Bella Coola. In establishing a link with the rest of the continent, the road marked the completion of an historic movement. It also marked the beginning of new era, as he well understood, since it opened the isolated, self-contained community to outside influences although, for him, that would have to be another story.

Engaged in other projects, my father did not write more about Bella Coola and then in 1978 he passed away. His community is still recognizable and the themes of adventure and exploration are still there. But it has changed too. Horses are now kept for recreation rather than work and a car ferry rather than a cargo ship cruises along the inlets. Satellite dishes and the internet connect people with the world beyond these mountains. This foreword outlines some of these changes in order to bring the reader up to the present and provide some understanding of the character of the Bella Coola community today.

While the book ends with the events of road building, this road was not merely the end of one story or the start of the next. It was also a turning point both practically and symbolically between two ages. Though not alone in summoning the new era, it was as if, when the blades of the two bulldozers met on September 26, 1953, they rang in a new world. That narrow track up the Young Creek valley, over Heckman Pass, and past Saddle Horse Meadow catapulted Bella Coola from a farther edge of the North American frontier to the brink of a new era. While fragments of that great continental frontier remain in the North, they, like Bella Coola, have been absorbed into the continental mainstream at an accelerating pace. Prior to the completion of the road, migrants came to

Bella Coola, like generations of pioneers before them, intent on building a new society. They were part of a process of settlement and an ideal of progress that had begun in North America 450 years earlier. Yet, in less than two decades, by the late 1960s, the valley had become a retreat for some people consciously wanting to get away from progress. Rather than building a new society they were bent on preserving features of the old.

Throughout this process of transformation and into the present day, however, Bella Coola has remained a unique and special place. Its uniqueness lies in its natural magnificence, its central place in history, and in the singular combination of groups who make up its population.

In the beginning, the Bella Coola Valley and many adjacent valleys and bays were populated by the Nuxalk people who lived only in this central coast area. While their language is related to the broader Salishan group, they are surrounded by the Wakashan-speaking Heilstuk and Owikeno to the west and Athabaskan-speaking Ulkatcho to the east. Other Salishan speakers are a long distance away to the east and south. In many other respects, too, the culture of the Nuxalk is distinct. For example, whereas red and black are common colours on masks and other works of art, for the Nuxalk, the use of sky-blue is distinctive.

But the Nuxalk culture was also deeply embedded in the natural world of cedar wood, salmon, and other sea creatures. Until the middle of the nineteenth century Nuxalk families lived not only throughout the length of the Bella Coola valley but also in the Dean and Kimsquit River Valleys to the north, Kwatna to the west, and Talio (now South Bentinck) to the south. While no one is sure how many people lived in these communities the total population was almost certainly well over 5,000. Then in the 1860s tragedy struck here as it did elsewhere along the British Columbia coast. Small pox and other diseases of European origin, for which Aboriginal people had no natural resistance, killed upwards of 90% of the populations. Within a very short time whole families were destroyed and the devastated communities had a difficult time providing for themselves.

Disease was not the only disaster. This destruction was made worse by government policy which restricted Nuxalk people, as with First Nations elsewhere in British Columbia, to small parcels of land and limited their access to the resources that had sustained them for eons. As a result of these catastrophes, most of the survivors of disease and disruption moved to the Bella Coola valley which soon became the only remaining community of the Nuxalk people.

The Aboriginal way of life never had a chance to recover when government policy attempted to further obliterate it and to assimilate the indigenous people into Canadian society. For example, in 1884 the Canadian government banned the practice of the potlatch, one of the centrepieces of coastal First Nations' culture. Further legislation in 1927 prevented any legal or political campaign on the part of Nuxalk or other Aboriginal Nations to reach a treaty about land, hunting rights or other concerns of Aboriginal life. These policies did not begin to change until after 1951 when the government rescinded its earlier restrictions. Then, in 1960 the voting franchise was extended to include First Nations people so that they could participate in Canadian democratic society. More changes were to come. One of the most significant was the 1973 Supreme Court of Canada decision on the Nisga'a land claim in which Aboriginal title received a degree of recognition that had been long denied. This and related political activities of British Columbia First Nations people, together with others across the country, meant that as the twentieth century drew to a close, the Nuxalk people have been able to throw off some of the constraints of a colonial system whose origins go back five hundred years.

In recent decades in Bella Coola, the Nuxalk Nation has taken control of the governing of their own community from government bureaucrats. They have established their own school where they teach their children and, among other things, teach the Nuxalk language to younger generations. Many of the traditional arts are being practised once again and the potlatch has been restored to its central place within the community.

Although there have been important initiatives to restore traditional practices and the basis for self-government, many issues remain outstanding. After years of rejection, the British Columbia government finally agreed in 1992 to recognize Aboriginal claims and to negotiate modern treaties. Even so, the process is slow and few treaties have so far been negotiated in British Columbia. At the time of writing, only the Nisga'a Treaty has been agreed upon by all sides and formally ratified. Nuxalk claims are, therefore, part of a very large and complex process.

Economic development and a relative degree of economic autonomy remain concerns for the Nuxalk, as they do for other First Nations. Since 1951, however, there has been, in sporadic increments, a dramatic shift away from the old paternal, colonializing measures of the past toward a new relationship where the Nuxalk have more control over their own lives and a redefined relationship with the broader community in Bella Coola and beyond.

Another component of the Bella Coola community are the descendants of the Norwegian settlers of the 1890s. Those settlers, like scores of other national groups in what is a time-honoured settlement tradition throughout North and South America, sought to establish their own religious community, in this case a Lutheran, Christian one. Most came from Minnesota in 1894 and 1895 but others came directly from Norway through to the 1920s and 1930s. Their mark and their memory are well represented in Bella Coola among the descendants of those early settlers but also in place names of the area such as Hagensborg, Mount Saugstad, Odegaard Falls, Nordschow Creek, and others. Some buildings such as the museum in the town of Bella Coola, the heritage house in Hagensborg and some private homes remain as fine examples of the wood working craftsmanship of the Norwegian builders. No longer evident are their wooden boats, but even into the 1960s the tradition of boat building that goes back to Nordic antiquity was still being passed from father to son. The Augsburg Lutheran Church, which ministered to the Norwegian congregation, joined locally with the United Church of Canada in 1949 and its fine building, first constructed in 1904, in Hagensborg now holds services for the United Church.

After World War II, the original settlers were decreasing while the assimilating influences of the English language, schools, and employment meant that by the last quarter of the century the Norwegian language was spoken only by a few individuals. At the turn of the millennium, Norwegian is effectively no longer heard in public. As with national communities across the continent, the Bella Coola Norwegians have become part of the Canadian mosaic. Traditions are still honoured and groups do sustain connections with the "old country" as demonstrated by an active chapter of the Sons of Norway. Despite this continuing presence, the travelling visitor must look carefully to find evidence of the Norwegian heritage in the valley.

The construction of the road did not directly cause these changes, of course, but it helped to bring in some of the influences of change. Until 1953, two venerable forms of transportation connected Bella Coola to the outside world. Ships carried freight and passengers to and from Vancouver, sporadically at first, but weekly as of the 1950s. The other mode of transport was the horse. Until the road was built – and even assisting in its construction – horses played a vital role in the transport system between Bella Coola and Anahim Lake and the Chilcotin Country. The automobile quickly replaced them and, as the road became established, overland transport began to compete with the cargo ship. In 1969 Hodgson Freightways, of Williams Lake, demonstrated that they could maintain regular freight service into Bella Coola and by 1976 all freight was coming overland.

Air transport also became more feasible in the late 1960s and early 1970s. In the years following World War II, air travel into Bella Coola was difficult and often irregular. Mallards and other amphibious aircraft served the coast and Bella Coola was part of their route. Bad weather and rough water often affected schedules or, at the last minute, prevented landings so passengers needed a flexible schedule to travel by air to and from Bella Coola. Later, in the same spirit of community endeavour that initiated the building of the road, the local Board of Trade brought together local volunteers and government money to build their own gravel-surfaced airstrip. For the first time, rough water did not prevent a small plane from landing in Bella Coola. In stages, this air strip was improved and, later, paved so that now it allows for frequent and regular air travel between Bella Coola and Vancouver or other destinations. At 4,200 feet in length, this air strip now accommodates small jets the most significant of which is the air ambulance which can quickly transfer patients from the Bella Coola Hospital to the specialized facilities in Vancouver.

Another innovation was the installation of a central diesel generating station in the valley by the B.C. Power Commission (later to become B.C. Hydro) in 1955. Prior to that year, the hospital, the schools, and fewer than half a dozen private homes had their own "lighting plant," small gasoline-powered generators that could power a few light bulbs but little else. Later, in the 1970s, a small hydro-electric facility was built on Clayton Falls Creek in order to reduce operating costs, but the diesel plant remains an essential part of the valley's electrical system and the modern life on which it depends.

Modernizing the telephone system soon followed in 1966 when the locally owned Bella Coola Light, Power and Telephone Company sold its system to the B.C. Telephone Co. (now Telus). The community graduated from crank-handle phones, party lines, and a central switch board to dial telephone and automated switching which had been introduced in New York and London more than a half century earlier. Today, modern telecommunications connect Bella Coola to the rest of the world by means of the internet, fax and other systems. It was also about this time that television was brought to the valley, again through local initiative. In the days before satellite service, the high mountains prevented the broadcast signal from reaching the valley floor. Therefore, it was necessary to relay the signal across several mountain tops before it could be directed down into the valley. Broadcasters and government agencies firmly believed it was not technically feasible to do this and so the local community formed the Valley TV Society to accomplish what the experts could not do. The relay and rebroadcasting project originally took place without the approval of the CRTC, the federal government's telecommunications regulator, and, for a time, the independent attitudes from the now-diminishing frontier combined with the modern world of electronic communication in an unusual alliance.

Throughout a half century of political, social and, technological change, forestry and fishing have remained the mainstays of the Bella Coola economy just as they had for the Nuxalk people for eons before European settlement. However, these traditional activities have not been static. Technological change has meant that both forests and fisheries can be harvested at much greater rates than in earlier times. These resources have been heavily utilized and new techniques have had to be developed for their management. Mostly, local and even provincial control of them has slipped away so that today decisions are made on other continents and in foreign business and political centres. These remote decisions quickly and dramatically affect both resource use and the lives of individuals and the community in the Bella Coola valley. It is not just rubber-tired vehicles in place of horses, modernized telephones and regular air service that have come to Bella Coola since 1953, but the rapidly integrating world has ever more closely incorporated this one-time frontier into its great orbit.

It was indeed appropriate for Cliff Kopas to end his book with the building of "the road." While the Bella Coola community has continued to take many independent initiatives, the road itself represents the end of the pioneering phase of Bella Coola's past and the beginning of the establishment of modernity.

Paul Kopas, *May, 2002*

Original Foreword

In presenting this book *Bella Coola* I make no claim to being an historian. Over a period of forty years I have collected a veritable treasure house of stories, reminiscences, diaries, clippings, letters, photographs – all dealing with the events that make up the Bella Coola story. To develop from the whole a continuous account, a fusion of fact and fancy, has been sheer pleasure. I love my adopted home and I would like others to know of its colorful past.

As I look back in memory, I recall the variety of my sources of this material. I can see myself in a Norwegian gillnetter's boat, struggling with a salmon net as I chat with its owner; or waiting for dawn in an old Indian smokehouse to see Clayton Mack, the famous hunting guide, chase grizzly bears "for the fun of it"; or seated on a pile of goat skins in a trapper's cabin in the wild hinterland of this coastal community. I am indebted to so many for the details that went to make up the fabric of my book – to Frank, Milo and Bob Ratcliff, intrepid trappers all; to Iver Fougner, scribe and teacher with the Norwegians of '94; to B.F. Jacobsen; to George Draney, Clayton Mack and Andy Schooner.

These all, by their personal recollections or by lending me precious records, made it possible for me to gather up the threads of a romantic history of a beautiful corner of British Columbia.

It was my privilege to follow Alexander Mackenzie's route up the Westroad River a hundred and fifty years after him, and to arrive in Bella Coola at a time when many of the Norwegian pioneers of 1894 were still alive and hale and hearty. It has been my further privilege to live in this bowl of unsurpassed natural beauty and to know the friendship of people of many racial origins. For me every individual became a living story, an actor stepping out of a legend rooted in the fiords of Scandinavia, or in the misty lands beyond the Bering Straits, or in the land of the Scots whence came many of the early traders and adventurers.

I can now boast that in my veins runs the blood of all these people, because in a time of recent illness, my blood donors were a young Indian mother and a young man whose father's family had come from Scotland and whose maternal grandfather arrived with the Norwegians in 1894.

My purpose has been to perpetuate the thrilling story of Bella Coola and its peoples. If you read it with interest and feel you know us better, my book will have served its function.

Cliff Kopas, *Bella Coola, B.C. , February, 1970*

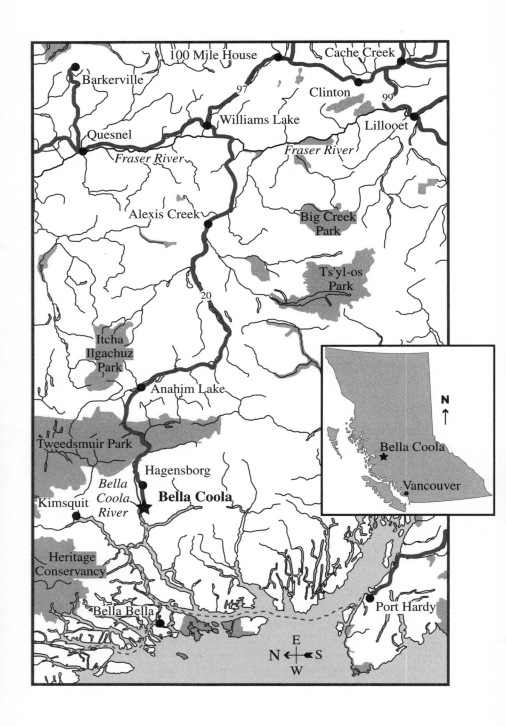

# **The Dim Past**

Up-coast, three hundred and fifty miles from the hurly-burly of Vancouver and the southwest coast, the Bella Coola Valley rises from the ocean floor eighty miles inside the island fringe at the eastern extremity of Burke Channel. Flanked on the north by high mountains and on the south by an up-ended tangle of still higher ones, the valley floor lifts gradually to create a broad green pass that extends almost entirely through the Coast Range. On the north the mountains are ice-scraped and worn, while those on the south are for the most part tall pinnacles indicating that they were lifted into existence after the ice ages, or that the ice-caps dipped only into the Bella Coola Valley before retreating.

After hours of flying over needle-sharp peaks and uninviting glaciers, the green valley far below stretches like an Eden. Or, if you have been struggling through the frosts and snows of the surrounding high country, the orchards in bloom, the heavily-treed forests, and the temperate ocean breezes come as a welcome surprise. The encircling ring of high peaks give the valley the protection of the bowl-like walls of a nest while, from aloft, either from aircraft or crag, little imagination is required to see as eggs or fledglings the homes and people on the valley floor.

This may not be too far-fetched for in Indian mythology the Thunderbird — that huge super-eagle whose beating wings caused thunder and whose snapping eyes created lightning, who fought with killer whales and featured in dozens of dramatic recitations — chose the Bella Coola mountains as his home, and spread a protective wing over the people of the valley.

It is of these people, the brood of the Thunderbird, that this account is written. Some of the story is history, some of it is legend,

1

some is a collection of tidbits exchanged around a campfire or in a fishboat as it tosses at the end of a net, while some of it is a personal journey back through the ways of the recent past. Since time has touched the area only lightly, these recollections are very much alive.

The stories deal with many subjects. Bella Coola has always been an objective of adventurous trips. Alexander Mackenzie, in the first overland trip in Canada to the sea, finished his epic journey there. At one time it was in competition with Burrard Inlet to be the terminus for the Canadian Pacific Railway. Over a two-year period, at another time, four railway companies announced plans to build a railway to either Bella Coola or its near neighbor, Dean Channel. It once was a gateway for entrants to the Cariboo goldfields and a portal through which the largest army to date in British Columbia marched to quell an Indian uprising.

None of the stories, however, go as far back as the coming of the Bella Coola Indians. How and when they came, and whom they replaced, is only conjecture, but there is one tidy explanation and this will be related. The Bella Coola Indians are of the Salish nation, which occupies also the Okanagan Valley and the Fraser delta area. How they came to be isolated some three hundred and fifty miles away from their kin, and surrounded on all sides by tribes who were often their enemies and with whom, either linguistically or biologically, there was remarkably little fusion, is cause only for further conjecture.

Anthropologists tell us the North American Indians are of Asiatic origin and that they ventured, tribe after tribe, across the Bering Straits whenever population pressures, political disturbances or man's restless nature impelled migration. With the Straits frozen for many months in the year and the Diomedes Islands visible from both continents, this route showed as an escape hatch through which moved southward wave after overlapping wave to become invaders in this new land. Like Moses of old they were looking for a Promised Land, and their legends told of the desirability of pushing ever southward, which some of them did, becoming the Navajos, the Sioux or the Apaches, and even the Aztecs and Incas of Mexico, Central and South America.

Undoubtedly the various tribes, coming at different times, originated at Asiatic points far removed from each other. It has been suggested that some of these people, far distant in ethnic origins, came from as far away as India — bringing their own gods, cultural distinctions and language. Some of the tribes reaching this continent perished and others were absorbed or destroyed by larger ones, but many found their places and prospered.

Some anthropologists theorize that part of at least two of these waves made their way to Bella Coola. The present Indians, they assert, have not long been here, as shown by lack of fusion with neighboring tribes, and by the presence of several areas of extensive rock carvings for which the Indians have no explanation. One anthropologist, Thor Heyerdahl, of Kon Tiki, Ra and Easter Island fame, has stated that he believes the present Indians of Bella Coola to have been here not more than five or six hundred years.

Heyerdahl's interest was kindled when, after spending a year studying the natives of the Marquesas Islands, he saw some photographs of Bella Coola rock carvings and was vastly intrigued with the likenesses between them and carvings in the south seas.

After spending many months in Bella Coola, Heyerdahl added a fresh theory to the controversy among anthropologists as to the origin of the peoples of the south seas islands. It was thought by some scientists that the oceanic people had island-hopped out from southeast Asia. Another group pointed to sufficient similarities in appearance and in methods of preparing food among certain south sea islanders and peoples of the Northwest coast to indicate that the Northwest coast people originated in the south seas. Heyerdahl agreed that the similarities were there and that the two peoples had a place of common origin, but stated that the south sea islanders came from the Northwest coast, rather than vice versa. Three hundred miles off the British Columbia coast oceanic currents flow toward the Hawaiian Islands, occasionally casting up drift logs on the beaches there. If forest flotsam, why not humans? It would be possible for humans to sail or drift southward, but never in the opposite direction.

And not only did the people of Polynesia come from the British Columbia coast, but very likely, he affirmed, right from the Bella Coola valley.

When the dust of inevitable contradiction had settled he had wrung from his opponents the admission that it was possible he was right.

His words inspired dramatic pictures.

The rock-carving race that once dwelt in the Bella Coola valley had grown fat and indolent in the plenty and security of their environment. Food was abundant, enemies scarce. None had ever come over the high mountains or through the deep forests; and along the channels to the west through which potential enemies could come were many of their own tribe, the Kwakiutl. The Bella Coola people felt secure.

History all over the world teaches that indolence plus security leads to trouble, and here was no exception, for suddenly enemies were upon the Bella Coola people. These enemies most certainly came overland, for had they attempted passage along the channels they would have been exterminated or absorbed by the intervening coastal tribes. Since their language ties them with a much larger group that got as far as the Okanagan and the lower Fraser valley, it seems plausible that the whole nation detoured inland from the coast and followed routes southward inside the coastal mountains. The portion of this tribe reaching Bella Coola was either an adventurous or wandering offshoot of the main body.

Of the battle or battles that occurred one can only guess, but the rock-carvers were driven from the valley. They might simply have gone to their neighbors or kinsmen to the west, but Heyerdahl has a more dramatic mission for them. He has the survivors escaping in their canoes, picking up recruits in lesser settlements and finally, with augmented numbers, settling near the clam beds of the outer islands. By accident, it is surmised, they got far enough off-shore to be caught in the drift of the strong southerly current and were carried to the islands of the South Pacific. Not all of them, of course, but some — enough to start a new race.

Heyerdahl said that the legends to which he listened in the far-off Marquesas group told of a long sea voyage from a land of tall cold mountains, to a landfall at Paradise, the Hawaiian Islands. Then there were stories of other journeys away from Paradise. And he went on to tell of words in the Polynesian tongue that sounded the same and meant the same as those along the British Columbia coast.

It is intriguing that the solution of the mystery of the south seas people can perhaps be found in the islands and channels of British Columbia, and that the glamor girls of the coconut beaches have their blood sisters on the edges of our salmon streams.

The new people of Bella Coola, with probably some of their conquered hosts as slaves, found their territory good. They revelled in the abundance of food, and out of the ever-present cedar forest they built their new civilization. These trees provided easy-splitting wood for their houses. The inner bark was shredded and woven into cloaks, hats, aprons, baskets, and mats. It was braided into fishing lines, or ropes with which to tie their canoes or tow logs. Their canoes also — the river canoes or the larger sea canoes — were fashioned with adze and fire from the trunks of the large cedar trees. Masks for their intricate winter ceremonials were carved from cedar, and crushed, fluffed-up cedar bark made the soft lining of their babies' cradles.

As well as their language the newcomers brought their religion and myths which in time became interwoven with the various geographic features of the district and served to rationalize nature's phenomena. And while they did not have a common language with their new neighbors, mythology and social customs were freely exchanged, even to the extent that a member of one village belonging to either or both of the secret societies — the Kusuit or the Sisook — was a member of the same society in other villages, even though the villages were enemies in other respects.

These new people adapted themselves rapidly. They became expert canoemen. They wove the ever-present stinging nettle into fine nets which elevated their fisheries to the point where an inter-tribal commerce was built on the products. They caught eulachon in great numbers, rendering oil from them, smoking vast quantities for food and using the fat bodies for candles. The eulachon run on the April full moon was the first return of summer abundance after the rigors of winter and attracted the Carrier neighbors from the eastern plateau country. These people brought with them for trade, furs and buckskin and returned with supplies of fish products. The paths they used were well-marked and called "grease trails". When white men eventually appeared, one of these trails extended two hundred or more miles eastward to the Fraser River. The first white man to use this trail called it a road and the river that it paralleled was called the Westroad River.

Besides a complex religion, complete with heavenly abode after death and one of discomfort below, these people had an elaborate social structure with an aristocracy, commoners and slaves, and strict social observances, the most noticeable of which was the potlatch.

There grew a pride in personal accomplishment and out of this a verbal literature and an art of delicate interpretation. They carved great houseposts and made paint by grinding colored rocks and mixing the resultant powder with fish oil.

The tribe increased. Villages appeared all along the river, which was the highway through the valley. Related villages appeared on the Kimsquit River, others on the Dean, at the head of South Bentinck Arm and down channel in Kwatna Bay.

In each of these villages there developed a slightly different language, a result natural to isolation. And different physical characteristics became evident. The Dean-Kimsquit villager was taller, the South Bentinck resident shorter than the Bella Coola. The Kwatna villages became a mixture of Bella Coola and Bella Bella people.

No political or military alliances developed. In fact, villages within the area frequently fought short-lived battles with each other. There was never any threat from outside the area to necessitate a military alliance. No dictatorial leader appeared and no large scale objective was ever set up.

It was into this setting that the white man made his exploratory incursions in the latter part of the eighteenth century.

2. The First White Men in Bella Coola

In 1793 a pincer movement of explorers closed in on Bella Coola from both east and west and white men came into this, the Thunderbird's Nest. There were two converging expeditions, and neither knew of the other's presence. It was not until two years later and half a world away that it was learned that travellers from the other side of the world with a common objective came within a few weeks of meeting each other on the Pacific shore off Bella Coola.

The search for the Northwest Passage was a partial motive for each expedition. For decades, growing into centuries, the maritime nations of western Europe had participated in the three-fold endeavor of trying to discover a route around the north of North America south of the Polar ice (or, as a very acceptable alternative, a water route across the continent), of finding new fur-bearing areas to exploit and, thirdly, of beating the others in exploration that would justify claims to large new areas.

Marine expeditions to the Pacific northwest coast were undertaken by the Spanish and the British to discover or rediscover the Straits of Anion, which were supposed to go entirely through the continent from the Atlantic to the Pacific. Several adventurers claimed to have sailed through this channel.

However, the English and Spanish were considerably behind the Russians who, under the leadership of Vitus Bering, a Danish naval officer in their command, after an incredible 5000-mile overland trip from St. Petersburg, built at Okhotsk the ship *Gabriel,* the first white-man-operated ship in the north Pacific Ocean. This was in 1728. After many months of exploration, Bering returned to St. Petersburg and after a second expedition had been sent to the Siberian Pacific Coast, in 1741, two ships *St. Peter* and *St. Paul,* sailed out into the Pacific waters, making landfall on the American Coast and doing some exploration among the Aleutian Islands.

While little in the way of charts resulted from the heroism of the men and crews of these vessels, they were forerunners of the sporadic efforts of the Russians to explore the north coast, which made them followers of our western North American in crossing the narrow straits from Asia. The Russian purpose was at first exploratory, but when the crews of the boats discovered a wealth of furs, particularly the pelts of the sea otter, exploration gave way to fur-trading. However, even though it had dropped to second place in importance, exploration of the far Northwest by the Russians did contribute much to the white man's knowledge of the area and, for good or bad, to the Indian's knowledge of the ways of the white man.

The Spanish, thoroughly established in California, responded to the threat of Russian advance southward by sending a tiny ship in 1774 which made a landfall off the western coast of the Queen Charlotte Islands, but bad weather forced the ship southward and she returned to California without actually effecting a landing. In the following years more ships from the Spanish colony sailed north and landings were made. At least one such shore party was ambushed and completely butchered and their ship narrowly escaped capture by the natives. So, while the Spaniards were gathering information about the coast, the Indians were also doing their own gathering.

Coming into the picture at this time, still in quest of the Northwest Passage through or around northern North America, were the English. England had ousted France in their mutual claim to Canada, and was aware that she might not be the winner in the inevitable struggle for the Pacific seaboard of America if she delayed until either Spain or Russia, or both, was firmly established in the area. She entered the competition in a vigorous way, by sending out from England two sufficiently large ships under the able and already famous British naval commander, Captain Cook. In this expedition were two other men who were to rise to fame for vastly different reasons — one was George Vancouver, who probably did more to promote knowledge of the Pacific coast than any other man. The other was William Bligh, whose story as commander of *H.M.S. Bounty* provided history — and Hollywood — with an outstanding naval character.

The expedition left England in 1776, and after stopping at New Zealand and several of the island groups of the South Pacific, became the first European visitors to the Hawaiian Islands. Captain Cook and his men reached Nootka Sound in March of 1778.

Friendly contact was made with the natives, and over a period of several years the expedition carried on a vigorous program of exploration and trade with the natives. The trade was not sponsored, as was the exploration, by the British Admiralty, but the sailors indulged in it, and the return to the civilized ports of Europe showed the British tars that they had been nibbling on a golden apple. When the report of the expedition was published in 1784 and indicated, along with the geographic data accumulated, the riches from furs to be reaped in the new land, a feeling tantamount to gold fever flourished in both Europe and America.

The almost immediate result was the appearance along the northwest coast of a score of American and British ships intent on garnering this fortune in furs. A Spanish expedition sent north from San Blas to establish a settlement and thus solidify claim to the territory came upon some of these ships. Some they captured and sent with prize crews to Mexico.

It is not the purpose of this story to trace the paths of the British and Spanish into near war or to tell of the amicable arrangement by which Spain agreed that Britain have absolute sovereignty over the territory we now know as the British Columbian - Alaskan Coast.

However, attention must be called to the perpetuation of the myth about the Strait of Anion. Captain Cook had not found it, and had expressed the opinion that it did not exist. Yet Captain Meares wrote that Captain Robert Gray had in his sloop, *Washington,* explored much of the Strait. Also an English map-maker had published a map of the Strait and asserted that the Spanish had sailed through it from the Pacific Coast to the Hudson's Bay in twenty-seven days.

The British representatives sent to finalize affairs with the Spanish at Nootka were Captain George Vancouver in command of the *Discovery,* and Lieutenant William Broughton in the *Chatham.* Captain Vancouver was asked to acquire accurate information on the coast between latitudes 30 degrees and 60 degrees north, and, in short, to find and explore the Northwest Passage.

His was a tremendous task. Southward from Cape Flattery the coast is almost an unbroken line with the exception of the mouth of the Columbia River. North of Cape Flattery is the area generally referred to as the Northwest Coast — a long series of indentations.

Moreover, each indentation is a multiple one, breaking into lesser channels and compounded with islands. Hidden behind any one of these islands or in any of the channels could have been the mouth of the Strait of Anion. Explorers had already passed the mouth of the Columbia River many times without seeing it, and Captain Cook had failed to note the entrance to the Strait of Juan de Fuca. It could easily have been that the Vancouver expedition was within gull's cry of the opening of a continent-splitting strait and was not aware of it.

There was also a language difficulty. Not only had the white man not learned the native language nor the native the language of the Englishman, but the northwest coast was broken up into at least five linguistic groups, each with its individual language.

Add to this the incidents which showed that the native was prone to sudden acts of unfriendly violence against Europeans, and it will be seen that any explorer of the Pacific northwest must have been possessed of the qualities of resourcefulness, thoroughness and courage.

There could have been no better choice for a leader than Captain Vancouver. He had sailed with Captain Cook and possessed great personal knowledge of the natives and the geography of the Pacific. His method of exploration was also very simple and very effectual, even though strenuous. Starting at the Strait of Juan de Fuca, the mother ships anchored in strategic places and the boats, each with a crew under an officer, were sent to search the bays and channels. Frequently these boat trips were of many days' duration. Occasionally the crews rowed day and night, and on more than one occasion, after a brush with the Indians, rowed for their lives.

Vancouver started his examination of the coast at the Strait of Juan de Fuca, and among the first geographical features he named were Puget Sound, after his Lieutenant Puget; Burrard Inlet, after Sir Harry Burrard, a companion in the Navy; and Johnstone Strait after Lieutenant James Johnstone, who discovered it.

The summer of 1792 was spent in circumnavigation of Vancouver Island and in meeting with the Spaniards at Nootka. The *Discovery* went south to the Sandwich Islands (Hawaii) for wintering, whilst the *Chatham* made a trip to England with reports.

Both ships were back on the northwest coast in the spring of 1793. This time the *Chatham* was under the command of Lieutenant Johnstone, Lieutenant Broughton having remained in England on other duties.

Northward the two ships worked their way, contending with fog and heavy tides, probing into deep bays and unravelling the labyrinth of channels. Cape Caution was named because the *Discovery* was nearly lost on a reef in the area.

And then, farther northward, Burke Channel was named after an eminent British statesman. Burke Channel, with its elongated North Bentinck Arm, is the longest inland-reaching channel of the whole complex coast. Through the narrows just east of its junction with Fitzhugh Sound (already visited by Captain Hanna in 1786) the two ships floated their way on a flood tide to anchor in Restoration Bay. From here Lieutenant Johnstone set out with a crew in one of the boats and explored Burke Channel, North and South Bentinck Arms, Labouchère Channel and the head of Dean Channel. On June 3 he visited the Indian village at Bella Coola.

It was the middle of June when exploration was complete in this area and the two ships lifted anchor and proceeded northward.

Their commanders and crews could not possibly have known that an extraordinary overland expedition was proceeding westward to the head of North Bentinck Arm to discover the first land route from Canada to the Pacific; nor could they have known that some of the Indians with whom they dealt would use them as an excuse to bully this small expedition and threaten it with extinction. Nor could they have known that this small troupe of erstwhile overlanders carried with them proof positive that there was no Strait of Anion, and that the Northwest Passage did not exist for ships of the sea.

The leader of the overland expedition was Alexander Mackenzie. On July 19th he arrived at the mouth of the Bella Coola River where it discharges into North Bentinck Arm, his canoe floating on the waters of the Pacific on July 20th to complete the first overland journey from eastern Canada to the Pacific.

Vancouver and his men continued their duties northward, completing the season of 1793 and continuing in 1794 until, at the end of August, not far from the present town of Petersburg, Alaska, Vancouver felt satisfied he had accomplished his mission. He had not found the Strait of Anion, but by the time his ships had returned to their home port in England the *Discovery* had made a voyage of more than sixty-five thousand miles. The work boats in which much of the exploration had been done had covered ten thousand miles, mostly by oars. And in the four-and-a-half year journey only six men had been lost. This was about one-third the mortality rate in England at that time. The northwest coast of America had been mapped and was no longer unknown. Many years would pass after Vancouver's untimely death in England before there was adequate appreciation of his ability as a commander of men and a thoroughgoing explorer and chart-maker. It is right that a famous city and a magnificent island should preserve his name in history.

East of the Rocky Mountains, the latter part of the eighteenth century saw the expanding tentacles of the fur trade caught in the powerful struggle of competitive fur companies. For many decades the Hudson's Bay Company had monopoly of the fur trade but in the latter half of the eighteenth century adventurous traders of the North West Company from Montreal began carrying their wares right into the homeland of the Indians. This forced the Hudson's Bay Company to abandon its practice of waiting for the Indians to bring their furs to the company's posts at Hudson's Bay. The rivalry thus brought into the trapping fields took the white man and his commercial efforts farther and farther westward and northward in feverish haste.

The extremely long supply lines thus created made more imperative the finding of the legendary Northwest Passage to reduce costs of transportation of trade goods. Even though the trip of Samuel Hearne in 1771 overland to the mouth of the Coppermine River should have illustrated that there was no Northwest Passage south of the Arctic ice, the white traders wanted it so desperately they closed their eyes to the obvious conclusion to be drawn from Hearne's reports.

Also to be considered was the large territory between the explored land and the Pacific coast which might be claimed for the fur traders who explored it and, of course, for their country. And on top of all this was the fur traders' spirit of adventure and ever present curiosity concerning the unknown.

Aggressive in all these interests, a young Scot, Alexander Mackenzie, came from Montreal to Athabasca in the fall of 1787, where he wintered with the veteran trader, Peter Pond. It was during this winter that Mackenzie formulated the plan to follow the river from their quarters at Fort Chipewyan to Great Slave Lake, thence down the outlet of that lake to the ocean. It was assumed the river must lead to the Pacific Ocean.

On June 3rd, 1789, with rubles in his pocket to help him trade with the Russians when he reached the Pacific coast, Mackenzie

12

started. For 1500 miles the exploring party traveled northward, led and finally driven by this tireless and infinitely determined young Scot. He had his men on the river at three o'clock in the morning each day and they paddled until nine or ten o'clock in the long daylight hours of the northerly latitudes. For 1500 miles the party travelled among strange and potentially hostile Indians who seldom could supply them with food, and never with accurate information of the dangers ahead. For 1500 miles starvation and other hazards threatened the voyagers, and all except their leader demanded return. But down the river they continued. For 1500 miles the mountains rose in an unbroken wall to the west, a stark, grey, formidable barrier, and the river continued ever northward. When he reached the delta of the river and encountered Arctic ice, and the tides indicated this could not be a lake, Mackenzie knew he had reached the sea. He knew also that it was not the Pacific Ocean, but his lack of competence in celestial navigation prevented him identifying his position closely.

He was bitterly disappointed. He had indeed carved himself a niche in the explorers' Hall of Fame. He had followed from its source to its effluence one of the greatest rivers of the continent. He had proved conclusively there was no easy, if any, water route from the plains to the Pacific Ocean. But he had not discovered the Northwest Passage.

Despite the fact that the journey outward and downriver had taken sixty days, the party was back at Fort Chipewyan in forty-two days, having completed a journey of over three thousand miles – a feat of endurance and enterprise that marked the young explorer as no accidental claimant to fame.

The unknown river he had followed to the Arctic Ocean became known as the Mackenzie. By coincidence, Mackenzie's disappointment at the end of his river-running would be repeated in the experience of Simon Fraser, who was to follow another great western river to its delta land at the sea.

Next summer, after wintering as a dutiful fur trader at Fort Chipewyan digesting the information he had gathered and formulating other plans for an attack on the unknown, Mackenzie went east with the fur brigade. En route he met a party sent out by the Hudson's Bay Company to explore and survey some of the northwest wilderness. The two parties camped together overnight and Mackenzie met the surveyor, Philip Turnor. In conversation with

Turnor, Mackenzie realized he had not been sufficiently trained in the art of location to make fully effective his efforts as an explorer. He determined then to get more education in that line, and the following winter spent six months in England studying navigation and astronomy.

Philip Turnor proceeded into the wilderness and spent some time at Fort Chipewyan. His astronomy-based calculations made there showed that the Pacific Ocean was much farther away than the fur traders had supposed.

While being acclaimed and feted in England, Mackenzie decided, since there was no down-river route from the plains to the Pacific Ocean, he would attempt a passage through the mountains. The Peace River, which the fur brigades used on the prairies and knew to within sight of the Rockies, cut right through this mountain chain, offering a water route. To the fur traders, with canoes and voyageurs, any water route was a highway, much to be preferred to the climb over the high ice-clad spine of the continent. On his return to Canada Mackenzie sent word ahead for a fort to be built well up on the Peace River. He planned on getting as close as possible to his antagonist in the fall of the year.

The fort was built near the site of the present town of Peace River.

Arriving literally on the eve of fall freeze-up, Mackenzie spent the winter trading furs, administering to the Indians who set up camp near the fort, and in querying the red men concerning the country to the westward. While most of this effort proved fruitless, two of them told him of the Fraser River, west of the mountains and of rapids in the Peace River.

"You make many portages," said the men, "and when you are through the mountains you will come to where the river forks. If you take the fork that flows in from the direction of the mid-morning sun you will come to a carrying place. At the other end of this carrying place you come to a stream that flows into big chief one that flows to the land of the mid-day sun many mountains away."

Mackenzie, hearing this of the Fraser River, was probably the first white man to learn of its existence. Had he been able to evaluate then the information given him, he might have pursued his subsequent journeying with greater confidence. Having listened to the many weird and untruthful tales told by these simple people of the forest, Mackenzie constantly calculated the relative merits and risks of believing or disbelieving. Total belief would have led to many futile if not deadly sorties, while disbelief might cause him to pass up a vital lead. Hence his winter was occupied with listening, checking, probing and cross-checking.

With the cessation of trapping in the spring, furs were packed for the long trip eastward. Every day the earlier-rising sun picked out scenes of determined activity in the trading post. Mackenzie had hand-picked his voyageurs, throughout the winter, and had been studying the men with him. When the ice had melted from the river and the geese were gone north the furs could be dispatched eastward. The trading post was handed over to the care of two men who were to supply the native hunters with ammunition during the summer.

The roll call of the canoe took place. There were Alexander Mackenzie and his cousin and lieutenant Alexander Mackay; six voyageurs, all small, muscular, very active and very volatile Canadians: Joseph Landry, Charles Ducette, François Beaulieux, Baptiste Bisson, François Courtois and Jacques Beauchamp. With them were two Indians as hunters and interpreters. Most noticeable was Mackenzie's dog – a canine of doubtful lineage but certain loyalties – who answered the roll call first and last.

The canoe, a 26-foot vessel, 26 inches deep with a four-foot nine-inch beam, was put into the water and loaded with three thousand pounds of provisions, arms, ammunition and trade goods. The bark craft was only paper thin, but in addition to the three thousand pounds it carried ten men and a tail-wagging dog.

There was a moment of pause. The Canadians prayed. The two remaining at the fort wept with their prayers. Then, at a word of command from Mackenzie, six paddles bit deep into the water, a song rose from the throats of the voyageurs and like an eager living thing the canoe leaped forward and shortly disappeared, still to the tune of the voyageurs' songs, around the first bend westward in the river.

The first few days were pleasant enough, through prairie country alive with buffalo – full days, too, for departure from camp first morning out was at 3.30; the second morning at four o'clock and again the third day it was at four in the morning. Travel continued each day until seven in the evening. Thus was the pattern of travel established.

They started on May 9th from their fort. On May 17th they came within sight of the Rockies, a high, snow-covered seemingly unbroken barrier ahead of them. They welcomed the sight for they had arrived at their first real geographic hurdle sooner than anticipated.

On May 19th they met with rapids, and although they saw a path that might have been the Indian portage, they ignored it and took up their fight against the river. They crossed from one side to the other, lining their canoe, and unloading and portaging.

Alexander Mackenzie wrote in his diary:

Mr. Mackay, and the Indians, who observed our manoeuvers from the top of a rock, were in continual alarm for our safety, with which their own, indeed, may be said to have been nearly connected; however, the dangers we encountered were very much augmented by the heavy loading of the canoe.

When we had effected our passage, the current on the west side was almost equally violent with that from whence we had just escaped, but the craggy bank being somewhat lower, we were enabled, with a line of sixty fathoms (three hundred sixty feet), to tow the canoe, till we came to the foot of the most rapid cascade we had hitherto seen. Here we unloaded, and carried everything over a rocky point of a hundred and twenty paces. When the canoe was reloaded, I, with those of my people who were not immediately employed, ascended the bank, which was there, and indeed as far as we could see it, composed of clay, stone, and a yellow gravel. My present situation was so elevated, that the men, who were coming up a strong point could not hear me, though I called to them with the utmost strength of my voice, to lighten the canoe of its lading. And here I could not but reflect, with infinite anxiety, on the hazard of my enterprise: one false step of those who were attached to the line, or the breaking of the line itself, would have at once consigned the canoe, and everything it contained, to instant destruction. It, however, ascended the rapid in perfect security, but new dangers immediately presented themselves, for stones, both small and great, were continually rolling from the bank, so as to render the situation of those who were dragging the canoe beneath it extremely perilous; besides, they were at every step in danger, from the steepness of the ground, of falling into the water: nor was my solicitude diminished by my being necessarily removed at times from the sight of them.

On May 20th, at four-fifteen in the morning, they continued their struggle against the roaring fury of the water.

We now, with infinite difficulty, passed along the foot of a rock, which, fortunately, was not of hard stone, so that we were enabled to cut steps in it for a distance of twenty feet; from which, at the hazard of my life, I leaped on a small rock below, where I received those who followed me on my shoulders. In this manner four of us passed and dragged up the canoe, in which attempt they broke her.

Providentially a tree had fallen from the cliff high above them so they had fuel for a fire to melt gum to patch their canoe.

Mackenzie's account cannot be surpassed for vividness:

When the canoe was repaired, we continued towing it along the rocks to the next point, when we embarked, as we could not at present make any further use of the line but got along the rocks of a round high island of stone, till we came to a small sandy bay. As we had already damaged the canoe, and had every reason to think that she soon would risk much greater injury, it became necessary for us to supply ourselves with bark, as our provision of that material article was almost exhausted; two men were accordingly sent to procure it, who soon returned with the necessary store.

Mr. Mackay, and the Indians who had been on shore, since we broke the canoe, were prevented from coming to us by the rugged and impassable state of the ground. We, therefore, again resumed our course with the assistance of poles, with which we pushed onwards till we came beneath a precipice, where we could not find any bottom; so that we were again obliged to have recourse to the line, the management of which was rendered not only difficult but dangerous, as the men employed in towing were under the necessity of passing on the outside of trees that grew on the edge of the precipice. We, however, surmounted this difficulty, as we had done many others, and the people who had been walking overland now joined us. They also had met with their obstacles in passing the mountain.

It now became necessary for us to make a traverse (to the north side), where the water was so rapid, that some of the people stripped themselves to their shirts that they might be better prepared for swimming, in case any accident happened to the canoe, which they seriously apprehended; but we succeeded in our attempt without any other inconvenience, except that of taking in water. We now came to a cascade, when it was thought necessary to take our part of the lading. At noon we stopped to take an altitude, opposite to a small river that flowed in from the left: while I was thus engaged, the men went on shore to fasten the canoe, but as the current was not very strong, they had been negligent in performing this office; it proved, however, sufficiently powerful to sheer her off, and if it had not happened that one of the men, from absolute fatigue had remained and held the end of the line, we should have been deprived of every means of prosecuting our voyage, as well as of present subsistence. But notwithstanding the state of my mind on such an alarming circumstance, and an intervening cloud that interrupted me, the altitude which I took has been since proved to be tolerably correct, and gave 56. North latitude. Our last course was South-South-West two miles and a quarter.

We now continued our toilsome and perilous progress with the line West by North, and as we proceeded the rapidity of the current increased, so that in the distance of two miles we were obliged to unload four times, and carry everything but the canoe: indeed, in many places, it was with the utmost difficulty that we could prevent her from being dashed to pieces against the rocks by the violence of the eddies. At five we had proceeded to where the river was one continued rapid. Here we again took everything out of the canoe, in order to tow her up with the line, though the rocks were so shelving as greatly to increase the toil and hazard of that operation. At length, however, the agitation of the water was so great, that a wave striking on the bow of the canoe broke the line, and filled us with inexpressible dismay, as it appeared impossible that the vessel could escape from being dashed to pieces, and those who were in her from perishing. Another wave, however, more propitious than the former, drove her out of the tumbling water, so that the men were enabled to bring her ashore, and though she had been carried over rocks by these swells which left them naked a moment after, the canoe had received no material injury. The men were, however, in such a state from their late alarm, that it would not only have been unavailing but imprudent to have proposed any further progress at present, particularly as the river above us, as far as we could see, was one white sheet of foaming water.

That the discouragements, difficulties, and dangers, which had hitherto attended the progress of the enterprize, should have excited a wish in several of those who were engaged in it to discontinue the pursuit, might be naturally expected; and indeed it began to be muttered on all sides that there was no alternative but to return.

Instead of paying any attention to these murmurs, I desired

those who had uttered them to exert themselves in gaining an ascent of the hill, and encamp there for the night. In the mean time I set off with one of the Indians, and though I continued my examination of the river almost as long as there was any light to assist me, I could see no end of the rapids and cascades: I was therefore, perfectly satisfied, that it would be impracticable to proceed any farther by water. We returned from this reconnoitring excursion very much fatigued, with our shoes worn out and wounded feet; when I found that, by felling trees on the declivity of the first hill, my people had contrived to ascend it.

This was the Peace River canyon, 300 feet deep, where the Peace River cuts through the wall of the Rockies — the only river to do so — in places only 50 yards wide.

The party fought its way about half-way up the canyon, then by scouting ahead determined that no boat could navigate such a water route. They camped for the night on a flat above the river, and on the morning of May 21st, because it was rainy and the men fatigued and disheartened, Mackenzie allowed them to rest until eight a.m. when he sent Mr. Mackay with three men and two Indians to look for a portage route.

The next day they cut a road up the mountain, and brought their baggage (3000 pounds less the food they had eaten) up from the waterside.

"This was likewise," said Mackenzie, "from the steep shelving of the rock a very perilous undertaking, as one false step of any of the people employed in it would have been instantly followed by falling headlong into the water."

After getting their baggage up, Mackenzie has stated:

"The whole of the party proceeded with no small degree of apprehension to fetch the canoe which in a short time was also brought to the encampment; and, as soon as we had recovered from our fatigue, we advanced with it up the mountain, having the line doubled and fastened successively as we went up onto the stumps; while a man at the end of it, hauled it around a tree, holding it on and shifting it as we proceeded; so that we may be said, with strict truth, to have warped the canoe up the mountain."

On May 23rd they advanced three miles, running into fallen timber and Devil's Club, which added to their already considerable difficulties. On May 24th they accomplished four miles. But they had passed most of the canyon and were down again on the water from where they could see the awesome force of Peace River as it fights for its freedom from this rocky straitjacket. "It was really awful to behold with what infinite force the water drives against the rocks on one side, and with what impetuous strength it is repelled to the other; it then falls back, as it were, into a more straight but rugged passage, over which it is tossed in high, foaming, half-formed billows, as far as the eye could follow it."

Even though once more able to take to their own element — the watery highway — they had their difficulties. One was the coldness of the temperature, possibly due to the snow and ice on the peaks above them. The river constricted into narrow channels at times. They portaged and now, at the end of May, they were contending against the spring floods in the mountains. Swollen streams pouring in from the side created, even for men of their ability, periods of extreme hazard.

They arrived at the junction of the Parsnip River flowing in from the southeast, and the Finlay River coming in from the northwest, which join to form the Peace River. Since Mackenzie's every instinct told him to head northwest, and the Finlay River coming from that direction was a smooth-flowing stream compared with the Parsnip River brawling in from the southeast, he was strongly tempted to take the former.

But the Indian back at the fort had told him that the river from the southeast was the one that led to the big river flowing to the land of the midday sun, and then to the ocean. All that he had told Mackenzie to date had proven to be correct.

"We will ascend that stream," Mackenzie commanded his steersman, pointing to the Parsnip River.

There was a grumble of protest from the men.

"The stream is too swift, M'sieu Mackenzie," one spoke up. "It looks unnavigable."

"You are the best of the voyageurs," Mackenzie replied, "and the stream does not flow that voyageurs cannot navigate."

The voyageur was almost right. A fierce struggle all afternoon against a powerful current took them only two or three miles up the stream. The next day was almost as bad. Mackay and the Indians walked to ease the load in the canoe. That night fear of an Indian attack caused them each to take station under a tree with loaded musket. Though no hostile Indians appeared, little rest was had. Followed two more days of struggle against freshet-proportion waters. Mackenzie and Mackay, with two Indians, went on a reconnoitering trip and when the canoe did not appear when it was expected the Indians assumed that it had been lost. However, a long hike downstream re-united the party. The Canadians stated they had broken the canoe and had to repair it. While Mackenzie believed they had been wasting their time when he wasn't with them. he was so delighted to be joined again safely with his men that he gave them a tot of rum.

The next morning they left at half-past four, and proceeded against the roaring current only by hauling themselves along by branches.

Several days later they came upon an Indian encampment. Both the Indians and the explorers were alarmed at first, but after some overtures contact was made. Mackenzie was not certain that they were on the right branch of the Peace River and was anxious to gain information from the natives. They camped with the Indians that night.

These people had not previously seen white men, but had some iron which they had procured by trade with other natives who had journeyed a great length to the sea. They did not know of any river that flowed to the ocean, they affirmed. Mackenzie did not believe they were revealing all they knew but decided to leave further questioning until next morning.

He wrote in his diary: "The solicitude that possessed my mind interrupted my repose; when the dawn appeared I had already quitted my bed, and was awaiting with impatience for another conference with the natives. The sun had, however, arisen before they left their leafy bowers, whither they had retired with their children, having most hospitably resigned their beds, and the partners of them to the solicitations of my young men."

The conference did bear fruit; Mackenzie found that the Indians knew of a large river that flowed to the south and promptly engaged one of them to go with his party as guide. The new guide appeared nonchalant about the dangers ahead but the remainder of his party expressed great concern for his safety.

Several days later, on June 12th, they found a beaten path leading between two lakes a distance of 817 paces apart — the carrying place over the height of land.

They were now on the watershed of the Pacific Ocean.

They were also in an entirely new world. Gone were the gently flowing streams of the prairies, the abundance of hoofed animals, the relatively submissive type of native. In their place were roaring cataracts as streams, fed from the fathoms-deep melting snows of great mountain ranges, tumbled down steep water courses in a race to return a winter's tribute to the sea in a few fierce weeks.

Their difficulties were thus three-fold. The Pacific watershed — British Columbia today — had no abundance of large hoofed game, and its native peoples were more numerous and more independent than those east of the Rockies.

But the explorers' greatest antagonist was the river they were using. Fallen trees criss-crossing the stream, gravel bars threatening their thin craft, roaring cataracts, were all obstacles the very first afternoon. They camped at five in order to cut a carrying place around a rapid. Scouting ahead, two men brought back fearful tales of rapids, rocks and windfalls. Their new guide stated he wished to return to his people. He had been alarmed in going down some of the rapids.

The next morning Mackenzie announced his intention to walk in order to lighten the canoe.

"Please come with us, M'sieu Mackenzie," one of the voyageurs cried. "If we perish, you should perish with us." The others shouted their agreement.

Mackenzie embarked with them. He records in his diary:

> We accordingly pushed off, and had proceeded but a very short way when the canoe struck, and notwithstanding all our exertions, the violence of the current was so great as to drive her sideways down the river, and break her by the first bar, when I instantly jumped into the water, and the men followed my example; but before we could set her straight, or stop her, we came to deeper water, so that we were obliged to re-embark with the utmost precipitation. One of the men who was not sufficiently active, was left to get on shore in the best manner in his power. We had hardly regained our situations when we drove against a rock which shattered the stern of the canoe in such a manner, that it held only by the gunwhales, so that the steersman could no longer keep his place. The violence of this stroke drove us to the opposite side of the river, which is but narrow, when the bow met with the same fate as the stern. At this moment the

foreman seized on some branches of a small tree in the hope of bringing up the canoe, but such was their elasticity that, in a manner not easily described, he was jerked on shore in an instant, and with a degree of violence that threatened his destruction. But we had no time to turn from our own situation to inquire what had befallen him; for, in a few moments, we came across a cascade which broke several large holes in the bottom of the canoe, and started all the bars, except one behind the scooping seat. If this accident, however, had not happened, the vessel must have been irretrievably overset. The wreck becoming flat on the water, we all jumped out, while the steersman, who had been compelled to abandon his place, and had not recovered from his fright, called out to his companions to save themselves. My peremptory commands superseded the effects of his fear, and they all held fast to the wreck; to which fortunate resolution we owed our safety, as we should otherwise have been dashed against the rocks by the force of the water, or driven over the cascades. In this condition we were forced several hundred yards, and every yard on the verge of destruction; but at length, we most fortunately arrived in shallow water and a small eddy, where we were enabled to make a stand, from the weight of the canoe resting on the stones, rather than from any exertions of our exhausted strength. For though our efforts were short, they were pushed to the utmost, as life or death depended on them. This alarming scene, with all its terrors and dangers, occupied only a few minutes; and in the present suspension of it, we called to the people on shore to come to our assistance, and they immediately obeyed the summons. The foreman, however, was the first with us; he had escaped unhurt from the extraordinary jerk with which he was thrown out of the boat, and just as we were beginning to take our effects out of the water, he appeared to give his assistance. The Indians, when they saw our deplorable situation, instead of making the least effort to help us, sat down and gave vent to their tears. I was on the outside of the canoe, where I remained till everything was got on shore, in a state of great pain from the extreme cold of the water; so that at length, it was with difficulty I could stand, from the benumbed state of my limbs.

After spreading their goods out to dry they had a good meal, and enough rum to raise their spirits before Mackenzie told them they were voyageurs whom nothing could daunt, that they were northerners who would writhe in disgrace if they returned home without accomplishing their objective.

A voyageur jumped to his feet with a shout. "Lead us, Chief," he said, "and we will follow."

There was a loud cry of assent, and the voyageurs all leaped to their feet and did a spontaneous dance and song around the fire.

The song did not last over the days. They had to patch their canoe. A scouting party sent ahead reported that the river was a series of falls and rapids, choked here and there with fallen timber. Their guide, whom they had taken from beyond the height of land, had become most dissatisfied and could give no coherent information on the country ahead. One night, in spite of Mackenzie's watchfulness, he escaped. They had to cut roads around waterfalls, and carry their now very heavy canoe through swamps and brush.

But three days later, on the evening of June 17th, they arrived on the bank of the great river — the Fraser. "At length we enjoyed," Mackenzie wrote, "after all our toil and anxiety, the inexpressible satisfaction of finding ourselves on the bank of a navigable river, on the west side of the first great range of mountains."

They sighted Indians on the river banks several days later, but the Indians fled.

A second group of Indians showed great alarm also, but stood their ground and demonstrated that they would attack if the white men landed. The explorers did land, but on the opposite side of the river, and Mackenzie walked out alone on a beach with trade articles. Eventually contact was made, and it was discovered that Mackenzie's Indian hunters and these Fraser River Indians could understand each other fully. Mackenzie distributed trinkets and treated the children with sugar.

These and subsequent peoples the explorers met within the next few days told Mackenzie that this great river flowed a long distance, through canyons where a canoe could not pass. The natives lower down the river were very antagonistic and would certainly kill the small party of white men. They said these down-river natives possessed iron, arms and utensils which had been obtained from other tribes who had traded with white people who came in huge canoes.

"Such an account of our situation, exaggerated as it might be in some points, and erroneous in others, was sufficiently alarming and awakened very painful reflections; nevertheless it did not operate on my mind so as to produce any change in my original determination." So Mackenzie writes in his diary.

If Mackenzie's original plan was to reach the western sea by water, it very soon had to be altered.

These people told Mackenzie that they traded with the people of the coast by travelling overland to the westward. It took six days of travel, they said, and the road was easy, without mountains, and had been travelled so often that the path was well marked. At the western end of this journey they met the people of a coastal valley with whom they bartered their dressed leathers and furs for metals, beads, etc. The Indians were telling Mackenzie of the route from the Fraser River up the Westroad River (or Blackwater River) to the Bella Coola River and the sea, the first commercial overland route in British Columbia.

Mackenzie traveled for three or four days with these and other Indians who joined them, descending the Fraser as far as the future site of Alexandria. Always he met with the story of the evil nature of down-river natives and of the impassable river. Finally the stories began to take effect. He realized that he did not have sufficient supplies for a prolonged journey; that even if he did not have trouble with the natives, the return up the river might take so long that he would be unable to return to Athabasca before the coming winter. He had little ball and shot for his muskets and his men were uneasy; they had been listening to the stories of the difficulties of going down this river.

Mackenzie made a major decision. He resolved to abandon the water route and take the west road to the sea. His men surprised him by agreeing quickly to his change of plans.

In order to pursue this course they had to return some miles up river. This was done to a pattern of Indian alarms and near skirmishes. Mackenzie's men were frequently in a state of near panic, necessitating his use of wiles never previously resorted to — he accused his men of imaginings and fears. He himself understood that at any time a situation might develop which would threaten the completion of his journey and the very thought of this caused him to express an agony of disappointment. However, these feelings never gained control beyond making him extremely alert.

His men came near mutiny and on one occasion they considered themselves in a state of siege.

They captured a blind old man whom hunger had forced from the woods, and by good fortune were able to communicate with him. He told them that the natives had been exceedingly alarmed by their change in plans and had considered their return up the river a hostile act. Mackenzie decided to carry this oldster with them for introductory purposes.

They had trouble with their canoe, which had been patched and gummed so frequently that it had become a crazy craft and was leaking badly. They landed on an island which seemed to offer sufficient raw material for a new canoe, and immediately set to the work of construction. During the course of this endeavor they were joined by some natives whom they had previously met. The blind man they had abducted helped their cause by giving a favorable account of their treatment of him.

The new canoe was soon ready — an excellent vessel, even exceeding in grace and favor the one they had started with and the sight of it, plus an extra ration of rum, put the men in a fine humor and they returned up the river through Cottonwood Canyon and, on July 3, came to the mouth of a small river. They were without a guide but judged from the information given them that this was the river the Indians followed in their journey to the western sea — Mackenzie called it the Westroad River. A young Indian who had agreed to be their guide joined them here.

On July 4 they left a bag of 90 pounds of pemmican, two bags of wild rice and a gallon keg of gunpowder buried in the ground. Over the disturbed earth they kindled a fire, the ashes of which served to conceal the hiding place and discourage wild animals from digging up the cache. They built a staging for the canoe, and hid all the goods they were not taking with them.

They started westward. For details of the trip, let us go to Mackenzie's diary:

We carried on our backs four bags and an half of pemmican, weighing from eighty-five to ninety pounds each, a case with my instruments, a parcel of goods for presents, weighing ninety pounds, and a parcel containing ammunition of the same weight. Each of the Canadians had a burden of about ninety pounds, with a gun, and some ammunition. The Indians had about forty-five pounds weight of pemmican to carry, besides their gun, &c. with which they were very much dissatisfied, and if they had dared would have instantly left us. They had hitherto been very much indulged, but the moment was now arrived when indulgence was no longer practicable. My own load, and that of Mr. Mackay, consisted of twenty-two pounds of pemmican, some rice, a little sugar, &c. amounting in the whole to about seventy pounds each, besides our arms and ammunition. I had also the tube of my telescope swung across my shoulder which was a troublesome addition to my burthen. It was determined that we should content ourselves with two meals a day, which were regulated without difficulty, as our provisions did not require the ceremony of cooking.

The explorers found the country west of the Fraser River to be an undulating plateau. Through the Rockies the challenge had been one of topography, while here there were no dark canyons, no towering mountains, no roaring waterfalls. The main difficulty was in retaining guides. Mackenzie tried again a stratagem he had used unsuccessfully in attempting to keep their unwilling guide from the Peace River summit to the Fraser; his diary of July 6th reads:

At four this morning I arose from my bed, such as it was. As we must have been in a most unfortunate predicament if our guides should have deserted us in the night, by way of security, I proposed to the youngest of them to sleep with me, and he readily consented. These people have no covering but their beaver garments, and that of my companions's was a nest of vermin. I, however, spread it under us, and having laid down upon it, we covered ourselves with my camlet cloak. My companion's hair being greased with fish-oil, and his body smeared with red earth, my sense of smelling, as well as that of feeling, threatened to interrupt my rest; but these inconveniences yielded to my fatigue, and I passed a night of sound repose.

There were many indications that they were on a highway to the sea. The path was well marked, following natural contours; dwellings were frequent, and meetings with groups of Indians more than occasional. Many of the Indians had been to the coast and one party included a woman of the coastal tribe.

"This woman," quoted Mackenzie, "was more inclined to corpulency than any we had yet seen, was of low stature, with an oblong face, grey eyes, and a flatish nose. She was decorated with ornaments of various kinds, such as large blue beads, either pendent from her ears, encircling her neck, or braided in her hair; she also wore bracelets of brass, copper and horn. Her garments consisted of a kind of tunic, which was covered with a robe of matted bark, fringed around the bottom with skin of the sea otter."

Mackenzie also discovered — the first of many white men to do so — that distances in that country were elastic. He met a party of Indians whose members declared they had been to the seacoast, some said it was a four day journey, others that the trip took six days, while others extended it to eight days. This information was gathered after they had been six days out on the trip from the Fraser River — a trip which, completed, would take only six days according to the original informants. Mackenzie found that as he travelled westward the Indians showed less fear, yet were less war-like. He travelled with one family group who took a much more leisurely pace than the explorers had been used to setting. Mackenzie, in fact, grew impatient the second day and exhorted the party to greater speed, pointing at their scanty provisions by way of a spur.

"There is no rush," replied the older Indian. "One more sleep and you will be through the mountains-that-bleed, and among the people of the seacoast. There you will be given more fish than all your men can carry."

The Indian was right. Mackenzie had crossed the plateau country west of the Fraser, crossing and re-crossing the Westroad River. The village of Algatcho had been passed, and they had from there seen the high white ramparts of the Coast Range rising south and west of them. From Algatcho they had plunged down swampy meadows to the banks of the Dean River, which they crossed on a raft, and continued westward through low country abounding in lakes and meadows. In camp on the north side of the Rainbow Mountains, the Indians knew that between Mackenzie and the Bella Coola Valley lay only those mountains and the high, rocky rim of the valley itself.

They started the ascent through the Rainbow Mountains, a small extinct volcanic range northeast of the Coast Range proper. The mountains were highly colored with ridges of red lava shingles. Some of the slopes were creamy white striped with red — Mackenzie understood what the Indian had meant by "the mountains-that-bleed." Their Indian guides shot some of the numerous marmots that vented their shrill whistles as the party trudged upwards to the snows. They brought down too a small caribou which they carried, rather than cache it as Mackenzie suggested. They went over a summit and, "it began to hail, rain and snow, nor could we find any shelter but the leeward side of a huge rock. The wind also rose into a tempest, and the weather was as distressing as any I had ever experienced."

From the slopes of the Rainbow Mountains they looked upon a great range of glacier-clad peaks, at the foot of which ran the river which would carry them to the sea. One stupendous mountain rose so high its snow-clad summit was lost in the clouds.

As soon as the explorers got off the snows and could gather sufficient wood for a fire, they dressed their venison and had a hearty meal. Also, Mackenzie changed his clothes and shaved. It was a procedure in which voyageur parties engaged whenever they were approaching a trading post or town. Mackenzie had learned enough of the nation in the valley below them to consider this mark of respect advisable.

We continued our route with a considerable degree of expedition, and as we proceeded the mountains appeared to withdraw from us. The country between them soon opened to our view, which apparently added to their awful elevation. We continued to descend till we came to the brink of the precipice, from whence our guides discovered the river to us, and a village on its banks. This precipice, or rather succession of precipices, is covered with large timber, which consists of the pine, the spruce, the hemlock, the birch, and other trees. Our conductors informed us, that it abounded in animals, which, from their description, must be wild goats. In about two hours we arrived at the bottom, where there is a conflux of two rivers, that issue from the mountains. We crossed the one which was to the left. They are both very rapid, and continue so till they unite their currents, forming a stream of about twelve yards in breadth. Here the timber was also very large; but I could not learn from our conductors why the most considerable hemlock trees were stripped of their bark to the tops of them. I concluded, indeed, at that time that the inhabitants tanned their leather with it. Here were also the largest and loftiest alder and cedar trees that I had ever seen. We were now sensible of an entire change in the climate, and the berries were quite ripe.

In the darkness of late evening their guides left them but the explorers managed to find their way. They could not have lost it, Mackenzie said, because of the tremendous cliffs — the like of which he had never seen before — which hemmed them in on both sides. Without ceremony they almost tumbled into an Indian village, where people were collected around fires preparing food. The white men were received without excitement by the natives who, after

Mackenzie had shaken hands with some of them, motioned him to go to the largest house.

After climbing some steps cut in a broad piece of timber, he entered the building indicated, where three fires were burning. By one of these sat a man from whose bearing Mackenzie recognized the chief. The explorers were seated and each fed with half a roast salmon. That night Mackenzie slept on a board provided by his host, with a block of wood for a pillow and "never enjoyed a more sound and refreshing rest."

He had arrived among the people of the Coast.

He had descended into the Bella Coola valley through the steeply precipitous valley of Kahylsk Creek, or Burnt Bridge Creek, thirty miles from where the Bella Coola River pours into the sea. In the last several hours of their travel they had gone from the rim of the valley, an altitude of six thousand feet, to the floor of the Bella Coola, here a height of 250 feet. From winter they had dropped to fullblown summer. Above them rose mountains to heights of eight or nine thousand feet, to altitudes of perpetual ice and snow. The feast to which their new hosts treated them illustrated that here was a land of abundance and stability, and before he retired to his wooden bed for the night Mackenzie realized he was among a people who had attained a high degree of civilization.

He awoke about five the next morning. The sun had not yet climbed the ridge north and east of them, but a fire had been kindled and the chief and several of his men were sitting beside it. When the natives saw that Mackenzie was awake they departed momentarily and returned with a slab of wood on which was a mound of berries, half a roast salmon and some dried fish eggs. As Mackenzie ate he saw the men of the tribe taking fish from traps placed in the river beneath a weir or artificial dam which created a waterfall. Mackenzie started to walk over to inspect it, but the chief stood in his way holding out an arm to prevent him coming close to the weir.

One of the Canadians threw a venison bone to a villager's dog, that sniffed at then bolted it. A native who had been standing by seized the dog, beating it upon the ground and pummelling it until the screaming animal disgorged the bone. The native gingerly picked up the bone, threw it into the fire and then washed his hands.

"That is a lesson to us," the Canadian said. "We do not feed bones to dogs." Then to a companion who was chewing the meat off another bone he said, "Throw the bone in the river so the dog cannot snatch it and be beaten again."

The voyageur threw the bone in the river. There was a shout of dismay from the natives, one of whom threw off his robe, dived like a flash of golden light into the river, came up and swam ashore, putting the second bone into the selfsame flame that had consumed the first.

"Name of a saint!" cried the vogageur. "It must be that their salmon gods will be offended if meat comes near their river."

He had stumbled upon a truth, for when Mackenzie asked their new-found friend, the village chief, for a canoe or canoes to take them down to the sea, the chief refused.

Mackenzie was surprised for nowhere had he been shown greater friendship.

The chief shook his head, pointed at the venison in their packs then at the weir, and made a motion as of everything falling out. The explorer understood — if they took meat in their canoes, the salmon deity would be offended and the fish would no longer come up the river — from a nation rich in food, the Indians would be reduced to starvation. Mackenzie cast round for a way out of the dilemma. He saw some Indians in a small group who appeared different from the Bella Coola natives.

"Are those meat-eating people?" he asked the chief, and when the answer came in the affirmative Mackenzie called them over, gave them the venison and by signs indicated they were to take it away from the river.

The chief was pleased. He gave a staccato command and in several minutes two canoes, one manned by four natives the other by three, thrust into the bank. "Your canoes," the chief indicated. "Your men."

Mackenzie looked at the Indian canoe men. They had cast off their cloaks, because by now the sun was well into the heavens and the morning warm, and they stood naked like golden statues, their muscles rippling under skins that gleamed with a thin film of perspiration. Several of them had curly hair while the rest were straight-haired, all of it gleaming black and short-cropped. As they stood for a moment gracefully braced against the slight bump of the canoe touching the bank, they were poised and carefree, with gleaming white teeth flashing in reddish-brown faces as they smiled.

The chief called a guttural command as the canoes landed, and all seven canoe men leaped lightly along the canoes and ashore. Deftly they assisted Mackenzie's Canadians in loading the explorers' baggage into the two canoes. As Mackenzie and his men were about to embark the chief gave them two roast salmon. He had asked for some in the raw state, but the giving of raw salmon to guests was contrary to their social rules. "You go now," the chief said. "Next village down river you get much fish."

Mackenzie did not understand why the chief wished their hasty departure, and was wondering how to ask when the captain of the canoe team gave a short command. Seven canoe men leaned on their poles. Two canoes backed out into the river current, turned deftly and darted downstream.

It was the commencement of a trip that at times caused the Scottish explorer to wonder if he were not dreaming. They were in dugout canoes, thirty feet in length, three feet on the beam and thwarted, and while the explorers' party were all seated their picturesque boatmen stood and plied poles in perfect team work so that the canoes leaped swiftly downstream. Along this gleaming waterway white with a burden of glacial silt, surging over riffles and stopping only briefly in calm pools, they dropped between columns of the tallest trees Mackenzie had ever seen. High above them the snowclad peaks gleamed in the sun. Eagles watched them from tall snags, and seagulls walked on gravelly beaches. On the river itself other canoes were being worked by crews of fishermen. Against the banks empty canoes were tied.

As they passed the fishermen, Mackenzie's escorts exchanged salutations but never ceased their efforts with their canoe poles; they came to a weir where the water had been dammed so that there was a waterfall some four feet high. The white men were landed above the weir, and the Indians shot their lightened vessels over the waterfalls without shipping a drop of water.

"By dam!" said one of Mackenzie's Canadians. "These Indians could teach us voyageurs how to handle a canoe."

Mackenzie agreed. Until this time he had thought his Canadians, whom he had personally picked for their water ability, to be the best canoe men in the world. Now he realized they were inferior to these Bella Coola Indian rivermen.

Downstream some ten or twelve miles below the Kahylsk Creek village they landed and followed their guides along a well-beaten forest path. Ahead of them they could hear a lot of clamor, and as they approached the edge of a village their guides dropped back and motioned Mackenzie to take the lead. Mackenzie realized the peril of the situation but without faltering or diminishing pace stepped out into the clearing. Immediately they were surrounded by a crowd of Indians, most of them armed with bows and arrows, some with spears.

"Your chief," Mackenzie demanded, drawing himself up.

It was as if his words were understood, for the crowd parted and a man with an undoubted air of command stepped through the crowd and embraced him. The crowd closed in, their clamor dying down. Then there was a shout and the crowd parted again, this time to give way to a younger man. The chief said a word or two to Mackenzie and pointed at the young man who was standing straight and imperious in front of them. The explorer saw a most obvious resemblance between the two Indians and gathered that this young man was the chief's son.

"Young Chief!" he exclaimed, naming him, and stepped forth and seized his hand.

With his other hand the Young Chief broke the string of a fine sea otter robe he was wearing and with it mantled Mackenzie's shoulder.

Mackenzie realized he had been accorded the highest mark of friendship and esteem. And as the young chief stood nude in front of him, he realized he had never seen a more magnificent physique. He had short curly hair, dark piercing eyes, lean features and a small growth of beard. His skin was golden, and rippling with muscles. Like the rest of the Indians, this young man showed no embarrassment at shedding his only article of clothing.

They were led to the house of the senior chief where they were entertained and feasted all afternoon.

In our front other mats were placed, where the chief and his councillors took their seats. In the intervening space, mats, which were very clean and of a much neater workmanship than those on which we sat, were also spread, and a small roasted salmon placed before each of us. When we had satisfied ourselves with the fish, one of the people who came with us from the last village approached, with a kind of ladle in one hand, containing oil, and in the other something that resembled the inner rind of the cocoa-nut, but of a lighter color; this he dipped in the oil, and, having eaten, indicated by his gestures how palatable he thought it. He then presented me with a small piece of it, which I chose to taste in its dry state, though the oil was free from any unpleasant smell. A square cake of this was next produced, when a man took it to the water near the house, and having thoroughly soaked it, he returned, and, after he had pulled it to pieces like oakum, put it into a well-made trough, about three feet long, nine inches wide, and five feet deep; he then plentifully sprinkled it with salmon oil, and manifested by his own example that we were to eat of it. I just tasted it, and found the oil perfectly sweet, without which the other ingredient would have been very insipid. The chief partook of it with great avidity, after it had received an additional quantity of oil. This dish is considered by these people as a great delicacy; and on examination, I discovered it to consist of the inner rind of the hemlock tree, taken off early in summer, and put into a frame, which shapes it into cakes of fifteen inches long, ten broad, and half an inch thick; and in this form I should suppose it may be preserved for a great length of time. This discovery satisfied me respecting the many hemlock trees which I had observed stripped of their bark.

Mackenzie distributed gifts to his new friends, a blanket to Young Chief, and to the senior a pair of scissors, explaining that these were for trimming his beard. The chief immediately and with obvious pleasure set about this task.

We were all of us very desirous of getting some fresh salmon that we might dress them in our own way, but could not by any means obtain that gratification, though there were thousands of that fish strung on cords, which were fastened to stakes in the river. They were even more averse to our approaching the spot where they clean and prepare them for their own eating. They had, indeed, taken our kettle from us, lest we should employ it in getting water from the river; and they assigned as the reason for this precaution, that the salmon dislike the smell of iron. At the same time they supplied us with wooden boxes, which were capable of holding any fluid. Two of the men that went to fish, in a canoe capable of containing ten people, returned with a full lading of salmon, that weighed from six to forty pounds, though the far greater part of them were under twenty. They immediately strung the whole of them, as I have already mentioned, in the river.

The explorers toured the village, which was by far the largest they had ever seen, and Mackenzie named it "Great Village."

Near the house of the chief I observed several oblong squares, of about twenty feet by eight. They were made of thick cedar boards, which were joined with so much neatness, that I at first thought they were one piece. They were painted with hieroglyphics, and figures of different animals, and with a degree of correctness that was not to be expected from such an uncultivated people. I could not learn the use of them, but they appeared to be calculated for occasional acts of devotion or sacrifice, which all these tribes perform at least twice in the year, at the spring and fall. I was confirmed in this opinion by a large building in the middle of the village, which I at first took for the half finished frame of a house. The ground plot of it was fifty feet by forty-five; each end is formed by four stout posts, fixed perpendicularly in the ground. The corner ones are plain, and support a beam of the whole length, having three intermediate props on each side, but of a larger size, and eight or nine feet in height. The two centre posts at each end are two feet and an half in diameter, and carved into human figures, supporting two ridge poles on their heads, at twelve feet from the ground. The figures at the upper part of this square represent two persons, with their hands upon their knees, as if they supported the weight with pain and difficulty: the others opposite to them stand at their ease, with their hands resting on their hips. In the area of the building there were the remains of several fires. The posts, poles, and figures were painted red and black; but the sculpture of these people is superior to their painting.

South of the village a giant mountain rose to an altitude the explorers considered must be two miles. Its sides were hung with glaciers and in the late afternoon sun its crevices and ribs looked like the muscles of a huge monster rearing into the heavens. Twice the heavy thunder of an icefall shook the air, and the Indians all stopped their activities and stared worshipfully up at the mountain.

"Noosgultz!" they cried.

Despite the language difficulty, the white men and their Indian hosts were by now managing to interchange some fairly complicated ideas. The mountain that thundered at them, the explorers learned, was treated with the highest reverence by these people. Long, long ago there was a tremendous rain storm. The rivers flooded and the valleys filled with water. Almost all the people drowned, and the one canoe load of survivors landed on the utmost peak, this Noosgultz, which appeared above the stormy waters as a refuge, a solitary post to which to tie their canoe. They looped their canoe rope around the peak, but the sawing caused by winds and tides cut loose their craft, leaving the people marooned. Eventually the flood waters subsided and the people descended to the valley floor, starting this Great Village, and from here their descendants spread to the rest of the world.

"Where come white man?" the chief was asked.

"White man, I don't know." he replied. "I tell story of my people. You tell how white man come," he concluded with a twinkle in his eye.

That night, Mackenzie had scarce retired when he was visited by the senior chief. "You come to my bed," he intimated. "I stay in your bed. Then my woman have white man baby. Your son. My son. I want white son. You come."

Mackenzie realized that he was again being given the highest mark of esteem, that this was more than a gesture of hospitality. But he declined the invitation.

"Why not?" demanded the chief, "You come. Your men they all go to women. Some two, three women."

"What my men do, their chief cannot do," the explorer replied. "If leaders go to women in a strange land, they cannot find their way home. Some time they and their men all perish because their god would be displeased."

"You are a man of courage," the chief replied. "I give you my son, Young Chief, to go with you when you travel."

Mackenzie stroked the sea otter robe the young chief had given him. "Your son is favored by your gods," he told the chief.

He gave the senior chief a burning glass, which the explorers used to make fire. The chief, forgetting his original errand, accepted the gift with delight and left Mackenzie.

Mackenzie writes in his diary:

At an early hour this morning I was again visited by the chief, in company with his son. The former complained of a pain in his breast; to relieve his suffering, I gave him a few drops of Turlington's balsam on a piece of sugar; and I was rather surprised to see him take it without the least hesitation. When he had taken my medicine, he requested me to follow him, and conducted me to a shed, where several people were assembled around a sick man, who was another of his sons. They immediately uncovered him, and showed me a violent ulcer in the small of his back, in the foulest state that can be imagined. One of his knees was also afflicted in the same manner. This unhappy man was reduced to a skeleton, and, from his appearance, was drawing near to the end of his pains. They requested that I should touch him, and his father was very urgent with me to administer medicine; but he was in such a dangerous state, that I thought it prudent to yield no further to the importunities than to give the sick person a few drops of Turlington's balsam in some water. I therefore left them, but was soon called back by the loud lamentations of the women, and was rather apprehensive that some inconvenience might result from my compliance with the chief's request. On my return I found the native physicians busy in practicing their skill and art on the patient. They blew on him and then whistled; at times they pressed their extended fingers with all their strength on his stomach; they also put their fore fingers doubled into his mouth, and spouted water from their own with great violence into his face. To support these operations the wretched sufferer was held up in a sitting posture; and when they were concluded, he was laid down and covered with a new robe made of the skins of the lynx. I had observed that his belly and breast were covered with scars, and I understood that they were caused by a custom prevalent among them, of applying pieces of lighted touch wood (punk) to their flesh, in order to relieve pain or demonstrate their courage. He was now placed on a broad plank, and carried by six men into the woods, where I was invited to accompany them. I could not conjecture what would be the end of this ceremony, particularly as I saw one man carry fire, another an axe, and a third dry wood. I was, indeed, disposed to suspect that, as it was their custom to burn the dead, they intended to relieve the poor man of his pain, and perform the last sad duty of surviving affection. When they had advanced a short distance into the wood, they laid him upon a clear spot, and kindled a fire against his back, when the physician began to scarify the ulcer with a very blunt instrument, the cruel pain of which operation the patient bore with incredible resolution. The scene afflicted me and I left it.

On my return to our lodge, I observed before the door of the chief's residence, four heaps of salmon, each of which consisted of between three and four hundred fish. Sixteen women were employed in cleaning and preparing them. They first separated the head from the body, the former of which they boil; they then cut the latter down the back on each side of the bone, leaving one third of the fish adhering to it, and afterwards take out the guts. The bone is roasted for immediate use, and the other parts are dressed in the same manner, but with more attention, for future provision. While they are before the fire, troughs are placed under them to receive the oil. The roes are also carefully preserved, and form a favorite article of their food.

After I had observed these culinary preparations, I paid a visit to the chief, who presented me with a roasted salmon; he then opened one of his chests, and took out of it a garment of blue cloth, decorated with brass buttons; and another of a flowered cotton, which I supposed were Spanish; it had been trimmed with leather fringe, after the fashion of their cloaks. Copper and brass are in great estimation among them, and of the former they have great plenty; they point their arrows and spears with it, and work it up into personal ornaments; such as collars, ear-rings, and bracelets, which they wear on their wrists, arms, and legs. I presume they find it the most advantageous article of trade with the more inland tribes. They also abound in iron: I saw some of their twisted collars of that metal which weighed upwards of twelve pounds. It is generally in bars of fourteen inches in length, and one inch three quarters wide. The brass is in thin squares: their copper is in larger pieces, and some of it appeared to be old stills cut up. They have various trinkets; but their manufactured iron consists only of poniards and daggers. Some of the former have very neat handles, with a silver coin of a quarter or eighth of a dollar fixed on the end of them. The blades of the latter are from ten to twelve inches in length, and about four inches broad at the top, from which they gradually lessen to a point.

Just before their departure downriver about one o'clock in the afternoon, Mackenzie was taken by the senior chief to see his large sea canoe. This craft was made of cedar and was forty-five feet long, four feet wide and three-and-a-half feet deep. It was painted black, decorated with white figures of fish and the gunwales, fore and aft, were inlaid with the teeth of sea otter. The chief, some ten winters ago with forty of his people, had made a journey many days southward and had seen two ships full of white men. The white men had received the Indians well.

"Those ships were probably Captain Cook's," Mackenzie surmised.

Down at the scene of embarkation a canoe was in readiness for Mackenzie. Their goods had been stowed and the whole party was waiting on the shore. There were four village men assigned to take them to the sea, with Young Chief, outstanding by his physique and bearing, as their leader.

"We cannot find our dog," one of the voyageurs told Mackenzie. "We call, we whistle, we search. No dog. Maybe too many lady dogs here."

"We will have to go without him," Mackenzie said. "We must go at once."

In a matter of minutes farewells had been said, and crew and explorers stepped aboard the canoe. The visitors sat as before, with the four native canoe men — with poles — standing. Deftly they backed the canoe out into the current and, shouting to those left on the bank, pointed it downstream and skimmed down the silvery white surface.

That afternoon was a repetition of the previous day. Some small villages they passed but at another, where the chief was a man of great importance, according to Young Chief, they landed and were feted and feasted. At others they stopped to observe the daily life and tasks of these people. They came later in the afternoon to where rapids impeded their canoe's progress. Leaving their vessel here and walking several hundred yards through the woods, they came to a village of six very large houses on 25-foot high palisades.

From these houses Mackenzie could see the termination of the river where it discharged itself into a narrow arm of the sea. He was looking upon the Pacific Ocean. The first overland journey had been accomplished.

Mackenzie expressed no jubilation. In fact, he felt the reverse of satisfaction. Except for four men and their families, this village at the mouth of the Bella Coola River was deserted in favor of up-river fisheries. Mackenzie tried to get some fish from these people, but either through want or misunderstanding was refused. In the last several days he had been treated as a visiting personage of the very highest rank, had been asked to sire a chief's son, and had been feted to the extent that it took two days to make a downriver trip that could be done in four hours. Now he had arrived at the natural culmination of his voyage and found himself in a semi-deserted village, among a scant handful of people who refused them even food.

The next morning two of the Indians from the Great Village refused to go any farther with them. "You wanted to come to the sea. Here you are. Now we go back," they stated.

"I want to go to the place where there is no more land west," Mackenzie explained to them.

"You wanted to come to the sea. We bring you here. Now we go back," was their final word.

Young Chief, however, stated his willingness to continue, and the fourth Indian likewise agreed. They got a larger canoe from one of the villagers, a sea canoe with a built-up prow and, despite the fact that it leaked, it was better for their projected trip on the salt water than the spoon canoes used on the river.

About eight o'clock they floated downriver out into the bay which a few short weeks before had been visited by Captain Vancouver's Lieutenant Johnstone. The bay was North Bentinck Arm, so named by Vancouver, and when Mackenzie saw it a vigorous west wind opposed them, and clouds scudded low on the mountain sides. Seals and porpoises played around.

The poles which had propelled and guided them the last few days were now put aside and the Canadians as well as the Indians wielded paddles. In spite of the high complement of manpower, the west wind and rising seas finally drove them to shelter in Green Bay, where they made camp at two o'clock in the afternoon. The Indians from Great Village decided they wanted to go home. Mackenzie consequently gave one of them a pair of shoes, necessary for the rugged hike, and sent him on his way. Young Chief went with him, but returned at dark with a large porcupine on his shoulder, which he dressed and, aided by two of the explorer's party, completely consumed.

Mackenzie called the spot Porcupine Cove.

Next day they were on the water at six in the morning, coasted along Burke Channel, around Mesatchi (Evil) Nose into Labouchère Channel, thence to Dean Channel.

They met three canoes carrying fifteen men, and when they closed with them the men entered into conversation with Young Chief. The Indians examined the explorers' baggage with an air of disdain.

"One moon ago," one of the Indians said, "two big canoes were here filled with white men. Bad white men. One man, Chief called Macubah, he shot at my friends and me. One other bad man, white man, called Bensins, hit me across back with long knife."

Mackenzie would have done the same, had he dared, when this Indian seized Mackenzie's gun, and then his sword, to illustrate the white man's felony.

"White man bad," the Indian chanted.

Mackenzie was further distressed when these Indians persuaded Young Chief to get into one of their canoes.

Historians believe that "Macubah" and "Bensins" were the Indians' interpretation for the names of Captain Vancouver and his naturalist, Menzies.

When the explorers continued their way along the channels, the three canoe loads of Indians accompanied them, and at one period the irksome character boarded Mackenzie's canoe and probed into its cargo.

"White man bad," he kept repeating. "That man Macubah shot at my people. Bensins hit me with long knife."

At the mouth of Elcho Harbor they found a rock which had the appearance of being fortified. They were now surrounded by ten canoe loads of natives of unknown temperament. Some of the natives appeared to be trying to annoy the white men, while others kept inviting them to visit their village which was nearby in the bay. Mackenzie, fearful there would be mischief if he were to go there, refused. About sunset all the natives departed, taking with them Young Chief. The explorers started a fire to warm themselves and cook their food. They had very little because the daily ration had been reduced to the point that it did not make up even one good meal.

Shortly after the departure of the main lot of canoes, another canoe load of men came to trade. They had with them a fine sea otter skin.

"They actually refused to take a yard-and-a-half of common broadcloth with some articles for the skin," Mackenzie exclaimed, "which proves the unreflecting improvidence of our European traders."

The natives refused to part with a seal, nor would they supply the explorers with fish.

When eventually the canoe left, the men retired. However, a double watch was established. Nothing occurred in the night to disturb them.

Next morning two canoes came from the village in the bay for trading purposes. Young Chief rode in one of the canoes, and when he landed he tried to convince Mackenzie that he should leave at once.

"These people are from another nation, the Bella Bella, that live among the islands in the setting sun. They are as thick as mosquitoes and will kill you. They are planning an attack now."

"Yes," a spokesman for the voyageurs exclaimed. "Let us go! Let us not remain here to become sacrifices,"

"I have work to do here," Mackenzie replied. "When it is finished we shall go back, and not before."

Two canoe loads of people were seen approaching, but they contained five men and their families rather than warriors. Mackenzie, however, was becoming apprehensive and commanded his men to load the canoe ready for an immediate departure. He managed to get an astronomic reading. Then, even in the sight of approaching canoes, he calmly mixed some vermilion in melted grease and inscribed in large characters on the southeast face of the rock on which they slept last night, this brief memorial —
"Alex Mackenzie from Canada by land
22d July 1793"

It was a classic understatement.

In order to relieve the tension, Mackenzie allowed a move up channel. They landed near the mouth of Cascade Inlet. Two canoes followed them there and when they were preparing to depart Young Chief stepped into one of them. Mackenzie hauled him from the canoe by sheer force and compelled him to stay with him.

"I thought it better to incur his displeasure than to suffer him to expose himself to any untoward accident among strangers, or to return to his father before us," Mackenzie stated in his diary. He was a powerful man, and this was not to be the only time on this trip that he resorted to physical force.

He managed to get a reading from the stars which gave him pleasure: "I had now determined my situation, which is the most fortunate circumstance of my long, perilous and painful journey, as a few cloudy days would have prevented me from ascertaining the final longitude of it."

It was ten in the evening when he had finished his recordings and gave his men permission to start the return journey. This they did with great enthusiasm. They avoided an adverse tide by keeping in close to the rocks. At four-thirty the next morning they were at the camp at Porcupine Cove and a few hours later they pulled up near the Bella Coola village.

Young Chief leaped ashore, telling them to draw the canoe above the reach of the tide, and immediately started off along a rough path, with Mackenzie following close behind determined that the young Indian would not get out of his sight. When they were in view of the houses two men dashed out with fury in their faces and with drawn daggers. When Mackenzie pointed his gun at them they stopped short and dropped their daggers to dangle from the cords holding them to their wrists.

Then several more Indians joined them, similarly armed.

Mackenzie heard a familiar, hated refrain — "White man bad. White man shoot at me" — and there was his malevolent tormentor once again. Mackenzie felt rage surging up within him. Here, indeed, was the cause of all his trouble! Could he have got his hands on him, the trouble-making Indian would rapidly have gone to join his ancestors.

One of the Indians managed to get behind Mackenzie and grasped him in his arms, but the explorer threw him off as if he were a child. At the same time one of Mackenzie's men appeared out of the woods, and the Indians ran for shelter in their homes.

One by one his men came along the path and in a space of ten minutes the white men had all joined their leader.

"They could have killed us one at a time," Mackenzie told his men, "but now that we are together we will teach these saucy knaves a lesson."

Mackenzie recognized these men, particularly the Malevolent One, as the occupants of the three canoes they had met in the channels, the men from the Bella Bella island villages.

"Prime your pieces and prepare for action!"

When they were ready he marched them near the house, and there marshalled them shoulder to shoulder with muskets pointed at the building. "Come out!" he cried. He appeared ready to attack any stronghold on the Pacific Coast.

Shortly Young Chief appeared at the doorway. "These men from Bella Bella have told their friends here you treated me very badly. You also killed four of their companions," he said.

"Those men tell untrue stories," Mackenzie retorted. "You are a chief, and the son of a great chief. You tell them the truth. You tell them that we will stay here ready for attack until they return the goods they have stolen from us." Mackenzie waited until the young man had passed on this message to the occupants of the house. "Tell them also that if they wish us to go they must supply us with fish."

Mackenzie's show of force, plus a reputation for strength and fierceness which he had built up in the channels, and in the tussle with the natives a few minutes past, had its effecᵗ. The men came from the house, bearing the explorer's hat and coat which they had taken in the scuffle, as well as several articles they had purloined from him out in the channel.

Young Chief watched the restitution with concern. "I go," he said to Mackenzie. "You bring my father's canoe, for sure, else there will be mischief." And without further ado he disappeared along the path up the river.

The explorer told the villagers that he needed more fish. They brought two salmon. Then he asked for poles with which to push the canoe against the rapids; immediately poles were produced. The Indians were very, very anxious for their savage and uninvited white guests to be quickly on their way.

Mackenzie waited until noon when he got a meridian altitude making this place (Bella Coola) 52.23.43 north latitude. He then named the place "Rascal's Village", and with his people close on his heels took the path leading around the rapids.

When they reached the canoe his men expressed a wish to go by land because of the fierceness of the current, but one of the Indian hunters was ill and so weak that he could not easily walk nor carry a burden. Four of the white men set off in the canoe, but it took them an hour to go a half mile. Mackenzie, with the rest of the party, followed the path through the woods. He saw a canoe poled by the Malevolent One and four companions push rapidly up a channel not taken by his men and their canoe.

When the canoe party and the walkers rendezvoused above the rapids, the canoe party declared they would go no farther by water. When Mackenzie told them he had seen the Malevolent One go upstream in a canoe, the men became exceedingly agitated.

"We cannot go up the river," one of the Canadians cried. "We will surely be killed — every man of us!"

"We might go up over the mountains and find the trail by the Mountains-that-Bleed," another said. "We will miss all these savages."

Others shouted their approval and almost immediately the Canadians started throwing all their baggage, with the exception of their blankets, into the river.

Mackenzie sat patiently on a rock hoping their frenzy would pass, but when it persisted he asked them to rest for a moment that he might talk with them.

"My people," he addressed them, "before you embark on a mad journey into those awesome mountains" — and he pointed to the lofty pinnacles rising to the skies above them — "consider that we have only two days' provisions. There will be no fish in those dark caverns or on those eternal snowfields. That way lies certain death. If we retrace our steps up this river, we will meet no greater problems than we have already overcome. Indeed, there may be no problems; we may have already overcome them.

"You are voyageurs. You are men of the north. If you flee into the mountains you will be deserting a man who has been with us through all our dangers and privations. This Indian hunter who is ill will surely languish and die if you leave him. That, you men of the north — if you live to be a hundred — will never boast nor sing about nor, in the quiet hours of the night, forget.

"You have come with me this long way. I have accomplished my object, and it is now my sole desire to see every man of you safely home. We must not go into those mountains."

The Canadians shuffled their feet.

"Chief," cried the steersman, "I have travelled with you for five years. I will now go where you wish to lead. But I will not, by the name of a saint, enter that canoe again."

So part of the group followed the path through the woods while Mackenzie, Mackay and two voyageurs struggled against the current with the sick Indian in the canoe. The current was so strong they progressed much of the way only by pulling themselves along by tree branches. Mackay's gun was swept out of the canoe and lost.

They came in sight of a house, and a canoe put out to greet them. In the canoe was Young Chief, an assurance in itself that the Malevolent One had hatched no mischief in this village. Young Chief led them into the canoe landing as his protégés.

At the next village, which they gained just about dark, Malevolent One and his four companions were there. But there seemed no mischief in them now for they were busy trading. Mackenzie learned they were traders from the Bella Bella islands and watched with professional interest as they traded with the villagers for roast salmon, hemlock bark cakes, dried salmon roe and soapalalie berries. For these they paid with cedar bark, fish spawn, copper, iron and beads, which they had got from white traders on their own coast.

Having tired of watching this commerce and having received enough fish for their wants of the evening and the next day,

Mackenzie sent all his men to rest, with one companion retained to stand watch with him. When Mackay and another of the men came to relieve at midnight Mackenzie decided there was no need of a guard, since all was tranquil.

Next morning, awakened at four, he sent Mackay to see if their canoe was where they had left it. In a moment Mackay was back.

"Chief," he cried, "the Islanders are taking our canoe. They have their boxes loaded in it and are ready to depart!"

Mackenzie was at the water's edge in a flash. Seizing the stern of the canoe he was about to twist and upset it, its merchandise and traders, into the river when an Indian, one of Mackenzie's hosts, stopped him, telling him that Young Chief had taken their canoe and departed.

In the momentary quiet caused by this interruption, several of the Bella Bellas who were still ashore leaped nimbly into their own canoe and fled in haste downriver from this strange, powerful and savage white man.

The explorers proceeded up river, hitch-hiking and being received hospitably at the numerous villages. Mackenzie again admired the skill of the Indian boatmen who were fishing and travelling on the river.

"These people are surprisingly skillful and active in setting against a strong current. In the roughest part, by way of sportive alarm to us, they almost filled the canoe with water," he said.

When they were following riverside trails they passed through the finest timber Mackenzie had ever seen. Some of the cedar trees were twenty-four feet in girth and tremendously high. Many of the larger cedars had been cut into, in search of canoe logs, but because they were hollow had been allowed to stand.

Mackenzie had been worried about the reception he would receive at the Great Village. Young Chief had preceded them, and the explorer could not hope that a favorable report would have been given to his father by the young man. As they approached the village Mackenzie had his men ready their arms. When they came to the village the people crowded around them, but Mackenzie drew a line and forbade them to cross it. Observing that none of the chief's family was in the crowd, he gave his gun to Mr. Mackay. With loaded pistols in his belt and dagger in hand he addressed his men. "I am going alone to look for the Senior Chief," he said. "You stay here. But if you hear the report of my pistols, fight your way out and get away. It will be useless to come to my help, as I will not shoot unless I am certain it is the end."

He found the chief, who had been in deep distress — from which he had not yet recovered — over what he thought had been the loss of his son — even though Young Chief was now with him once more. He had cut off his hair and blackened his face because he imagined either that the explorers had killed his son or that they had all perished together. When the chief had stopped talking Mackenzie took his hand and his son's hand, and invited them down to where his baggage was. The white men were very happy to see their leader again, and when Mackenzie gave the chief and his son many gifts happiness was restored all around.

"The presents," he said, "had the desired effect of restoring us to their favour; but these people are so changeable a nature, that there is no security with them."

Senior Chief informed them that their dog had been howling around the village ever since they left. Mackay was sent in search of the animal but couldn't find him. However, shortly after leaving the village they caught sight of the animal. It was very frightened and would not approach until they had dropped some food. It was starved to skeletal proportions, and food was the only thing which would overcome its fear.

That night, doubtful that they had established a lasting friendship at the Great Village, they made a fireless camp somewhat removed from the path, each man fully clothed and armed, ready for action. But they were undisturbed.

They arrived at eight o'clock next morning at the first village they had come to on their outward journey. The people and their chief, Soocomlick, received them with the same friendliness they had experienced here before. In a wave of relief and joy Mackenzie called the spot "Friendly Village."

For three hours the explorers visited with their hosts then, laden with all the salmon they wished to carry, they set out on the trail up the mountain. Every man of Friendly Village accompanied them for the first hour, then parted from them with signs of regret.

Despite the fact that their progress was slowed by the sick Indian, they left behind them the summer of the Bella Coola valley and camped on the edge of the snows. They were so tired they could barely crawl about to get firewood, but gather it they did, and after a hearty supper of roast fish they sat about the fire and talked of their adventures, delighting in the feeling of being almost out of danger and well on their way homeward. As they sat the darkness welled up from the valley floor so far below them, gradually chasing the golden sunset colors to the very peaks of the mountains, which for a few moments stood like gleaming islands of rock in a dark engulfing ocean. The colors climbed to the clouds and disappeared, the skies darkened and the only light came from the gay flames of their fire high on the wall of the mountain.

"Such was the depth of precipices below," commented Mackenzie in his diary, "and the height of the mountains above, with the rude and wild magnificence of the scenery around, that I shall not attempt to describe such an astonishing and awful combination of objects: of which, indeed, no description can convey an adequate idea."

That was the evening of July 26. On August 17 they made the portage from the Fraser to the Parsnip River. On August 22 they were through the mountains and out onto the prairies. On August 23 they were on the river before daylight, travelled hard and camped for their ceremonial approach to the home fort the next day.

On August 24 — "At length, as we rounded a point and came in view of the Fort, we threw out our flag, and accompanied it with a general discharge of our fire-arms: while the men were in such spirits, and made such an active use of their paddles, that we arrived before the two men whom we left here in the spring, could recover their senses to answer us."

3 Early Pathfinders and Roadmakers

For a decade following Mackenzie's journey most of the Indians living between the Rocky Mountains and the sea might have thought that all the white men in the world had come and gone. In 1797 James Finlay went up the Peace River to the forks, explored the Finlay River far enough to determine that there was no route by that stream to the western sea, retraced MacKenzie's route up the Parsnip River, then retreated down the Peace River to the prairies. Until 1804 no other exploration party squeezed through the high dangerous passes of the Rockies.

East of the barrier the North West Company had run into trouble. Since its inception in 1783 its aggressive policies of putting the fur buyers right out among the Indians on the trapping fields, and of exploring new fields, had permitted them to set the pace in the fur rivalry. Then opposition between Alexander Mackenzie and Simon McTavish caused a civil war and bitter enmity in the partners' ranks. They had neither time nor resources to spare for the exploration or exploitation of new lands. Then the death of the autocratic Simon McTavish led to the resolving of their troubles, and the partners reunited to fight their original rival, the Hudson's Bay Company.

Stories from the south indicated that the Americans were organizing an expedition under Lewis and Clarke to explore a route into the Oregon Territory, which action would bring into the territory west of the Rocky Mountains a host of trappers and traders.

If the North West Company were to capitalize on Mackenzie's efforts and establish their right to the Pacific watershed, immediate action was required.

In 1805 they sent Simon Fraser up the Peace River in Mackenzie's footsteps. On McLeod Lake he built Fort McLeod, the first fort west of the Rockies. In honor of his homeland he called the area "New Caledonia". It was a territory reaching from where the Rocky Mountains reared their heads high above the clouds to where the Pacific Ocean growled and gnawed at the foundations of the continent. It embraced an expanse reaching into the unknown north on one hand to the still undiscovered Columbia River territory to the south. Yet the naming was a doubtful honor to his homeland for this region became almost a punitive district, the Siberian saltmines of the Pacific fur trade.

In 1806 Fraser and his lieutenant, John Stuart, dropped down to the Fraser River, descending to its confluence with the Nechako. This stream they ascended to Stuart Lake where Fort St. James was established. Then Stuart explored southward and on Fraser Lake established still another fort, Fort Fraser.

In 1807 the fur brigade returning from Fort William brought with it a communication Fraser had been awaiting. Calling his lieutenant to him he said, "I have here" — tapping the thick pile of papers — "instructions to follow the big river to the sea. We cannot go this fall, but we will direct out attention to being fully prepared for a departure in the spring."

Part of the preparation was to build a fort at the junction of the Nechako and the main river which everyone confidently considered to be the Columbia.

Fort George was thus established.

In May, 1808, a flotilla of four canoes carrying Fraser, Stuart, Jules Maurice Quesnel, nineteen voyageurs and two Indian guides set out from Fort George. Their journey down the big river, which was to be named after Fraser, was a classic defiance of death in dark and roaring chasms, of clinging to the sides of vertical rock walls on crude native ladders, of travelling under the hostile attention of swarms of natives.

But they won through the problems of dark canyons and inimical natives to float down the peaceful lower Fraser River after it emerges from the mountains. When they felt the regular rise and fall of the tides they knew, despite the wall of mountainous islands in front of them, that they had come to the western sea.

Fraser felt no jubilation. The known latitude of the Columbia River mouth was 46° 20′ N., while Fraser's instruments showed the mouth of this river to be at a latitude of 49° N. There was only one conclusion — Fraser had followed the wrong river to the sea. Also, he was looking for a feasible canoe route by which to supply from the Pacific Coast the forts of New Caledonia and those immediately east of the Rockies. This would avoid the long overland haul from Montreal. But there was no water route here — no route at all, in fact — and Fraser felt he had wasted his time.

On July 2 he turned back. They had made one landing near the present site of New Westminster, and another not far from the place that was to become the campus of the University of British Columbia. The food situation was very bad, and at every move they were surrounded by Indians of the Musqueam Tribe threatening to impale them with spears and arrows. The return was almost a flight in its precipitous haste. The party arrived back at Fort George on August 6, intact but with a disappointed leader.

The highways for furs that shortly developed from New Caledonia and the forts just east of the Rockies took neither of the direct routes explored by Mackenzie and Fraser. One route established Kamloops as a fur capital and used the Okanagan Valley and the lower Columbia River to get to the sea. Another, from the forts east of the Rockies came through Athabasca Pass and down to Boat Encampment on the Columbia River. Then, instead of going down it went up the Columbia River, Kootenay Valley and finally down the lower Columbia to the sea.

In both cases, also, the conveyance used for part of this way was one most strange to the voyageur — it was the pack horse.

The educated wanderings of David Thompson, starting in 1807 and continuing for eight years, led him through various passes in the Rockies, up and down the valleys west of the Rockies, through the mountain ranges of New Caledonia, and resulted in the territory becoming almost suddenly generally known.

The establishment of John Jacob Astor's Pacific Fur Company with its base at the mouth of the Columbia River spelled real competition for the North West Company. The Astorians built forts as far north as Kamloops and each company did its best to outwit the other. The vigorous North West Company won the battle for, in 1813, the Astorians sold out to the North Westers, giving the latter a complete monopoly.

This monopoly was challenged by the Hudson's Bay Company, and in 1821 the two companies merged under the name of the latter. In New Caledonia many of the partners of the North West Company became loyal and, in some cases, very famous officers of the

Hudson's Bay Company. Among these men, James Douglas was the outstanding example.

The rule of the Hudson's Bay Company in New Caledonia was complete and unchallenged for several decades. In the Columbia region, however, the establishment of the International Boundary put the principal post, Astoria, under American control, necessitating a move on the part of the Hudson's Bay Company into British territory. Fort Langley had been built in 1827 but was declared unsuitable as a company headquarters because it was not on an acceptable route to the Interior, and the navigation of the Fraser River from Langley to the ocean was tricky and unreliable. The Hudson's Bay Company had forts on the coast. Fort Simpson had been established in 1831 and Fort McLoughlin at Bella Bella in 1833. By agreement with the Russian-American Company, the Hudson's Bay Company took over the Russian post on the Stikine River and established Fort Durham on the Taku River in 1840. They also had a fleet of ships, not the least of which was the *Beaver,* one of the first steamers to ply the Pacific Ocean. A headquarters post had to have easy access at least to the coast. The spot finally chosen was Camosun Bay on which a fort was built — first called Fort Albert, then Fort Victoria, and finally, in 1852 when the townsite was laid out in streets, Victoria.

It was from Victoria that the Hudson's Bay Company ruled New Caledonia. From here company orders went east to the Rocky Mountains and north to the edge of Russian territory in Alaska. In that area the company posts were the only evidence of white man's sovereignty. It was estimated that in 1858 the mainland of what is now British Columbia had a population of two hundred white people.

A sudden and violent change was in the making.

Gold! Gold! Gold!

The whisper started in 1851 when small finds of gold were reported from the Queen Charlotte Islands. The world was waiting for such a whisper, for the gold rush to California had played out, and thousands of people who would sooner adventure than plough or clerk in a store were looking for new fields of activity. It was disappointing then, to these and to hundreds of thousands of others who had not taken part in the California rush, that the Queen Charlotte Islands weren't surrounded with golden sands.

This first whisper, however, did show the Indians, from the Queen

Charlotte Haidas to the Shuswaps of the Okanagan, that the white man was interested in something else besides furs. The dull yellow dust and small pebbles were such that white men would give even more rum and muskets than they would for furs.

Though the first whisper died almost a-borning, a second, more emphatic repetition came about. In 1852 the trader at Kamloops accumulated 200 pounds sterling from the district Indians in the course of trade. More reports of gold came from near Walla Walla. In 1855 Fort Colville was reporting gold, and in 1856 an Indian near Lytton picked a large nugget out of the Thompson River.

In 1858 the first real rush was peaking in tumultuous frenzy. That gravel on the Fraser near Fort Hope.

In 1858 the first real rush was peaking in tumultous frenzy. That year as many as 30,000 people left San Francisco, augmenting other sources of potential gold seekers bound for the Fraser River, an area which just a few years previously had been so scantily populated by Europeans that they could be counted by the dozen. This influx of people, anxious to get farther than the lower Fraser River, brought about the need for a road reaching above the Fraser Canyon. Governor Douglas looked the situation over and declared that an alternative route lay up the Harrison River, across Harrison Lake, thence along the Anderson and Seton Lakes and out a few miles to Lillooet.

A group of miners volunteered to build the trail, free of charge, if the government supplied transportation for them to the site. The miners moreover each deposited $25.00 guarantee that the work would be finished. They extracted a promise in return that the road would be closed for any other traffic for two weeks. This would give them an advantage in finding and staking their claims.

On August 8th the work started on the trail. There followed days of struggle with the swamp, of struggle with delay due to lack of provisions and of tension because of fear of Indian attack.

But in October the trail was completed. Some £14,000 had been expended on the project. It was called the Douglas Road.

It was laid out by amateurs and built by amateurs at an amazingly low cost. It was also condemned by the first professional road-builder to report on it. It was not the last one to be so built and condemned in British Columbia. Nevertheless the road was for several years of inestimable value.

In 1859 excitement in the gold fields was waning rapidly. The bars were becoming worked out. The number of miners coming out over the Douglas Road was in the thousands, many times the number going in. Bitter crowds left New Westminster and Victoria, denouncing the Fraser River digging as "Humbug!"

Only a hardy few remained. These belonged to the class that believed the true riches were farther up the streams, waiting to be discovered. These Argonauts pushed northward and wilderness-ward, some up the Thompson River, some up the Bridge River, some up the Quesnel River to Cariboo Lake. These men found gold, richer deposits of it than had yet been discovered, and when the reports of their findings trickled south the fires of the gold fever were rekindled.

They were fanned to a fierce flame by the strikes on Keithley Creek, Antler Creek and Williams Creek. A few men who feared neither starvation, loneliness nor the rigors of a Cariboo winter kept at their ceaseless search. They staked claims that in one case paid $53,000 in six days; another, Cariboo Cameron's, yielded gold to the value of $385,000 in six months. The gold flames were raging in inferno proportions! Tens of thousands were pouring in over the Douglas Road, and only a scant handful coming out.

Now the centre of mining interest was much farther up in the province. New problems of transportation arose. Many more people had to be supplied, at a greater distance, and because the mines were deeper than those in the lower Fraser River, the miners needed more equipment. It was not possible to make a quick dash into the gold fields and out again. Time was required and more permanent structures took the place of crude camps.

New routes into the gold fields were being sought.

One of these routes led through the Bella Coola Valley. Here the long inland-reaching Burke Channel offered a short land-haul to the gold fields. The area was not unknown. Mackenzie's discovery had been supplemented by Captain Vancouver's, and in the decades that followed adventuring marine traders had come into the bay at the mouth of the river to trade furs. This bay enjoyed a variety in names, being first called Mackenzie's Outlet, then successively, Bela Kula, North Bentinck Arm and New Aberdeen, finally receiving the name of Bella Coola. Among the traders who visited the spot was John Dunn, trader and interpreter at Fort McLaughlin. Aboard the then new steamship, the *Beaver,* he probed into the countless bays and inlets looking for Indian villages where he could obtain furs. In Dean

Channel he saw the vermilion notation left by Mackenzie. This was in 1836 and Mackenzie's brief message was still discernible. This trader from Bella Bella, unlike his predecessor of Mackenzie's time, didn't go up the Bella Coola River in a spoon canoe. Instead, he stayed aboard, blew a sharp blast on his ship's whistle, and after the echoes had bounced from crag to crag, allowed the Indians two at a time to board the ship for trading purposes. The Indians welcomed the ship because by it and other trading vessels (with sails for motive power, however, since the *Beaver* at that time was the only steamer on the Pacific Coast) came trade goods direct, and not through their neighboring middlemen, the Bella Bella Indians. Trade goods which they received were cloth, muskets, powder and shot, knives, axes and rum. The goods they readied for trade were eulachon grease, furs, dried salmon and dried berries put up in cakes.

Far east across the mountains on a plateau sloping to the Fraser River, a fort had been built in 1821 by the Hudson's Bay Company at the spot on the Fraser where Mackenzie had turned back in his journey. The fort was called Alexandria and was an important junction-point, receiving and storing furs from the canoe brigades of the north on their way to Kamloops and south by way of pack horses, and at the same time holding trade goods and supplies from the south for transhipment by canoe northward. A post was established also in the Chilcotin River Valley, a post which was to be closed because of isolation, expense, and the troublesome disposition of the natives.

Journeys eastward from Bella Coola among the natives, for trading and for war were frequent, and the several routes were occasionally travelled by parties of white men seeking new lands and new travel routes.

But until the gold rush and the coming of a heavy population (relatively) no settlers dared tangle with the changeable disposition of the numerous natives. It was still the unquestioned domain of the Indians.

Despite the fact that footpaths had existed before the coming of white men and the first horse-trails from the interior of the province to the coast came to Bella Coola, there was no thought of a road until 1861 when Ranald MacDonald and John Barnston left Alexandria on May 24 of that year and reached the Bella Coola Inlet on June 19. MacDonald, son of a Scottish trader of the North West Company and a beautiful Indian princess, applied for a contract to build a mule road from Bella Coola to the mouth of the Quesnel River. For building the road he was to have the right to charge tolls at the rate of three farthings per pound of merchandise and two shillings per traveller. The agreement between MacDonald and the government was signed in April, 1862. MacDonald hoped to form a company to build the road — but neither the company nor the road materialized.

Then in July of 1862 Lieutenant H. S. Palmer of the Royal Engineers with Sappers Edwards and Breckenridge and a packer arrived at Bella Coola, commissioned to make a reconnaisance of the road route from Bentinck Arm to Alexandria. The government was looking for new routes into the gold fields and Bella Coola, with its far-inland reaching inlet, was one of the possibilities.

The Lieutenant was one of the body of Royal Engineers sent out from England to help in establishing the newly-formed colony of British Columbia. Less than two hundred strong, the Royal Engineers applied trained knowledge to the problems of the infant colony. They provided military protection; they laid out the townsites of New Westminster, Lytton, Clinton and Quesnel; they designed churches and founded the government printing office; they originated the coat of arms for the colony and the pattern for the first British Columbia stamp. They built the North Road from New Westminster to Burrard Inlet; they rebuilt the road from Douglas to Lillooet and helped in building two sections of the Cariboo Road. Now Lieutenant Palmer was to assess the route from Bentinck Arm to Alexandria for road purposes.

Ashore at Bella Coola, Lieut. Palmer found three white men established in a small community adjacent to the Indian village and carrying on trade with the natives. One of the trading posts was a little larger than the other two and bore the sign that this was the property of Barron of Quesnel. The operator inside, however, was a young man, Peter White, who invited them to set up their camp in the clearing outside his store.

Palmer left on a short inspection trip around the harbor after giving instructions for the erection of camp, leaving the packer shoeing horses, preparing saddles and packs.

When the sun was high in the heavens, White came from his store and invited the three men in for something to eat. In a back room they saw a young Indian woman preparing food over a fireplace. She continued stirring the food in the kettle as Peter White showed his guests to the table, seating them on the hewn benches. From a shelf he got a plate each and a tin cup, into which he poured a generous portion of whisky.

"The lifeblood of the fur trade," he said, "the Indians love it. They live for it and they die for it. And it kills them too, almost as fast as the smallpox."

He spoke to the Indian woman at the fireplace. Still with her back to them she reached and took the pot off the hook, and turned towards them. The light from the window by the table showed a face of almost ivory hue, with dark brown eyes framed by shiny curly blue-black hair. When she saw the three visitors watching her she smiled, revealing a set of gleaming white teeth. A simple cotton trade dress that reached almost to her ankles was gathered around the waist by what appeared to be a fine rope woven of different colors of cedar bark contouring a shapely figure in the first full bloom of womanhood.

It took a second look for young Edwards to note the type of rope holding the dress snug around the waist of the young woman. He breathed deeply.

"She's a pretty one, alright," Peter White said. "But don't do anything but look at her, for she's all mine. I picked her out of the village. I taught her to speak English. Taught her to cook, too. She taught me some things, too," he chuckled. "It's a good deal."

His guests paid attention to their meal, which was a stew of potatoes, carrots and a meat which the sappers did not recognize.

"It's beaver," Peter White said. "Here, have some more salt on it. It tastes better a bit salty."

"Hum grease," he said to the Indian woman. She placed a plate of crystaline grease on the table, along with some ship's biscuits.

"This is eulachon grease," Peter said. "It's the Indian's butter, his gravy and his syrup. He just about lives on it. Here, try some of it on your biscuit."

The visiting white men smeared a small portion on their biscuits. It had a strong rancid smell and a heavy, greasy taste. Breckenridge almost gagged on it.

"Hum Grease — that's Chinook for strong smelling grease," White laughed. "The eulachons are a small fish, something like a herring. Every spring about the first of April they appear in the river in hordes — so many of them the river turns black. The Indians catch them in nets by the millions, store them in vats for a week or two to ripen and then they render the fat off by cooking them in big boxes. They heat rocks and dump them into the big boxes full of fish. The fat comes to the top and they scoop it off and put it in other boxes and store it.

"It's quite a time. If it's been a hard winter, it's the first real abundance of food again. There's a gathering of the tribes in river mouths like this one. Tribes from the outer coast, and tribes from the interior come down over the grease trails to eat and trade and make war and make love. Maybe it wasn't too bad before white men came along with his liquor, but now, Holy Mother!"

He stopped for a moment, rolled his eyes.

"I came here last year, just in time to get this shack up and start trading for the winter's catch of furs, when the tribes began to come down from the top country, and canoe loads of them came in from the islands. The population of the village just about doubled. You'd see the local natives out in their canoes on the river driving stakes in the riffle. Then they'd attach a purse-seine net between pairs of stakes. When the fish came up the river the rising tide would carry them up the riffles, then, when the tide went out the fish would be carried out, a lot of them being caught in the nets. In the morning the bucks go out and collect the fish. A whole canoe load may be caught in one net. A ton or two.

"You know, it's quite a sight. The seagulls are so thick you'd think it was a snowstorm, and they are screaming and complaining around. Those dark boys with their canoes might have been spawned in the river, themselves. They skim over the water and disappear into the shadows against the rising sun, and suddenly you wonder if you had seen them at all, or if you were only dreaming.

"When the fish are caught, and the feasting starts and the Indians get wild with drink, the whole tribe could kill each other off. It's a wild country! Last spring they bought me right out of liquor. I could have made twice as much if I'd been smarter and got more supplies in, or if I had not been so generous in trading. Three men were killed in one of the drunken fights they had."

Peter White had not heard that in September of 1858, almost four years previously, when the colony of British Columbia was scarce a month old, Governor Douglas had issued a proclamation forbidding the gift or sale of liquor to Indians. In one of the brief breaks in the flow of White's conversation Breckenridge told him of this.

The trader studied Breckenridge for a moment.

Left: Sir Alexander Mackenzie.

Below: The Bella Coola Valley, looking eastward, with Mount Noosatsum dominating the scene. Photo – Leslie Kopas.

Left: The inscription painted on Mackenzie's Rock in Dean Channel, about 40 miles west of Bella Coola.

Below: A view of the Bella Coola Valley from across the inlet.

Above: Mae Lake, 1940. High in the Coast Range near Bella Coola, this alpine lake is typical of the spectacular scenery of the region. Mae Kopas, pictured here, is the lake's namesake and wife of photographer and author, Cliff Kopas.

Right: Mount Noosatsum, which the Nuxalk people called Noosgultz, just above the Big Village.

Left: Mount
Noosatsum and a
'slough' of the
Bella Coola River.

Below: God's
Goblet and
Thunder
Mountain on the
north side of the
Bella Coola Valley.

"A law for British Columbia is alright for Victoria and the Fraser River," he said, revealing that behind his friendly chatter, a hard-headed analysis of the situation was going on. "Those fellows down there haven't time to think of a half dozen or a dozen white people away out here. Except when the *Labouchère* makes her calls, we're on our own. I'll sell liquor as long as I have it."

In a few minutes the men rose from the table.

Edwards stepped across the room to where the young Indian woman was washing some dishes.

"Thank you for the meal," he said. Then drawing a scarf from around his neck, he gave the bright cloth to the woman. "Here, take this."

The Indian woman looked at him in surprise but took the gift.

Across the room Peter White turned livid with anger.

"Damn you," he shouted. "I told you to stay away from my woman. You go over to the Indian village and get one for yourself."

Nonplussed for a moment, Edwards turned to his angry host.

"No offence, sir," he said primly as if addressing an officer, "I wished only to pay for the fine meal I have received,"

"That's fine," White returned, "but leave my woman alone." Then suddenly calming he said, "Let's forget it."

Late that afternoon White arranged two canoe loads of goods to be sent up the river with Indian canoe men. Helping him, because they had finished their assignments, were the two Sappers. White was his talkative self again, and the incident of the scarf apparently forgotten.

"You should take canoes up the river to Barron's camp," he said. "The Indians do it in about eight hours with a loaded canoe. The trail is a quagmire in places and it will take you three or four days with horses."

"If we know the lieutenant, it will take us longer than that," Breckenridge replied. "He's a thorough one. He has to see the other side of every hill and get the contours down on paper."

Next morning the party with four saddle horses and four pack horses started up the valley. It was a sunny morning and a half dozen natives had gathered at Peter White's store to watch the departure. As the small pack train disappeared into the shadows of the forest they questioned Peter White about his late visitors.

"Boston men, those people?" they asked. The Indians had learned that the white men visiting the valley were mostly of two different loyalties, either Britishers or Americans. The Britishers to them were King George men, while the Americans were Boston men. They recognized Peter White as a Boston man because he was from the United States, even though San Francisco, his home, was a continent away from Boston. When White told them the Royal Engineers' party was British, they asked about its errand.

"Make hunt for wagon road?" they said. "Why for they hunt? Hiyu white man already go that way." Hiyu was Chinook word for many, and the Indians could not understand that with so many white men having gone over the trail to Alexandria, another party had to go simply to inspect the route.

"Crazy white men," they summarized, laughing.

In the forest the "crazy white men" were being initiated into the trials that awaited them in this lush rain jungle. The trail was merely a slightly improved version of the footpath Mackenzie had trod seventy years ago. For the Indians the trail was an alternate route to their main highway, the river. When white men started using the trail for horse travel they cut out some of the smaller trees and went around the larger ones. In the lower areas in the forest, the water level, which rose in the summer with the river level, was almost at the surface of the ground. Previous passage of many horses had broken the surface crust and churned the mud into a quagmire laced with tree roots. The trail became a nightmare for the men and beasts of the Palmer party. Horses were mired down, had to be unpacked and laboriously extricated from the mud. Where large trees had fallen across the trail, and no way could be found around them, smaller trees had to be cut and piled against the larger trunk, parallel with it in such a way that the horses could walk up over the large trunk. Where side-streams flowed from lateral valleys they spewed wide alluvial fans with occasional huge boulders that lamed the horses in their passage. At times laborious detours were necessary to find a crossing of a swollen stream. Grass was not abundant and travellers found it necessary to stop frequently to let their horses crop any small patches of grass they came upon.

At the same time Lieutenant Palmer spared no effort in gathering information for his subsequent report on this as a road route. Portions of this report were published in New Westminster by the Royal Engineers Press in 1863, and state:

The Nookhalk Valley, which averages from one-half to one

and a half miles in width, opening out considerably at the confluences of the principal tributaries, is walled in by giant mountains of from two thousand to six thousand feet in height, presenting the usual varieties of scenery met with in mountain travels in this country. Some of the slopes, particularly those between Soonochlim and Nookeetz, are perfectly devoid of soil, timber, or covering of any kind, and rise very abruptly from the valley, massive, unbroken walls of granite and trap in stupendous contrast to the forest scenery on the river bank and islands.

The line of the most elevated crest of the Cascade Range crosses the Nookhalk near Nooskultst, 22 miles from its mouth, maintaining apparently a direction parallel to the general coastline. But although a principal crest, this is by no means a principal watershed, for, in these latitudes, the rains and snows which fall on either slope of the range are quickly conducted to the Nookhalk and the other similar arterial streams near the coast, and restored by the most direct path to the sea. Two peaks of this range, Mt. Pope and Mt. Deluge, standing on opposite sides of the river and respectively about 5000 and 6000 feet in height, attract attention by their massiveness and their superior altitude.

Other magnificent mountains and clusters of mountains are met with on the journey, embracing most of the elements of grandeur that can be imagined in scenery of this description, and the numberless waterfalls which are seen in many parts, though more particularly towards the upper end of the valley, and which, on the melting of the snow, precipitate themselves in considerable volume down the crannies and crevices of the mountain sides, are worthy of notice as adding much to the sublimity of the scenery.

Names and altitudes have changed somewhat since Palmer's report. What he called the Nookhalk Valley and Nookhalk River have become the Bella Coola Valley and Bella Coola River. The two peaks he called Mt. Pope and Mt. Deluge became Mt. Saloompt and Mt. Noosatsum and their altitudes have been determined to be 6138 feet and 8444 feet. The mountains that hem in the Bella Coola Valley are known to have altitudes of from 6000 to 9000 feet rather than from 2000 to 6000 feet as he suggested.

They stayed overnight at Boat Encampment, where they crossed to the north side of the Bella Coola River. Men and goods were ferried by Indian canoe while the horses swam, snorting and blowing. Once across, the horses were rubbed down and their backs given a short time to dry, before the packs were replaced and the journey resumed.

The second day from the river crossing they unwittingly rode between a mother grizzly bear and her two cubs. The horses had given warning of the presence of the ursine family by snorting and prancing in distress; but since their horses had occasionally done that before and investigation proven that it was only because of the smell of carrion, the men paid little attention.

Now, a sound of scratching in a tree beside the trail attracted their attention.

"There's a bear cub," one of the men cried. "No, two of them!"

Then from the other side of the trail came an enraged roar, and a large bear, with its ears back and froth flying from its mouth as it champed and snapped and snarled, came tearing out of the bushes. The horses, three of which bore packs and were allowed to travel free, bolted. The saddle mounts took the bits in their teeth and for a moment or two there was a scene of the most violent confusion. The pack on one of the horses rolled and as the animal fled it bucked and kicked until it had scattered the pack and its contents along the trail.

Fortunately the mother bear was content to drive these humans away from her family. As soon as she had done this she spanked the cubs as they made their way in the opposite direction and disappeared.

The men were busy for an hour collecting the scattered goods, repairing gear and repacking.

They came to the confluence of the two main tributaries that join to form the Bella Coola River, the Talchako (or White-water River) and the Atnarko River. The Talchako River flows in from the southeast, being born under Talchako Glacier some twenty miles distant on the lofty sides of 11,714-foot high Mount Monarch. From these glaciers it emerges a small trickle in the winter but in the summer it is a formidable silt laden stream that creates the major flow of the Nookhalk.

At the confluence of the Talchako and the Atnarko Lieutenant Palmer wrote:

"At Shtooiht, a small Indian village situated in the heart of piles of majestic but strikingly bleak and forbidding mountains, the trail leaves the Nookhalk and travels up the Atnarko, a large clear-water tributary, here nearly equal in size to the Nookhalk. The latter river, which from this point upwards received the Indian name Talchako, runs in from a southeasterly direction, its course being traceable for about ten miles."

Shtooiht was the uppermost point of practical navigation, even for the skilled Bella Coola Indian canoe men, and except for summer fishing camps, there were no more Indian villages in the valley. The stream was rapid and picturesque, and the valley floor rose rapidly. The journey from Bentinck Arm to Shtooiht, Palmer describes as the first section of his journey; from Shtooiht to the Great Slide, fourteen miles distant, the second section of the journey.

"Here the first serious obstacles to road making are met with," he wrote of the Atnarko valley. "From the crossing of the Cheddeakulk to the foot of the Great Slide, mountains crowd closely in upon both sides of the stream; frequent extensive slides of fragmentary trap rocks of all sizes run either directly into the river, or into the low, swampy lands bordering it, which are liable to inundation at the freshets, and the Indian trail which winds along their faces is difficult and almost dangerous for travel. These slides vary from 300 to 600 feet in height, and are capped by rugged cliffs extending to an average altitude of 1500 feet above the river, and, since they are unavoidable, the labour of trail-making between Shtooiht and the Great Slide will be considerable and entail a probable expense of 1000 pounds."

Eight miles above Shtooiht at Taparntowoot, Palmer camped. The day had been a bad one. Where the trail wound over some rough rocks on the hill side the pack train had disturbed a nest of hornets, and when the yellow-jacketed balls of fire struck the horses, each one of them turned into a kicking plunging bronco. Packs were scattered and men kicked. Several hours were lost as a result of this incident and the eight-mile journey took six hours to accomplish. As soon as he had eaten, Lieutenant Palmer walked ahead along the trail to reconnoitre. He found fallen timber and rocks.

"Tomorrow," he announced on his return to camp, "we will take minimum requirements on our backs and proceed afoot. The packer will wait until the pack train from Barron's store comes through, and bring the horses and the rest of our baggage in their company."

Thus far they had travelled 57 miles from North Bentinck Arm and the time consumed was eighteen days. Palmer blamed the slow progress on three causes: bad weather, trouble with natives and the difficulties of the route. He was by nature a pedestrian so that the troubles into which horses got themselves and the party were magnified by his prejudices against them as a mode of travel.

The next morning, July 27, they commenced the climb from the

Atnarko Valley to the summit of the Precipice. It was the third section of the journey, and one of great exertion.

From Cokelin (or Taparntowoot) he described the broken country from there to the Bella Coola (or Atnarko) Valley:

At Cokelin, 1110 feet above the level of the sea, famous among the natives for its raspberries, which grow in great profusion, the trail leaves the Atnarko running about southeast, and strikes to the northward, directly up the face of the Great Slide, at a high angle of elevation. The slide, similar in character to those frequently met with in mountains, though perhaps the stones composing it are smaller than is usual, is simply a mountainside of disintegrated trap rock about one mile in length, forming the northern slope of the valley of the Atnarko, and separated from the slides lately passed by the glen of a mountain torrent. The height of the actual loose rock is about 1120 feet, the barely discernible trail wriggling almost directly up the face in would-be zigzags bitterly trying to pedestrians. Above this it is lost among cliffs and hollows dotted with small timber, and rises more gradually until, 5 miles from Cokelin, an altitude of 1780 feet (2890 feet above the sea) is attained.

Corresponding to this increased elevation is the change in the character of the vegetation and the scenery. The trail now emerges on an elevated, rolling district, where the mountains, with whose summits we are nearly on a level, seem of inconsiderable height and lose much of their rugged appearance. Small, stunted firs take the place of the large pines and cedars of the valleys; the trail, though here and there rocky, improves, the soil becomes sandy and light but firm, brush less plentiful, and grass, though of poor quality, appears in patches.

Down by a gradual descent of 500 feet to the brook Hotharko, a tributary of the Atnarko, and up its valley 7 miles in an east-north-easterly direction to its forks, meeting with no serious obstructions but fallen timber and occasional small rocky slides. The space between the forks of the Hotharko, which run in southeasterly and west-northwesterly directions, is occupied by a peculiar mountain mass of basaltic rock, 1350 feet in height, which has received the name "The Precipice." The ascent of this mountain is excessively steep, the trail at first running up the backbone of a singular spur, farther up winding among crumbling fragments of rock, and, finally, reaching by a dizzying path the summit of the perpendicular wall of rock, 100 feet high, which crowns the mass, and from which it derives its name.

The cliff is composed of blocks of columnar basalt in the shape of multiangular prisms averaging, in their perfect state, about two cubic feet in size, usually stained of a dull red color and somewhat vesicular. , The blocks are fitted together as perfectly as if by human agency, and the layers are horizontal; thus, on the summit, which is perfectly level, patches are met with in which, the scant soil having been washed away, the jointing of these singular stones, almost resembling mosaic pavement, is clearly visible; and, towards the edges of the cliff, large portions of the rock have crumbled away, leaving standing in many places abrupt, columnar masses of as much as fifty feet in height, which, viewed from a short distance, assume the appearance of massive artificial and battlemented structures.

If a trail be made over North Bentinck Arm route, the two serious obstacles spoken of in this section, viz: the Slide and the Precipice, may be easily avoided — the former by not leaving the Atnarko until reaching the mouth of the Hotharko, the latter by following the south fork of the Hotharko and attaining the level of the Precipice at any easy inclination.

They followed the Indian trail, recently cut deeper by the passage of the Barron pack trains, up the gradual climb of the valley southeast of the Precipice and came in several days to the large Indian village where the Dean River flows out of Nimpo Lake.

A clamor of dogs announced their arrival, and as they walked into the village they were surrounded by a group of tall, athletic Chilcotin Indians.

"You trade?" one of the Indians asked.

"No, we don't trade," Lieutenant Palmer said. "We are looking out a road route."

"Root?" the Indian queried. "You mean road grows from it?"

"Maybe," Palmer replied. "Now we would like to buy some fish." He pointed to the long rows of fish being smoked by the women.

"You got rum?" the Indian asked.

"No rum. Gold. Make road."

"We give you fish."

"No give," Palmer said. "We buy."

They were at the Indian village of Nancootloon, on the shores of Nimpo Lake. The Indians had constructed a fish trap at the outlet of the lake, and because of the wealth of food thereby derived had become one of the most important villages away from coastal waters.

When the white men asked for fish, they were loaded with as many as they wished to carry for a small gold piece.

As they proceeded on their way they ascended the gradually sloping Dean River Valley, turned their backs on the huge backdrop of coastal mountains and dropped to Punzi Lake.

At Punzi Lake they realized that their trials were almost over. They had yet a hundred miles to go to Fort Alexandria, but it was a country of rolling hills. There were white men everywhere looking for gold. The trail was well marked, the terrain gentle. A boat would take them across the Fraser River.

It was Lieutenant Palmer's task to compile a report on the Bentinck Arm route into the gold fields. He had made an exacting examination of the route as they travelled. He and his men had experienced difficulties and had overcome them. There were two obstacles only to the building of a wagon road from Bentinck Arm to Alexandria, and Palmer had pointed out a detour around each.

Rumor grew that the government was going to build a road from Bella Coola to Alexandria, then a distribution centre, the capital of the fur trade.

The importance of Fort Alexandria, its people, its very buildings, was to disappear before a wagon road existed. And when the road was brought into being it was not the government but the brood of the Thunderbird that mothered and nurtured it.

The Royal Engineers had put the Bentinck Arm road on the map, then destroyed the need for it to be built. They built instead a road through the Fraser Canyon in 1862 and 1863 and all other routes died of neglect.

4 Overland to Bella Coola – 1862

The excitement concerning the Cariboo gold fields rose and fell with the years. It was at its peak in 1862. During that year interest was fanned vigorously by transportation companies who, events showed, were advertising extravagant claims about the ease of getting into the Cariboo. Farmers, doctors, clerks and schoolteachers sought routes to get to this land of glowing gold.

Three main avenues were offered:

(1) By train to New York, thence by ship to the Panama Canal Zone, across the Isthmus of Panama by rail, thence again by ship up the Pacific Coast. River steamers ascended the Fraser as far as Yale from which transportation to the Cariboo was by wagon road.

(2) By train and boat to St. Paul, thence across the prairies of the United States, over the Oregon Trail, then up the coast by steamer to British Columbia.

(3) By train and boat to St. Paul, by stage to Georgetown, by river steamer to Fort Garry, thence a long trek across the Canadian prairies to Fort Edmonton, through the mountains to the Fraser River down which argonauts could float to the gold fields.

The first one was the most costly, and the second the most dangerous because of the possibility of Indian attacks. The third, particularly from Edmonton westward, was virtually unknown, but because it was from Fort Garry, the end of public transportation, entirely in Canadian territory and through the domain of friendly Indians, it appealed to many Canadians.

In the spring and summer many hundreds of gold seekers augmented the population around Fort Garry as they prepared for the long struggle across the prairies and through the mountains. Of the initiation of city men into the ways of oxen, the vagaries of weather and the savagery of mountain rivers, many stories have been told. The survivors of these overland trips to the Cariboo gold fields could have authored many for every day they were subject to circumstances new to them. They pioneered paths that were to be used by millions — or discarded as being too hazardous. They faced death by starvation, they froze, and some drowned in the raging rivers of British Columbia. A few turned back, and a few stopped east of the Rocky Mountains to try their fortune in seeking the gold that was reported in the North Saskatchewan River.

Of those who did win through, many did not even take a look at diggings; others took a quick glance only, and almost all joined the throngs of miners who were leaving the mining territory to escape the harsh winter that was imminent. Victoria and New Westminster offered winter homes to some of these, but others returned to their homes in distant places. Some sought out the area of the gold fields the following spring, established homes and laid the base for permanent settlements.

The first major party to come through from Ontario and Quebec had separated at Tête Jaune Cache into a party attempting to drive their livestock through the Cariboo mountains and another one which, with several casualties, ran the Fraser River with rafts as far as Quesnel. They arrived there on the afternoon of September 11, 1862.

We pick up the report of James Young, a newspaper correspondent from Ottawa who accompanied the expedition partly to dig gold and partly to write the story of the trip. The following pages are quoted from Young's account:

> That afternoon we saw groups of Chinese working in the river gravel, panning gold, and that night we moored near one of their camps. When we asked them if they were making any money, their replies were noncommittal.
>
> We romped through the really dangerous waters of China Rapids and Cottonwoods Canyon and meandered among gravel bars and shallows and arrived at Quesnel on the afternoon of Thursday, September 11th. We had started from Tête Jaune Cache on September 1st.
>
> That evening, for the first time in many months I ate with my feet under a table. There was quite a settlement at Quesnel, with

two stores, and many eating houses and some number of small cabins for miners, and huts of the Indians. It was the first settlement west of Fort Garry that was not built for and dependent on the fur trade. And it was the first time since leaving Fort Garry when there was an abundance of food. Considering that food had to be hauled by primitive means for over four hundred miles from New Westminster, prices were not bad. Flour was fifty cents a pound, tea $2.00 a pound, bacon 75 cents to a dollar a pound. And I got a big meal for $1.50 at one of the stores.

We are at last at the door of the Golden Cariboo.

But no one called it that. Most of the men were returning from the mines broke, soured and were making their way on foot back to the coast to escape the rigors of what were reputed to be terribly severe winters.

Friday was a day of argument and decision. All but four of us decided to go to Victoria without even looking at the mines. I was among the four to stay.

Of the four of us who decided not to rush for the gentler climes of the coast without taking a look at the mines, there was A. L. Fortune, who throughout the trip had been a quiet leader or a supporter of the leader, and the two brothers James and William Wattie, and myself.

We managed to find an abandoned log hut and stayed there overnight. The next morning William Wattie decided to remain at Quesnel rather than accompany us to the gold mines.

"I am going to talk to some of these men and see what I can learn second-hand. I'll have a good pot of mulligan on the fire when you come back."

There were four of us started, nevertheless. The fourth member was James Wattie's ox which he had bought at Red River and which had accompanied him through all vicissitudes of prairie, mountain and river travel. We packed our supplies on his back and he followed along as steadily as a well-trained dog.

The trail might have been good in the beginning but so much travel had gone over it that in the low places it was a miry waste. Occasionally we had to wait while strings of horses and mules met and passed us.

"How are things at the mines?" we asked, and what we were told was in direct support of what we had learned at Quesnel. It seemed the Golden Cariboo was only a myth.

The most exciting meeting was the second day out when around a bend in the trail appeared a string of six camels. We had heard their grunting and their shuffling a moment or two before their appearance and had been trying to label the sound.

We were surprised at this near apparition but our poor ox was terrified. After gazing at the approaching animals — and it was amazing how speedily they moved — a whiff of their odor came to us. Our poor ox let out a bellow of terror and fled precipitously into the woods, crashing into trees and scattering his pack.

We took after him in mad pursuit, probably to the entertainment of the drivers of the camel-train, and when we had overtaken our ox and collected our scattered goods, the camels were no longer to be seen. But the ox still snorted in dislike and fear when an occasional whiff of the vile-smelling animals came to his nostrils. We learned later than an enterprising German, Launmeister, had imported the camels with the idea that the beasts could out-pack and out-travel mules, horses and oxen. He was correct, but the sight and smell of the camels struck such terror into the other beasts using the trails that he was beset with lawsuits and eventually turned the camels loose.

That evening we came upon the camp of two men who were feeding a large herd of cattle on the range, and decided to leave our ox with them. Next morning the ox was peacefully eating with his kind when we shouldered our packs and continued our way to the mines.

We spent eight days among the mines, visiting the miners. Some of them talked freely, some were reticent. All wore the signs of hard toil, and their cabins were little more than dark huts. One miner who had struck it very rich had his wife with him. But he was a very unhappy man, this man, Cariboo Cameron, for he had lost his only child, an infant daughter, less than a year ago and now his wife was very ill.

"It's no country for a woman," one miner told us. "If you aren't anchored to a good claim, get out of here yourself. Why, the temperature drops to fifty or sixty below zero, and the snow piles up six feet deep. Man, we have to live like we was crossed with a ground-hog but had lost his coat of fat and his hairy skin to protect us. I'm right sure no sane ground-hog would change places with us."

Because we didn't have a mine to anchor to, nor a layer of fat, nor suitable supplies for a winter in this dread spot, we turned our faces again to Quesnel.

"You know," Mr. Fortune stated emphatically after we had been around the mines for four or five days, "I am convinced that this is indeed a golden Cariboo. There is gold here. But it takes work and courage and luck to get it. Few will succeed. Many will fail, but tens of thousands will try."

Just to show us the fates might not smile on us, we awoke to a heavy snowfall on September 27th. We hurried our departure.

Our return to Quesnel was faster than our outward trip. We picked up the ox from his bovine friends, and were back outside the hut in one day less time than we had taken in going to the mines.

A halloo brought James Wattie to the door, a cry of welcome to his lips.

"Come into your castle, returning knights," he cried, "and report!"

He had acquired some rough-sawn boards and had built a table and two benches against one side of the hut, and two sets of bunks against the walls so we didn't have to sleep on the earthen floor.

The table and benches were particularly appealing, for civilized man does not readily take to continuously sitting on the ground. One of the delights of returning to civilization is to sit at a table, however rough it may be. James busied himself preparing food while we talked.

"I got a job whipsawing some lumber for a fellow and doing some carpentering for a couple of days. He paid me partly in lumber, so here we are, snug as beavers."

When we gave him our report of the trip to the mines, and our decision not to stay in this northland over winter, he came forward with some information that changed the course of our lives for the next several months and led to some almost incredible adventures.

"There's a man in Quesnel here, a storekeeper, who packs in his supplies from North Bentinck Arm on the coast about three hundred miles west of here. He has a trail and he says it is a lot better way than most of the people use, down by Lillooet and the Fraser River. Maybe we should go that way. We could go see this man. His name is Barron."

So we went to see Mr. Barron in his store. Between serving customers he told us of the trail to Bentinck Arm.

"The trail goes west from Alexandria, south of here," he said, "and is well marked because of the many horses that have travelled it. There are quite a few people coming and going, so you might be able to replenish supplies and maybe even have company once in awhile.

"Since I did considerable trail work, it has been called the

Barron Trail up until the last little while. Now an engineer, a Lieutenant Palmer, has surveyed it and some people call it the Palmer Trail.

"And in the last week I have heard that the government is going to build a wagon road through North Bentinck Arm. It will certainly avoid a lot of scary travel through the Fraser River country. It's a much better way."

Mr. Fortune was the leader of our little group. When he stated that he would like to see this new part of the country, we expressed our desire to go with him.

"Be cautious in the Chilcotin country," Mr. Barron cautioned us. "The Chilcotin Indians are a proud, tumultous bunch and trouble is brewing. One of these days there is going to be an explosion and there are going to be people killed ... and they won't all be Indians. The Hudson's Bay established a post at the junction of the Chilcotin and Chezko River some thirty-five or forty years ago and gave it up after ten years. If the Hudson's Bay Company can't make it stick, it's a pretty tough country!"

The next morning we were busy at daybreak constructing a raft big enough to float our four selves, our faithful and fearless ox, and two passengers who wanted to ride with "capable river men." Our adventures in coming down the Fraser River had been told around, and we were looked upon as experienced men. One of the Indians who came down with us from Fort George kept pointing us out and saying "Skookum Tum Tum" which is the Chinook for strong mind or brave mind.

We charged our passengers ten dollars each and sold our raft for thirty dollars after an uneventful six-hour ride from Quesnel to Alexandria on Saturday, October 11th.

The next day we attended church service held by the Rev. John Sheepshanks in the fort on the west side of the river. Alexandria, the fort established at the southern point at which Alexander Mackenzie had reached in 1793, was almost a capital of this territory of New Caledonia. Canoe brigades came down from the tremendous country at the headwaters of the Fraser River and the furs were transferred to pack horses and taken south by way of Kamloops and the Okanagan route. The same pack animals brought back the supplies needed in the northern posts. A large Indian village of some five hundred souls sprawled on either side of the river.

On Monday, with our few, very few, worldly goods packed on our ox, we waved good-bye to the people with whom we had become acquainted and climbed the long, high hill to the plateau stretching endlessly westward.

Beyond the plateau was a warm, lush coastal valley ending at the head of a long bay. Into this bay, called variously "Bella Coola" from the tribe of Indians living there, nostalgically "New Aberdeen" by the white people, "Bentinck Arm" by marine explorers or "Mackenzie's Outlet" because the explorer had reached the Pacific there, ships came with supplies to be hauled over the trail we were following. This bay was our destination.

Our conditions now were markedly different. Indians, we were told, would be a menace. When we had travelled through Indian territory on the prairies, we had been a considerable force. Now, numbering only four, diplomacy and evasion were to be our weapons.

For the first few days nothing exciting happened. The trail was indeed well marked and ran across an elevated plateau of large open tracts and dense forests of pine and fir. There were clumps of deciduous trees also, but these had lost their leaves already, a reminder that winter was not far away. We believed we were making good time, as there was no bog, fallen timber or mountains to contend with.

The fourth day out of Alexandria we passed, late in the afternoon, a place where Indians had been camping and obviously catching fish in the nearby stream and drying them. The racks were still standing.

"I believe we have the Indians behind us," James Wattie said, after studying the camp.

We were shortly to be disillusioned.

Not an hour later we were following the trail through a dark copse of spruce trees. We crossed a stream, picking our way carefully from boulder to boulder, paying more attention to our footing than to our surroundings when I, in the lead, looked up and saw we were surrounded by a band of Indians. They were standing as still as statues watching our efforts to get across the stream dry-shod.

"Indians!" I said, loudly enough for my companions to hear.

"Don't hesitate," Mr. Fortune commanded immediately. "Show no surprise or fear."

So we continued our crossing, then marched right up to a giant savage clad in furs, with a brass ring in his nose and a long musket standing on the ground, its butt beside his moccasin-clad feet.

Mr. Fortune thrust out his hand. The chief, for we were sure this big savage was such, took it. Smiling slightly, he said,

"White man poor warriors."

"White man no warriors," Mr. Fortune said, emphasising the *no*. "We travel, we come as friends."

"No guns?" half asked, half stated the chief. Meanwhile, I had looked around. Ten tall, dark savages, each partly clothed in white man's garments, partly in long-haired fur that looked like wolf-skin, stood around, awaiting their chief's command.

"One little gun," Mr. Fortune said, drawing our one firearm, a revolver from his small pack. Handing it by the barrel to the chief, he turned his back on the savage, as if this encounter were as casual and harmless as mailing a letter. After a brief interval he turned back to the chief and held out both hands to show them empty, then withdrawing one hand, held out the other for his revolver. The chief gave it to him.

Mr. Fortune swung open the chamber, showing only one loaded cell.

"How far you come?" the chief asked.

Mr. Fortune told him we had been travelling since spring, that we had covered a distance of possibly four thousand miles.

"Skookum tum tum" the chief commented. "Come," he said.

We were taken to their village some half mile away, the chief leading his warriors behind us.

"Are we prisoners?" I asked James Wattie, walking near me.

"We will act as if we are guests," was his reply.

We were treated as guests. In their main village we were shown to the chief's house and there, around the fire were regaled with a feast of roast fish, berries and then haunches of what I first thought was sheep, but which had a different taste. The smell and the associated taste reminded me of dog.

"What kind of meat?" Mr. Fortune asked the chief.

"Leloo," the chief replied, then at our puzzled expression, "Wolf, Delate Klus."

We gathered that we were being treated to a delicacy, but we had to choke the meat down.

In the long evening talk we were informed that the Indians had spotted us at their fishing camp and had parallelled our course to the stream-crossing where they had waited while we walked literally into their musket barrels. But the fact that we did not seem concerned, that we had come a long way, and were leaving the country added up in our favor. We were well treated, and that night slept in the chief's house.

The next morning we went on our way, with our revolver and one round of ammunition, and our faithful ox. We did not ask the

Indians for food to take with us because we feared they might give us more of their delicacy.

The second day from the Indian camp we used the last of our flour; the last round of ammunition was expended in shooting a duck on which we feasted around our camp-fire that night. What we would eat the next day, we could not tell. If it came to a life and death matter, we could slaughter our ox.

The next day we had a small breakfast of oatmeal, and were feeling desperate about our situation when we saw coming across a meadow, late in the afternoon, a string of about twenty laden horses in the care of two riders. The train stopped when it met us at the edge of the meadow. We introduced ourselves and learned this was Barron's pack train from Boat Encampment in the Bella Coola Valley, en route to the gold fields.

The leader, a leather clad muscular fellow, introduced himself as Bob McLeod, his companion simply as "Slim."

"Better make camp with us tonight," Bob McLeod said. "Not too many people in this country."

"We haven't much food," Mr. Fortune said. "We'd like to buy some from you."

"Tonight the food is on our account. And tomorrow we'll sell you enough to take you through to Bentinck Arm."

They turned all their horses loose except their saddle horses, which they left saddled and picketed close by. We had an evening meal, deer liver and onions and bannock, with gallons of tea.

While we ate, Bob talked.

"Smallpox is a real killer out west. You'll run into it in a few days. Up by Nancootloon, where the Dean River leaves Nimpo Lake there once were four or five hundred real lively Indians. We used to worry about going by there, thinking they would way-lay us. But this time the only thing to be alarmed about was the smell. The ones that haven't died have run away into the hills to get away from the smallpox. Must be half of them dead, anyway."

We had scarce finished eating when he looked over the meadow.

"Company coming," he said. "Take back what I said about not being too many people in the country."

Coming across the meadow was a very tall man, walking rapidly, while behind him a few paces trotted two men with obviously heavy packs. The tall man in the lead had on his back a heavy pack also, from which protruded survey instruments.

"Palmer, the engineer," McLeod said. "Lieutenant Palmer to

ordinary fellows like us. And his two human pack horses. Palmer doesn't like horses."

When the three men approached our camp, McLeod invited them in for food.

"We are going to camp here, but we have food of our own," Palmer told the packer. McLeod went back to his mug of tea, scarcely glancing at Palmer's party as the two sappers set up a tent, and a table, before starting preparations for supper.

The two sappers came over to our camp when they had finished their duties and exchanged views.

"We're still tying down this road route from Bentinck Arm to Alexandria," one said. "I am beginning to know almost too much about this country. In fact, I'm beginning to like it."

One of them drew me to one side.

"You are going to Bella Coola," he said, and drawing a bright silk scarf from his pocket, added, "When you get there will you give this to the girl who cooks for Peter White?" When I looked puzzled, he explained, "Peter White is the storekeeper for Barron at Bella Coola. Don't let him know about this."

Of the mind that I was getting into a conspiracy, I accepted the scarf.

Before nightfall McLeod and Slim went out, retrieved all their stock, and tied them to trees about their camp. Then, each with a musket and revolver, made his bed outside the ring of horses. McLeod explained that they weren't afraid of Indians massacring them, but they did have to take precautions against them getting off with their animals.

Morning dawned clear and cold, and we went on our way, this time with our ox carrying enough food to see us through to Bella Coola.

That evening we came to the camp of a group of a half-dozen men who were putting up hay on the extensive swamp meadows for the wintering of the Barron pack horses. The man in charge was a soft-spoken man who introduced himself as Linn, and invited us to stay the night. Since they were putting up hay for wintering the stock, it made this a permanent ranch, the only one west of Alexandria. Their nearest neighbor, except Indians, was a hundred miles eastward at Alexandria, or a hundred miles westward in the Bella Coola Valley. We observed that they carried muskets with them.

"Maybe we're just trying to bluff the natives so they won't try anything," Linn said. "We'd be outnumbered a hundred to one if they ever got the idea that they wanted to clean us out. We hope that by being ready all the while we'll snuff out any such ideas."

We bought some powder and shot from them for our revolver.

We left our faithful ox with them the next morning. McLeod had told us, and Linn confirmed it, that there was no winter forage in Bella Coola.

"I can't guarantee he'll survive the winter here," Linn said. "It gets fifty-sixty below here and lots of stock dies. But we'll do our best."

We learned later that Bob McLeod and Slim were killed by the same Indians who had given us food and lodging for the night. Why the Indians let us pass and then attacked the pack train we supposed was the comparative wealth in food and liquor the horses were carrying. The murderers went unpunished.

We also learned that our ox didn't last long. About two weeks after we left him, some miners from the Cariboo came along, desperate for food — as we would have been had it not been for Bob McLeod — and finding the hay crew in bad straits, not knowing when more food might come (Barron's routine had become disturbed with the loss of one of his pack trains), killed our ox. Linn had protested but the miners had insisted that Fortune would not object, since it was to save human lives. They left $85.00 with Linn to get to Mr. Fortune for the ox. It was probably the most travelled bovine in British Columbia, having come all the way from Fort Garry.

We pushed on with heavy packs, over an undulating plateau, going through endless miles of pine forests and threading hundreds of meadows on our thin gossamer line of a trail. The days were brilliant autumn ones, with cold nights. There was ice in the ponds and streams. We frequently kept a fire going to keep warm.

One afternoon we were skirting the edge of a lake, on the other side of which rose a wall of snow-clad mountains, when a nauseating smell assailed our nostrils. A breeze swept the offensive smell away, and then when it dropped, we again smelled it. Puzzled, we walked along the trail, and came upon a large Indian village, of some twenty or thirty houses. No dogs appeared to warn the occupants of our approach, nor came any of the inhabitants to greet or question us.

We stopped at the sight of this silent village.

"We are approaching a village of the dead," said Mr. Fortune. "Look," and he pointed at two heaps of earth that looked much like a grave. But more demonstrative was a heap of brush piled over another Indian corpse, and beside this yet another partially wrapped in a blanket, his face turned to the sky and his shrunken eyes drawn into the skull. When I saw flies crawling over those sightless and decaying bodies I almost retched.

Speechless, we realized that this was Nancootloon. Bob McLeod had told us about it, but we had not been able to picture it.

The trail skirted the village, but as we moved on, Mr. Fortune said, "I am going to look in some of these houses."

We followed, and saw in many of the houses corpses that had been deserted when their owners were still alive. We saw signs of a fight against a relentless enemy, a sudden conquering fear, and a flight by all those who could flee, leaving their dead unburied, and their sick to become dead, uncared for.

Shortly we could stand no more, and departed as fast as we could. The trail turned around the north end of the lake and pointed to the snowy mountains.

At the north end of the lake the smell of wood-smoke caught our attention, and by a little stream a man sat by a fire in front of a brush hut. He was horribly pockmarked but there was no fever upon him. He had survived the tragic epidemic.

When he saw us he rose to his feet. He had a knife in his hand, and from the look of anger and hatred in his face, I wondered if he would attack all four of us.

"Cultus white man," he shouted. "Cultus white man bring smallpox, kill all my people."

We tried to talk to him, but without avail. Finally Mr. Fortune left some food for him and we departed, rather hurriedly, for an arrow in one's back was not desired. But the Indian was busy with the food and didn't use an arrow.

That afternoon we dropped down into a high valley which we traversed for several hours then descended rapidly a darksome canyon, so narrow that the trail had to cross the brawling stream a dozen times in order to make passage. At the bottom of this canyon we came out into a cathedral-like grove of huge fir trees. On the bits of shrubbery that grew at the bases of these tremendous columns, the leaves still clung, bright patches of red and yellow.

"It's warm," one of us remarked. "We must be in that long-sought coastal valley."

We camped, and next day followed a growing river down a widening valley under huge peaks hung with eternal ice. The trail was rough, and we camped under a huge cedar tree instead of reaching Boat Encampment, as we had expected from Bob McLeod's briefing.

Next day about noon we arrived where the trail stopped by the river bank. Across the stream were several buildings, some corrals and a clearing of some acres. We hallooed and a man came out of one of the buildings, stepped into a large skiff moored nearby and rowed over to us.

"My name is Alex McDonald," he said. "I have been expecting you."

We introduced ourselves, then asked, "Who could have told you we were coming?"

"Remember the Indian up on top you gave some food to, a couple of days ago? Well, he arrived here yesterday afternoon."

"But he looked pretty sick to us," we said, remembering open pustules.

"If they live through the climax, they recover in a hurry. He waited a whole day after you passed him. He travelled pretty fast, without a pack. Passed your camp before you were up yesterday morning."

He told us that there were several dozen Indians encamped around his store, and as many had died from smallpox.

"It's not my store," he said. "It's Barron's. The regular keeper is sick. He's got the smallpox too. If you've never had the stuff, maybe you had better not stay in our cabin. There's a couple of canoe-loads of Bella Coolas up here and for a little money they'd run you down to the water-front."

We didn't want to see any more smallpox so we engaged a crew of four Indians to take us down the river in their huge dug-out canoe for $5.00 a head.

When we were dickering with our crew a group of eight Indians stepped into another canoe and started out on the river. Some of them were so drunk they could hardly walk, but they did better with their canoe. It was more their natural habitat.

Our crew was sober, and we were amazed at how they handled their craft. Standing up, using a pole in the shallow parts, squatting to use a paddle in the deeper parts, they turned the grey dug-out log into a fleet and eager water-bird. We flew down a silvery avenue between banks of green conifers and golden, yellow deciduous trees.

We had to stop once in our flight. Our canoe captain, standing at the stern, gave a guttural command and the canoe turned swiftly to where three Indians were struggling for life. Our men hauled them aboard. The drunken Indians had not been as good on the water as we had thought and had caused their canoe to upset. Five were drowned.

Dark was already starting to flow into the low parts when we rounded a jutting point and looked at a bank of fog that was rolling in from the west. The moon, rising behind us in full autumn glory, painted the river and fog and trees into a picture of mystery. We plunged under the fog, which was beginning to erase the tree tops, and travelled as in a tunnel. Darkness was almost complete when our canoe turned into the bank and its bow grated on the gravel.

"This place, this man's house Peter White," our canoe captain said. "You call white man's talk."

We saw a building a few rods away from the river bank, the light of candles flickering yellow in the window pane. We hallooed and the light was extinguished. A door opened and a man's voice called, "Who is it?"

"Strangers," Mr. Fortune answered. "Four of us, from Alexandria."

"Come up," was the invitation.

We grabbed our packs and were scrambling up the path when a long mournful wail split the evening calm. Another joined the first and the forest and the river vibrated to the savage dirge. Several pairs of yellowish-green eyes caught the moonlight as their dark owners moved restlessly.

"Mother of God!" ejaculated William Wattie. "It's wolves!" and he pulled out the revolver and levelled it in the direction of the beasts.

There was a cry from one of our canoe men.

"Halo! Halo! Halo shoot!" and he dashed forward and struck Wattie's arm with such violence that the revolver flew into the bushes.

As Wattie gazed at the man in amazement, a voice called out.

"Get his gun and give it back to him, Billy!" and the Indian dived into the bushes and retrieved the revolver, then gave it to Mr. Wattie. We were all still dumbfounded by the turn of affairs, when the same voice came out of the shadow of the house, "Now, you fellows, come up."

Gathering our wits and our packs, we went in the direction of the voice. A shadow within the shadow moved, hinges squeaked slightly and we could smell the warm interior of the dwelling.

"Go on in, men, and we'll close the door behind us and light the place up."

When we had stumbled in, the door closed. There was a rattle of tin, and the light of two candles appeared as the man lifted a pail off them.

"Sorry to appear nervous about things like this," he said easily, "but I have an aversion to being silhouetted against the light. Somebody might just try out the sights of his musket about then."

While he was talking, he put shutters against the two windows. They were strong shutters, and I noticed then that the door was made of two-inch planks.

He introduced himself, "Peter White, agent for Barrons, and for James Furene. And you men?"

When we had introduced ourselves and told where we had come from, he whistled a low whistle and said,

"Maybe you should go out the channel and inscribe on a rock 'From Canada, By Land', same as MacKenzie did. And leave a few descendants in the place."

Then he bustled about preparing some food for us.

"Haven't got much of a variety," he said. "The boat has been overdue for a couple of weeks and we're reduced to salmon and whisky. Lots of that, though. Salmon is a local product and the Indians have been too busy dying to consume the usual amount of liquor."

"Smallpox?" we asked.

"Yes. If the white man wanted to kill off the Indian without much cost, he sure brought two number-one weapons in smallpox and whisky. This summer smallpox has cleared out entire villages. The biggest village in the whole valley, up by Noosegultz between here and Boat Encampment, has been cleaned out except for about a dozen people. And that was a village!"

He set food before us, potatoes and coffee as well as roast salmon and whisky which we attacked with a will. While we ate, he talked.

"Maybe the smallpox is good. It sure took a bunch of potentially bad Indians to where they won't do anything but raise a smell." (After Nancootloon we were not sure we liked that humor.)

"And whisky?" we prompted our host.

"The Indians love it," he said, "and it kills them. They have never developed a stomach for it, and the amount it takes to make a white man just glowing puts an Indian out. And he keeps right on drinking. He forgets to trap or fish and he's no good to himself or anybody else. There's been fifty deaths in the last two years from Indians burning their homes or drowning when they're drunk. And it's the main article of trade with them."

We asked him why the Indian canoe-man had stopped Mr. Wattie from shooting at the wolves.

"It's one of their beliefs that when someone dies he is re-incarnated as a wolf. Maybe you would have been shooting at Billy's brother or son or father. They never kill a wolf, and if he accidently gets killed in one of their deadfalls, they leave him right there, and that trap is never used again."

"Don't they ever attack the Indians?"

"Not if the Indian keeps on his feet. If he is down, then it is a different story."

We slept well that night, and awoke to a day that was to bring us to an amazing civilization. A "cedar and salmon civilization," Peter White called it.

Nearby was the considerable village of the Indians, the houses along the river in one single street, large houses built some six or eight feet from the ground, and housing three or four families, sometimes several generations. The houses were elaborately ornamented with carved posts. Several of the carved posts were so big that they formed the entrance of the building. Smallpox was in almost every house, and we avoided going in.

We learned why the wolves were around, and so numerous. One day we were walking along a path when we heard a little child crying piteously. We followed the sound and found the child, a mere baby, in a little brush shelter. It was horribly broken out with smallpox and seemingly deserted. We hurried back to Peter White, who by this time had become our mentor as well as our host, and asked him whether anything could be done about it. "Not a thing," he said tersely. "Unless you have enough vaccine to treat a whole tribe. Right now the only cure for smallpox is death. Tonight death will come to that poor little savage in the form of a yellow-eyed wolf."

We didn't sleep well that night. There seemed to be noises and rustling and the sound of crunching of bones outside the walls of the shack. Peter White's breathing continued steadily anytime the rest of us were awake and listening.

In the morning I was up a few minutes earlier than the rest, took the shutter off the window, and looking out, saw a horrible sight. An Indian lay on the ground twenty feet from the window, dead, very dead indeed. A blanket was lying near by and in the strengthening light I could see that the man had been disembowelled and partly eaten.

"Peter," I called. "Look outside."

Peter was pulling on his breeches. He looked out the window.

"Yeah, we'll have to get some of the braves to bury him. They might only throw him in a hole or stick him in a tree box."

"But how'd he get there, and what tore him open?" I queried, amazed at Peter's nonchalance.

"He probably died on my door-step last night. You heard some noises, didn't you?"

Peter had heard them, too, and with his knowledge had interpreted the noises, and had kept on sleeping, or trying to. "The Indians have the idea that they will go to their lushest paradise if they die on a white man's doorstep, or better still, right in his shack, and ever since this smallpox hit there has been an almost nightly seige of potential corpses crawling to my doorstep."

He sounded weary.

"The wolves do a pretty good job of cleaning up. Most of the time they leave just a few bones, maybe the skull. That poor buck out there didn't come early enough in the night to get properly disposed of."

That morning a canoe pulled into the landing and Alexander McDonald, the man whom we had met at Boat Encampment stepped out of the canoe.

"Bad news," he said, briefly. "Bob McLeod and Slim were jumped by the Chilicutneys the other side of Puntzi and killed. The whole pack train is lost."

Questioning revealed that both the killer and the killed had been our hosts a week or so ago.

"Why did they let us go?" we asked.

"You weren't worth robbing, maybe," suggested McDonald. "And the Indian grapevine tells that the chief was intrigued by your lengthy travels."

"Will the government try to apprehend the murderers?"

"We are too far away for the government to be interested in our troubles," Peter White said in a tone that indicated he had parroted this remark many times before. "They won't do a thing about it."

"But surely they will punish the murderers. No man's life will be safe."

"We are too far away," said Peter with finality.

Bob McLeod had been Alexander McDonald's cousin, and that afternoon Alexander left, up-river, to gather several companions and the best horses he could get to ride to the hay-camp at Puntzi, there to gain other companions and ride through to tell their employer at Quesnel the fate of the pack train and its attendants.

It must have been that afternoon, also, that we decided that the government had no plans to build a road through from Bella Coola to Alexandria. There was no sign of any plans at the Bella Coola end, and no reports by Indian grapevine.

Instead of waiting for a job to develop, we started watching for a ship to appear. The *Labouchère* was overdue from the North and Peter White hoped each day to see it come steaming up the inlet, for it would bring with it new supplies waiting for transhipment at Bella Bella.

When we had decided to go on the *Labouchère*, a commitment I had undertaken, that of delivering a scarf to a young Indian girl, was fulfilled. I had kept my ears and eyes opened but had not seen or heard any signs of the girl whom the sapper had said was White's housekeeper. Finally one evening I brought the scarf forth from my pack and told my errand frankly to White. He showed signs of mounting rage as I unfolded my story.

"Ha! I knew there was something between them," he said. "But he can't have her. Lord Smallpox took her. She was as red as an old coho before she died. Here, let's see the scarf," and almost snatching the scarf from my hand, he looked at it close, and crumpling it, threw it in the fireplace.

For another two weeks we waited for the *Labouchère* to come down from the North. We watched Peter White trading, and detected under his surface hardness an affection for the Indian. He studied him and sometimes even respected some of his better qualities.

There were two other men in shacks nearby, both of them conducting trade with the Indians, Angus Macleod and Jim Taylor. These men were heartless and cunning in their treatment of the Indians, considering them on the same basis as animals. They dealt in whisky, too.

"It'll only last a few years at the rate things are going," McLeod said, "and liquor and smallpox will have cleaned up the village. We are going to make some money while the going is good."

We stayed three weeks in Bella Coola. We saw the snowline of approaching winter come down the mountain, return again to treeline. The sun dipped behind the peaks and shone for brief hours through a glaciated gap, and disappeared. Finally with Peter White's assistance, we hired an Indian crew with their high-prowed sea canoe, and along with several other white men who had come through from Alexandria, we paddled down the channel to Bella Bella to intercept the steamer. At Bella Bella we learned, again by that incredibly swift and sure means of communication, the Indian grapevine, that the *Labouchère* had actually been seized by some Indians, the Chilkats, up north of the Stikine River. Captain Swanson and his officers were held at knife point while the crew was locked below. For two hours the Indians had command of the ship before leaving peacefully. The Chief of the Chilkats, as he stepped over the side of the *Labouchère* told Captain Swanson to leave immediately. The ship and its machinery had been unharmed, and Captain Swanson did as the chief advised.

When the ship didn't turn up at Bella Bella, we hired another crew, and this leg of our journey took us out onto the rolling open Pacific Ocean. We crossed Queen Charlotte Sound and arrived at Fort Rupert, where after a short wait, the *Labouchère* did indeed overtake us. We boarded her and eventually arrived at Victoria, the ultimate Mecca of British Columbia travellers.

Here the tale of travels across Canada must needs come to an end. At Bella Coola we had looked down a long arm of the Ocean, truly the Pacific. At Bella Bella we were several hundred miles west of Victoria, and in going from Bella Bella to Fort Rupert we had been most of a day on the open Pacific swells. Victoria, the largest civilized centre in British Columbia, and its commercial capital, offered the major amount of comfort, even though by eastern standards it was little better than a sprawling collection of huts, surrounding the Hudson's Bay Company's establishment.

Here we stayed.

5 Of Blood and Gold

The winter of 1862-1863 came early and with severity. The Bella Coola Indians were caught with empty cedar chests — they had not taken and smoked sufficient salmon because of their struggle with smallpox and liquor, and many, already weakened, died of starvation. When the run of eulachons came in the spring, a scant handful worked the nets and feasted and recovered their strength. More white people came to the Bella Coola Valley, and several of them were killed by the Indians — Robert McLeod, Sergeant Fisher, John Holmes, and a fourth, a German, whose name has been lost to history. A customs house was established at Bella Coola with a man named Wallace in charge.

Southward, events were taking place that might have spelled the doom of the infant settlement of Bella Coola.

The completion of the road up the Fraser canyon to the point where wagons could use it took the majority of the people going into the gold fields through New Westminster, and away from Victoria. This city felt the loss and one merchant, a man who came to the city in his fifties, Alfred Waddington, urged that a shorter land route to the gold fields be established from one of the up-coast inlets. There were several of these that came within two hundred miles of the gold fields and, if a road were built from one of them, it would give the miners quicker, cheaper access, it would lessen freight rates, and it would give trade supremacy back to Victoria.

The route Alfred Waddington preferred and promoted was from the head of Bute Inlet, up the Homathko River, past Tatlayoko Lake to Puntzi Lake, thence to Quesnel.

In the spring of 1862 Waddington's men, under Henry Teidemann, inspected the route from the head of Bute Inlet to the point where the Chilcotin River flows into the Fraser. The report arising from this inspection contained descriptions and measurements of one of the wildest mountain countries in all Canada. Some road work was done, but heavy fall rains carried out the bridges; and a deep blanket of snow in November smothered possibilities of further road work until next year.

In the spring of 1863, hobbled by financial difficulties, the endeavor carried on slowly and by the time work ceased in the fall a horse trail existed over the whole route. The contract, however, called for a wagon road sixteen feet wide rather than a six-foot pack horse trail.

In 1863 two of the traders at Bella Coola, Angus Macleod and Jim Taylor, disappointed in the return of a desperate winter among a band of Indians starving to death and dying of smallpox, went inland to Nancootloon. There, seeing the blankets on the graves of the Indians who had died of smallpox, they gathered them in, themselves immunized by inoculation, and sold them to the Indians again. The white men realized a tidy profit. Two hundred Indians died of the smallpox epidemic thus brought about, and the few survivors became careless of life and embittered toward white men.

In 1863 the mines of the Cariboo paid off richly and there was a marked increase in traffic over the Barron trail.

That fall, freshets carried away most of the bridges Waddington's men had built — more than forty of them — and unrelenting Mother Nature dropped another heavy blanket of snow on these men who dared invade this territory of huge mountains and roaring avalanches.

Through the winter of 1863-64 Waddington sold enough shares in the enterprise to give him sufficient capital to go ahead vigorously with his work. Lots were being sold in the townsite already surveyed at the mouth of the Homathko River.

In the spring of 1864 Waddington sent a crew of seventeen men into the canyon of the Homathko to proceed post haste with the execution of the road plans. At the same time a contract had been made with Alexander McDonald of Bella Coola to start building the road from Puntzi Lake by way of Tatlayoko Lake into the Homathko Canyon.

Harried by spring freshets but high with hope, the men worked with a will, replacing the bridges, building the road under the roaring snowfields. They were well equipped, even to muskets and revolvers. The latter they traded off to the Indians who had a camp nearby and who were hired to help the road-builders. The Indians had little by way of provisions, having to supply their own camp with food. The white men gave them some used tea leaves and scraps from the table. It amused the white men to see the Indians scrambling for scraps of food thrown them.

"Coyotes is what they are," one of the men said. "No courage! They are scavengers!"

There were some Indian women in the camps of the Chilcotins and these were frequently induced into the road builders' camp as hostesses, being sent home in the morning with a handful of food as payment for their services. Occasionally they were sent back empty-handed.

Late afternoon of April 29 Klattasine, a fierce looking chief of the Chilcotins, still wearing the wolf-skin garb of his ancestors and with a ring in his nose, and accompanied by two hunters, came out of the woods at the ferry operated by Timothy Smith of the road crew.

"We hunt," Klattasine said. "We hunt hard all day. No animals stop. You give us food?"

"No food," Smith replied curtly. "You dirty coyotes can die of starvation. This food is for white men."

Klattasine was a proud chief, and no insult greater than that of being called a coyote could have been given him.

"You white man, Cultus, delate cultus," he said, fury in his face. "You die!"

Seconds later Smith gasped out his life on the ground, blood frothing from his nose and mouth and pouring from the gaping hole in his chest where Klattasine's shot had torn it open. The big bored musket was horribly deadly at a distance of ten feet. As Smith died the Indian jumped on his head that his moccasins might be stained by the blood of the hated white man.

Klattasine and his companion left him where he lay, broke open the caches of food and carried a load into the forest to hide it. When about a half ton of provisions had thus been secreted, they ate briefly and, each with a small pack of plunder on his back, trotted up the road. After they crossed the river on the ferry, they cut it loose so that pursuit would be discouraged. They detoured around the camp of the white men, which they passed without detection and arrived, not un-noted, at the Indian camp several hundred yards away.

Without comment, Klattasine and his companion dumped their

packs at the feet of Tellot, the chief of the Chilcotins who had brought his people down to work on the road.

Tellot looked at the food, then hard at Klattasine.

"White man's food," he said.

"White man's blood," said Klattasine, holding up first one moccasined foot, then the other so that Tellot could see the reddish brown stains on the buckskin.

The Indians ate of the food and talked of their hatred of the white men, of the glories of their tribe before the white man came with his greed, his smallpox and devastation. As words mounted, so did the fire.

Suddenly Klattasine seized a hatchet, slashed his arm to draw blood, and smeared his face. Then he leaped high in the air screaming, and started a frenzied dance around the fire. At the end of the first round Tellot joined him, and by the end of the second circle twenty-five males were doing the war dance behind their chief.

The sound of their frenzy carried over the still night air to the ears of the thirteen white men who were resting after their day's labor.

"By dam," one of the white men said, "the Indians are howling tonight."

"Coyotes always howl when the moon is filling," said another scornfully.

"Do you suppose they would ever get up courage to attack us?" the first asked. "Do you think we should take turns at guard duty tonight?"

"Set up for guard duty against coyotes? Don't be crazy, man."

The spring night was cool and short. The river sang below and youthful cataracts leaped noisily down the mountainsides. Occasionally the rumble of a snowslide or the thunder of an icefall disturbed the silence.

Twenty-seven Indians, carrying hatchets and knives and with their faces painted with blood, did not make enough noise to disturb the other creatures of the forest, nor yet the little terrier, the pet of the white men, who sometimes received all the scraps of food so that the Indians had none. They made no noise while they surrounded the camp, so close to the tents that the sounds of snoring from several of the sleepers came to their ears.

Then, as the light of coming day started flowing down from the peaks, Klattasine and Tellot leaped out of the shadows, each with a musket in one hand and a hatchet in the other. Simultaneously, their arms went in the air, a mighty scream echoed by twenty-five other throats in the shadows springing from their lips. Falling hatchets severed tent ropes, and the canvas structures collapsed on the recumbent road-builders. Planned pandemonium resulted as twenty-seven men shot into bundles of heaving canvas, or struck blows with axe or knife. The excited screaming of the little terrier mixed with the cries of the Indians, the shouting of the trapped white men and an occasional heavy groan as a fatal thrust tumbled a man into oblivion.

A ridge pole fell upon one of the men, and protected him while on either side his companions were sliced to death. When the tide of activity ebbed for a brief second, he slipped from beneath the tent, tumbled down the riverbank and escaped. Another flung himself clear of the canvas shroud, dodged a flailing axe, downed his assailant with a blow in the face, received a bullet through the arm and leaped into the river and was swept along by its current. These two white men joined each other a half mile down stream.

A third white man, Irish Buckley, a sailor-turned-road-builder, awakened by the shouting and screaming, opened his eyes to see four knife-wielding savages almost astride him. Escape by flight being obviously impossible, he decided to play dead. This was done at the expense of his cheek being cut open by a hatchet-blade and several knife stabs in the ribs before his assailants went away. When it seemed he could stand no more, a command from the chiefs brought the Indians to attention. The chiefs spoke a few words and the Indians gathered up any arms that had been dropped and trotted in a group after them. Buckley lay for a few minutes listening intently for sound that would indicate a return of his attackers, but none came.

"May the good Lord who listened to my prayers from my mother's knee be with me now," he murmured. Cautiously he moved several feet, aware that the Indians might have left one of their number to keep guard. But no further attack came. As his hopes rose, he crawled faster, and reached a shadowed area. He applied some moss to his wounds to stop the bleeding, and finding a little rivulet he drank eagerly. Total quiet reigned in the camp. He crawled to his feet and found he had strength to walk, even run.

"Where have the Indians gone?" he kept pondering. Not to their camp, for they would have taken plunder with them. They were always hungry. They would have taken the food with them. Then suddenly the answer came.

Four miles up the stream Brewster, in charge of the road-making, and two companions had established a small camp and were doing some preliminary road-work. The Indians, Buckley knew, had gone to attack these men. A score or more against three, thought the Irishman. Maybe he could warn them, or help them. Too bad they had traded off their muskets and pistols.

He made his way quickly but with caution up the road, now merely a trail. When fatigue caused by wounds and loss of blood overtook him, he retreated into the woods to rest. It was during one of these periods that he saw the Indians, still travelling at a trot, return down the trail. They passed within a few yards of where he crouched behind a fallen tree.

"Have the devils done their murderous work?" he questioned as he saw them trot silently by. Their faces were smeared with blood and paint and he could read no story there.

But two hours later he did. Around a bend in the trail he came upon the mutilated bodies of Brewster and his two companions. Buckley had seen violent death before, but this sight nauseated him. The two companions had been killed . . . shot from ambush, Buckley thought . . . and their bodies slashed, but Brewster's body had been so mutilated that had it not been for clothing and the fact that he expected to see him, Buckley would not have recognized him. His throat had been cut so that the head was almost severed from the body, the cheeks had been cut so that all his teeth shone in the morning sun. His eyes had been pierced; and the body disembowelled, the entrails pulled out and spread on the ground.

Buckley turned away and removed himself from the scene.

"I've got to get out," he said, "or the bloody bastards will do the same to this mother's son."

Doubly cautious, he followed the trail back from whence he had come. When he approached his camp he could hear the sound of loud shouting from the Indians' camp. He listened, assessing the sounds.

"Celebrating their victory, the bloody murderers," he surmised, and made a big circle of the camp to regain, after careful study, the road below. "If they are holding a party, no one will be out on the trail," he thought, and forsook caution for a greater measure of speed.

As he approached the ferry, he saw two men leap into the bush. He recognized them as white men, even from the fleeting glimpse he had of them.

"It is I, Buckley," he called.

When he came to the spot where the two men had plunged into the woods, he stopped, and from their hiding place the two stepped forth.

"It's you, Peterson, and you, Mosley," he said. "Are we all that are alive?"

"Nobody else has shown up here," Peterson replied. "We can't raise Smith on the other side. We've been here for about three hours and haven't seen a sign of life."

"Maybe the Indians are making a general clean-up" — and Buckley told them of Brewster's fate. "We'd better get out of here if we want to save our own scalps."

"I hope you're good at swimming," Mosley said. "The raft is gone."

The cable was still intact. If the Indians had tried to cut it with their hunting knives they had given up the vain attempt. With a few scraps of line lying around, Buckley the ex-sailor rigged a sling which bore him across the river.

As he leaped to the bank on the far side, a prostrate human form lying on the ground drew his attention. It was Timothy Smith!

"Peterson said he didn't see a sign of life," he murmured as he covered Smith's face with a piece of cloth that was lying near by. "This is the reason."

When Mosley was over the river, followed by Peterson, they carried Smith's body under the trees and covered it with some limbs.

"It's no use us trying to bury everybody," Peterson stated their thoughts. "If the savages go on the war-path again, we don't want to be around here."

So they left the dead man and hurried down-valley. At the Indian village at the bay they hired a canoe and fled down channel, thankful that the killers in the canyon had not overtaken them or beaten them to the village and inflamed the Indians there.

Smith had been killed late afternoon of the 29th of April, while the men in the main camp, and Brewster and his men, were killed on the morning of April 30, 1864.

When the three survivors reached Victoria on May 11, the population was shocked and startled. Was there to be a general uprising? People in outlying settlements blockaded their homes and every Indian appeared as a threat of insurrection.

Word was sent to Governor Seymour at New Westminster on May

13. On May 15, *H.M.S. Forward* sailed for Bute Inlet with a force of volunteers under Chartres Brew, Chief Inspector of Police.

In Waddington Canyon the expedition found that the Chilcotins, rather than coming to incite the coastal Indians into an uprising, had retreated to the interior, systematically burning all the bridges behind them to discourage pursuit. In the face of this difficulty, and further hampered by every miniature stream now grown huge and dangerous from the snows melting on the high peaks above, Brew gave up the attempt to follow the murderers along the Waddington trail, and returned to New Westminster.

When he announced he was going after the Indians by another route, via Bella Coola, he was besieged by volunteers. The Westminster Volunteer Rifles and the Hyack Fire Brigade were finally chosen. Governor Seymour himself decided to accompany the expedition, and *H.M.S. Sutlej*, a 51-gun frigate was to carry the force. For waters that until recently had seen nothing larger than an Indian dugout she was indeed a floating fortress. She displaced 3,007 tons, had a complement of 510 officers and men, and more firepower than all the Indians of British Columbia. She had twenty-two 68 pounders, four 110-pound Armstrong guns on the main deck, and eight 40-pound Armstrong guns and one 110-pound pivot gun on the forecastle.

The *Sutlej* arrived in Bella Coola on Saturday morning, June 18.

The *Beaver,* carrying four brass cannons, and muskets and cutlasses in racks around the mainmast, with hand grenades in safe places, arrived on Sunday.

The *Labouchère,* with more cannon and manpower, arrived on Monday.

For the first time in history the Indian population of Bella Coola was outnumbered by the white population.

The 17th of May at Canoe Crossing, now an accepted name for Boat Encampment, was a sunny day. Barron's Store had become the Hamilton Ranch. Clearing had been extended by laboriously pushing the forest back and digging out and burning many of the stumps. The set of buildings now served as home to a family, for Graham Hamilton had brought his wife and his nineteen-year-old daughter, Katie, to be with him.

Katie, blue-eyed and flaxen-haired, was helping her mother prepare some saddle packs of food. Outside, Graham Hamilton was checking lists of supplies that were being ferried across the river.

"Sorry we can't fill Mr. Waddington's order completely," he said to Alexander McDonald, who was checking with him. "The rest of the goods will be in on the *Labouchère* and will be waiting for you when you come back in a month or so."

"Good enough," McDonald replied. They watched for a few moments as several of his men drove a large number of horses into the river, which they swam with much blowing and splashing. They were received on the other side by more of the crew who caught the animals and tied them to hitching racks. "Forty-two head of horses," McDonald said. "Enough for spares and light packs. We'll dust through the country fast."

"I hope you don't have any trouble with the Indians," Hamilton said. "The Chilcotins haven't become any friendlier in the last year and too many killings have gone unpunished for my liking."

"We are a stronger party than most," McDonald said, "and we are pretty well armed."

He mentally checked his crew. There was himself, who had taken over Barron's hay camp at Puntzi Lake and had spent three years packing from Bentinck Arm to Alexandria and Quesnel. His lieutenant was Malcolm McLeod whose cousin, Bob McLeod had been killed by the Indians the other side of Puntzi two years ago. There was Peter McDougall who worked for him on some of his trips and had taken an Indian woman as a companion. She was with them now, a wiry young woman who had one withered hand. She was a Chilcotin chief's daughter and was called Secum Mamaloose which in Chinook means Part Dead. But even with one withered hand she could pack a horse as well as any man, and McDougall gave her the handling of his money. There was Barney Johnson here in the valley for two years and considered one of the pioneers and permanent residents. There was an Englishman, Clifford Higgins; Fred Harrison and two easterners, Charles Farquharson and John Grant whom Mr. Waddington had sent up from Victoria and about whom he knew nothing. But none of them acted as if they were afraid of the Indians.

Of that, however, he might never have to know more.

"We'll be careful," he told Hamilton.

"Do that," Hamilton replied. "We don't want to exchange the wedding for a funeral. And," he added in a low voice, "we don't talk of this in front of Katie or her mother."

McDonald stepped into the house. "Goodbye," he said to Katie kissing her lightly on the cheek. "Take some more lessons in cooking from your mother," and turning to Mrs. Hamilton, "I don't think there is a better cook than you, even in heaven."

"No sacrilege, now, young man," Mrs. Hamilton replied looking pleased with the compliment.

And a half hour later, as he mounted his horse to lead the pack train up the trail, mother and daughter were at the door of their house waving Godspeed to him.

At the river the crews of two Indian canoes who had brought supplies for the pack train up from Peter White's store at the mouth of the river passed a few remarks to each other in their guttural language as the white men disappeared into the forest.

"Maybe they will be with their ancestors before the coming of another run of salmon in the river," said one as he prepared his canoe for the trip downriver.

For the first few hours the horses of the pack train jockeyed for position, then settled to a mile-eating pace. The second day saw them into the pine forests of the plateau country. They camped that night on the edge of a large lake.

"Funny we haven't met any Indians," McDonald said to McDougall. "I wonder if we're headed for trouble."

"My woman will tell me if she gets wind of anything," McDougall assured him. "These boys would have to whip themselves up to the necessary excitement before they started anything. We'll likely be able to get back to Hamilton's unless things happen unusually fast."

"Where's the gold?" McDougall had carried a considerable amount of gold to buy supplies in Bella Coola. Furs he had collected through the winter had been traded for more gold. Had there been supplies in Bella Coola the empty pack horses would have been loaded.

"She's got it," McDougall said. "Carries it with her just in case I get too much liquor and lose it."

Next morning they were on the trail when the sun lifted over the hill to the east. By ten o'clock they were moving along the east side of the lake by which they had camped. They met a small group of mounted Indians—four men, five or six women and some children. McDonald, in the lead, assessed the party as the gap between them closed.

"No mischief here," he thought. "Warring Indians don't take their families with them."

When the Indians got off the trail and gave way to his hurrying pack animals he waved a friendly greeting to them and did not stop. Then, in about five minutes, McDougall came tearing up whipping his horse and confusing the pack horses.

"Alec," he shouted. "My woman tells me we're for it. The Chilcotins are on the warpath. There's a party of forty or fifty planning to ambush us."

"Those Indians we just met didn't look like they were out to ambush anyone," McDonald said as he studied his companion's face.

"Not all the Indians are on the warpath, but plenty. Listen! Klattasine went down the Homathco and joined up with Tellot and the crew that were packing for the road builders. They jumped Brewster and his men in the night and killed them all. Maybe two or three whites got away. Then . . . and this is going to be hard to take, but we haven't time for gentle words . . . they headed across country gathering supporters as they went and went in and killed Manning at our place at Puntzi."

"We'll have a talk," McDonald said. He stopped in a tiny meadow and beckoned the others to him while the horses started to graze.

He told them the news. "It looks bad," he said, "really bad. These fellows are killers. There's been a dozen white men murdered before this affair. Now they have their heads down and running. They've already got numbers. Maybe they'll inflame the whole country."

"It's no use us going through to the Homathco if the other crew has been wiped out, is it?" the Englishman Higgins asked.

"This will have to be cleaned up first. Every Indian in the country will be after our scalps. They dream of driving the whites out."

"Let's go back," Higgins voted. "But take the pack horses with us." Someone had suggested they cut the packs off the animals and, leaving them, make a run for it.

"That's it, then," McDonald said.

Fifteen minutes after McDougall's woman had told him what she had learned the pack train had been turned and was trotting briskly toward Bella Coola. There was no shouting but when a horse showed a tendency to lag a whistling rope burned him across the rump.

Two miles were accomplished in safety.

Then, from the bushes in front and on either side, arose a shouting, waving, shooting ring of Indians. The pack horses milled in confusion. Several of them, badly wounded, fell squealing in pain and fright.

Peter McDougall and Clifford Higgins fell under the first volley from the Indians. If they weren't dead when they dropped from their horses the wild maelstrom of pack horses completed the job.

McDonald and Farquharson attempted to drive the animals onto the encircling savages. Crossfire shot horses from under each of them. But the effort was successful and Farquharson escaped on foot into the woods. McDonald grabbed the reins of a riderless mount which he recognized as McDougall's. He felt the fresh slippery blood on the saddle. Then, seizing the musket from its scabbard he fired at an Indian and saw him fall. Using the musket as a club he charged at a group of Indians, split open one painted head and knocked down another before his horse collapsed under him.

He then leaped for the shelter of a tree from which his revolver barked every time an Indian showed.

He saw McDougall's woman fall off her horse; the term "Sitkum Mamaloose" became an understatement.

Through the dust and confusion he saw Johnson.

"Get out if you can," he shouted. "Get to Bella Coola!"

McDonald lasted only for a few moments. Three Indians crept up on him from the rear and before their combined attack he went down. His revolver was empty.

At this particular moment Chief Inspector of Police Chartres Brew was experiencing difficulties in Waddington Canyon with his New Westminster Volunteers in his attempt to apprehend the murderers of the Waddington road crew.

At Boat Encampment in the Bella Coola Valley Hamilton was busy opening a parcel of goods that had come up the river from Peter White's. His man-of-all-work was a Chilcotin who had attached himself to the place when Hamilton had saved him from drowning a year or so ago. Many times he had shown his loyalty and on occasion, Hamilton had sought his advice in dealing with problems of Indian contact; he had found him most discerning and reliable.

Now the Chilcotin was laboring with some thoughts he wanted to express.

"I think more better you go down river in big canoe, delate soon," he said, using a mixture of broken English and Chinook. "My people, some cultus men, say they kill every white man. They want no white man in country all same. They kill all white men in big canyon. They going to kill McDonald and all packer man. They going to kill everybody like white man."

The Indian stopped to collect words to express himself more emphatically. His earnest laboring impressed Hamilton almost as much as his words. These people were not exhibitionists and he knew that it was only with great difficulty that this near-savage could give such a warning.

"Any time, maybe right now they come. I think you go right away by that canoe. Hurry!" and he pointed to the river where a large dugout canoe shouldered the bank as the current swept by.

Hamilton suddenly decided the Indian was right. He had a wife and daughter to protect and if, indeed, the Chilcotins swept down on them he would not be able to hold out long.

"You come?" he questioned his Indian.

"No come. No good in canoe. I go into woods," the Indian confessed his inadequacy with river craft. "But you go. Now."

Hamilton strode into the house.

"We're going down to the river mouth immediately," he told his wife and Katie. Our Chilcotin has convinced me we are in danger here. His people are on the warpath and the nearest help for us is thirty miles away."

In a few moments the three stepped from the door.

As they left the doorway the sound of pounding hoofs drew their attention. A lathered horse leaped from the shadow of the forest and dashed across the clearing as if devils were in pursuit of it. Suddenly it stopped short and the rider leaped to the ground. His face was streaked with dried blood and his clothes bloody and torn.

"Grant! John Grant!" Hamilton recognized the man. "What has happened to you?"

"Shot . . . Shot!" Grant shouted. "They jumped us! Scores of the red devils. Ambushed us at Nankootloon. I think I am the only one that got away."

"Mr. McDonald?" queried Kathie Hamilton fearfully.

"A hero, Miss, a hero!" Grant replied. "When the devils jumped us McDonald took on more than half of them himself. I saw him charge into a pile of them and kill two and scatter the rest. He had two horses shot under him and was busy blowing the savages to bits with his revolver. He yelled at us to save ourselves, to get out of there. The last I saw of him, God bless him, he was standing behind a tree popping savage heads off."

"I'm going to stay here," Katie Hamilton said. "He might get down here and need help."

A loud chorus of shouts punctuated with the sound of hooves pounding up the trail announced the need for immediate action.

"To the canoe," Hamilton ordered. Seizing his wife's arm and then his daughter's he started for the river.

Katie objected.

"Let me stay here," she screamed. "I'm going to stay here!"

"Don't be a fool," Hamilton barked at her. "He wouldn't want you killed or captured by the Indians."

He almost dragged her and in seconds the three of them, with Grant immediately behind, tumbled into the big river canoe. Just as they were flipping the rope off the stump eleven Indians armed with muskets and riding on paint-daubed horses appeared.

When they saw their victims in the canoe they screamed in fury and spurred their horses on toward the landing. But the canoe, thrust savagely forward under the poles wielded by Hamilton and Grant and aided by the river current, sped almost as swiftly as the Chilcotins' horses and kept out of the range of the Indians' muskets. The Indians turned their attention to the house as if easier prey and certain looting would be there.

The Hamilton's Chilcotin had disappeared into the woods.

The constant traffic on the river in the last few years had caused the removal of most of the snags and all of the sweepers so that Hamilton, a man of much experience with Indian river craft, met with no difficulties in descending the river. Grant helped. After a period of unabashed sobbing in her mother's arms Katie seized a paddle and worked furiously and, for her own nervous system at least, effectively.

In six hours they grounded their canoe just below the Wallace store. Mr. Wallace was Customs man as well as storekeeper. His wife was with him and when she saw the distraught faces of the Hamilton women she shepherded them into her living quarters while the men talked to her husband.

"They have been getting saucier all the time," Mr. Wallace said. "About a week ago some Ausanies, about a half dozen, came into the store and demanded powder and shot. I told them I didn't have any for sale. This seemed to anger them and one made a swing at me with a knife. Fortunately he missed. I retreated into my warehouse and came out with a cutlass and when I rushed them, brandishing this, they left so quickly they almost enlarged the doorway." He laughed at the recollection. "But a day or two later a small schooner anchored in the bay. There were four men aboard and despite our protests they sold these same Indians all the powder and shot they wanted."

The settlement of white people, named by them New Aberdeen in memory of the homeland of one of the families, consisted of sixteen people including the Hamiltons. Four were women and when messengers went from the Wallace store for the whites to assemble there, all came, for the men would not leave their womenfolk unguarded. Each man wore sidearms and Peter White came with a shiny new repeating rifle, the newest invention in firearms.

The women went into the Wallace living quarters for the problem of defence against possible Indian attack was one for their menfolk. In the trading room the men were briefed on what had happened.

"We'd better be prepared for an attack," one of the men said. "These Bella Coolas are friendly enough but the damned Chilcotins and Ausanies have been working on them and when news gets around about this Nankootloon affair it might be the spark in the powder-keg. We'll have to send a canoe up the river in case any more of the McDonald party got down to Boat Encampment."

Two canoes, each with a picked crew of four Bella Coola Indians, started up-river. In the prow of one kneeled Peter White, his shining repeater across his knees. "With this I have the strength of ten men." In the other Graham Hamilton crouched, four muskets within reach and two revolvers in his belt. They saw neither man nor light and as they went around the last bend and saw Boat Encampment Hamilton cried out, "By gad, they didn't burn it after all."

As the canoes nosed into the landing Peter White leaped ashore telling his canoe captain to come with him. "He'll be a hostage for my safe return," he said quietly to Hamilton.

He was away for only a few minutes.

"No horses," he reported on his return. "Gates down and tracks headed down-trail. No Indians. Can't smell any. Let's go look at the house. You come, too," he said to Hamilton's canoe captain.

They found the house empty; it had been ransacked but not noticeably plundered.

Answering a call from the edge of the clearing, they were asked to show themselves, to demonstrate they were white men. Because the voice calling belonged to a white man they complied and two men rode out of the shadows, muskets in hand. They were McLeod and Fred Harrison.

"That makes three of you to escape," Hamilton said. "Do you suppose there are any more?"

"I don't know," McLeod answered. "It was a game of hide and seek with a hundred braves and I did most of my travelling at night. Even so, Harrison caught me with my guard down and could have had my scalp."

They stayed at Boat Encampment overnight, Hamilton and White alternately standing guard. When dawn broke without incident they pushed their canoes another ten miles against the boisterous current.

White's canoe captain pointed . . . "Man there," he said. "Sick man too."

Looking in the direction indicated, they saw a man walking along the river bank leading a saddled horse on which slumped the figure of a man.

"Not Indians," Hamilton thought, and shouted, "Ahoy."

The man with the horse stopped in startled attention.

"My god, it's Barney Johnson and Farquharson," McLeod said as the canoes closed the distance. "Now it's five of us."

Farquharson, the first to escape at Nankootloon, had fled into the bushes unseen and worked his way back toward Bella Coola. He had avoided the trail since he thought Indian pursuers would be on it. Wandering for many days afoot without food, he was so weak he had become careless and this morning Johnson had ridden upon him without detection.

"We had better get these scarecrows down to the river-mouth," White smiled. "If we hurry we might be in time for another Indian war."

All was quiet at the small collection of white man's buildings; no one moved and doors and windows were heavily shuttered.

A shout got attention; a peephole was opened, then a door, and Mr. Wallace appeared. "Come in," he cried, "and welcome to a besieged city."

In the Wallace house a discussion of plans took place.

"A group of Chilcotins, Mr. Grant's pursuers in fact, arrived here last night with the tale of Waddington Canyon and Nankootloon. They didn't take part in either fight and are thirsting to share in the glory. They say the upper country Indians are going to kill every white man who uses either the Bute Inlet or Bentinck Arm route into the fields. They are trying to arouse the Bella Coolas against us."

"They might mob us if they got started," Peter White said, "but they will never attack us with any plan. They haven't any leadership. Six well-trained men with repeating rifles could conquer the whole country between here and Alexandria. But as there could well be three hundred and fifty Indians men, that is — against the fifteen or sixteen of us I would say even their mob attacks could crush us. We'll have to teach the ladies how to load muskets."

They prepared for a siege. While Peter White from an attic eyrie, covered their activity with his repeating rifle some of the men filled every possible container with water. Three buildings were occupied, windows and doors barricaded, and logs hoisted under the eaves so that, in case of an attempt to fire the buildings, logs could be dropped on the arsonists in a manner calculated to crush them.

Several times Indians came around and were warned away. Once when a group of them commenced to taunt the whites Peter banged off two shots from his rifle in rapid succession. The bullets sprayed sand in the Indians' faces and they left.

"Though we may be afraid of the bastards," he said to McLeod, "it will be an easier war if we keep a ready trigger-finger."

That evening the sounds of shouting came from the Indian village.

"Tomorrow at dawn will be the critical time. They are having a war dance. That's the Chilcotins trying to work the Bella Coolas into a state of frenzy," Peter White explained.

Northern nights in the summer solstice are brief — only a few hours of grey-out. This was a period when days were sunny and nights clear and dew-laden. Guard for the dark hours was trebled, one man being posted in each house in such a manner that the three combined commanded a clear view of the little clearing and its collection of buildings.

About midnight the shouting from the Indian village had quieted down and the mountain and valley seemed to be given over to sleep. Inside the barricaded houses the white people lay down to fitful rest while the guards maintained their vigil.

Dawn was just announcing the imminent birth of a new day when, from the bushes at the edge of the clearing, the call of a wolf rose to the sky. From one of the buildings a musket roared. The wolf-howl ended in a human scream of surprise and pain, and a man staggered from the shadows and dropped to the ground.

Inside the buildings every man jumped to his post, gun-ports were cautiously opened and in thirty seconds time an attack would have been met with fire from almost a score of guns.

But there was no attack. Silence followed the scream and dawn came without further excitement. When the morning sun warmed the little village some of the men went out to the figure lying prone a few yards from the bushes. It was daubed with paint and only scantily clad with a wolf-skin.

"One of those damned Ausanies," Peter White exclaimed. "When you cut his howl short last night you disturbed their plans to rush us. That howl was a call to others to come and get in on the kill. It was a bad omen for them that the call was cut short."

They unceremoniously threw the body in the river and, later in the morning when some Indians came, made a point of advising them that henceforth Indians must not come near the trading posts between sunset and sunrise or they would be shot.

"Maybe we've won the first battle," Hamilton ventured. "The Bella Coola just aren't ready to take on a war and we have stopped an Ausanie surprise attack before it got going."

It was the beginning of almost a month of suspense. The white people did not venture to return to their homes for from the interior came repeated pressing invitations to the Bella Coola Indians to rise up and drive the white men from the country. From the Chilcotins came stories of the Bute Inlet massacre and of the Nankootloon disaster. McDonald's death, previously only guessed at, was confirmed and it was told that McDougall's Indian woman, Sitkum Mamaloose, had been shot by her own father, a Chilcotin sub-chief because he had known she was carrying considerable gold on her person. And almost daily, it seemed, came reports that insurgents were planning on storming Alexandria and killing all the white people there. The Bella Coola Indians vaccilated, inclined to one direction by fifty years of friendly dealings with white people, and to the other by the insolent encouragement of visiting Chilcotins.

Peter White told his companions, "We're in a spot where things would be worse if the Chilcotins were anything but a pack of wolves. They aren't warriors. Look, at Waddington they outnumbered the whites two to one and the whites weren't armed, yet three got away. At Nankootloon the whites were outnumbered fifty to eight, yet five of those eight white men escaped."

Trading was resumed, but with caution.

Then, after the frictions of fear and tension and living in too close quarters had reached a serious point, the *Sutlej* arrived and immediately the whole situation was eased. Not only was the lot of the white people alleviated, it was made almost desirable. After a month of near imprisonment they were made much of by their rescuers and the socially-minded had the opportunity of entertaining the Governor of the colony of British Columbia, Fredrick Seymour. This gentleman, three months in office, was an enthusiast in dealing with Indians.

Faced with what appeared to be a general uprising, his first action in Bella Coola was to assess the Indians' attitude toward the insurrections. Finding they were amenable to advances, he accepted thirty or more volunteers from the tribesmen and equipped them with uniforms and muskets. The evening of June 18 saw more than a score of the Bella Coola braves strutting around in their uniforms in entertaining mimicry of the white man's soldiery.

... And the person who likes to write letters to an editor — for there is no assembly complete without one — had a field day; for indeed here was something to write about. The Victoria *Colonist* in an edition of Tuesday, June 28, 1864, carried the following letter:

Editor, British Colonist, Sir,
I have had this letter waiting for you for some time, but have had no opportunity of sending it, having missed the Amelia on her last trip down. The Indians here have been very saucy ever since they heard of the Bute Inlet Massacre. . . . The Interior Indians are coming down here among the Bella Coola, to try and persuade them to follow their example with the white men on this route. Some of the Bella Coola are willing and some are not. . . . We are in great danger of losing our lives here at present; we number 16 souls all told. If the present governor takes no more heed of our dangerous position than Governor Douglas did, we had better start all together in canoes for Victoria or New Westminster, or some other place of refuge, as one will not be long safe here. We are in hopes, however, that we now have a representative of Her Majesty who respects the life of a white man more than Mr. Douglas did, for when there were three white men murdered here three months ago, the only satisfaction we had was a visit from one of the gunboats, and the gallant commander, on two of the murderers being pointed out to him, coolly remarked that he did not come here for the purpose of apprehending murderers! One of those savages was the man who brutally murdered John Holmes, the other the man who shot poor Sergeant Fisher.

I could spend a whole summer day writing to you on this subject but I will only send these few remarks, on the truth of which you may fully rely.

A resident.

And, again in the same issue of the *Colonist:*

"Those who are well acquainted with the Indians of the North-west Coast express great surprise at the course adopted by governor Seymour in arming and taking with the expedition some thirty or forty of the Bella Coola Indians. Setting aside the well-known treachery of the savages, it is a notorious fact that this tribe is closely connected both by blood and marriage with the very rascals whom the volunteers are in search of. Besides, it will be seen from the letter of our resident correspondent, who is intimately acquainted with the Indians, that some of them at least were prepared to join the Chilcotins in cutting off every white man on the coast routes. Mr. Waddington, whose knowledge of the Indians in that region is very considerable, is also of the opinion that the course pursued has been far from prudent, and thinks that both Governor Seymour and the whole party are in very serious danger. It is not at all unlikely that the Bella Coolas may lead the expedition into ambush, where every soul may be cut off; or with their habitual treachery they may, in the skirmish that occurs, turn suddenly around and attack the very party they have been engaged to assist. It is to be hoped that the marines from the *Sutlej* may arrive to swell the numbers of the little band before any possible treachery can be accomplished."

Thus was the stage set for Act II of the Chilcotin War in which a number of shots were fired and one man killed.

On Sunday the New Westminster volunteers, thirty-eight in number, with their commander Chartres Brew, were landed from the *Sutlej* and, picking up their thirty-plus Bella Coola reinforcements, started eastward toward the scene of hostilities.

On the same day the Hudson's Bay Company steamer, the *Beaver,* with her four bright brass cannon dropped anchor alongside the *Sutlej.*

Monday, June 20, the anniversary of the Accession of Queen Victoria, *H.M.S. Sutlej* fired a royal salute of twenty-one guns, the roar of which echoed back and forth from the towering mountain walls with such cumulative force that seagulls fell into the water from the vibrations and had scarcely recovered when a further salute of seventeen guns for Governor Seymour shook the great trees of the forest as if they were willow wands.

Governor Seymour landed at nine o'clock in the morning to commence his journey meaning to overtake the army which had preceded him. The Bella Coola Indians, collecting themselves from the forests to which they had fled when the gun salutes thundered, called him "God of the Mighty Thunder", and to a man would have followed him to the death had he then commanded it.

When Rosabelle, a laughing young woman whom Peter White had taken from the Indian Village to allay his loneliness − "I just have to have someone to talk to", he explained, − saw Governor Seymour, she said, "He is the mightiest Thunderbird that ever shook our mountains. I thought the sky was falling in."

Accompanying Governor Seymour as aide-de-camp was Lieutenant Stuart of *H.M.S. Sutlej.*

That same Monday there was further activity when the *Labouchère,* 202 feet long, dropped anchor alongside the *Sutlej* and the *Beaver.*

The following day a contingent of fifty marines from *H.M.S. Sutlej* was dispatched and when they joined forces with the two companies of men preceding them, the total constituted a small army, the largest ever to be on the move in the Colony of British Columbia. And while this little army never fired a shot, their presence had a profound effect on subsequent events.

As these men moved through the country the enemy fell away before them, and evidence was found that the insurrectionists had planned to resist. At Nankootloon, for instance, where two lakes force traffic through a natural gate, there was a fortress strong enough to prove very embarrassing had it been manned by insurrectionists. But the Indians had fled, reluctant to make contact with an enemy who could out-number and out-gun them. The fortress was demolished.

At the scene of the ambush of McDonald, the story of the conflict could be read in the remains of packs of tools, kegs of nails, broken pack saddles and the rotting carcasses of six horses. But there were no signs of the bodies of the men who had fallen in the conflict.

Farther east an army of somewhat lesser proportions had bogged down in an almost untenable position. A reward of two hundred and fifty dollars for each of the murderers had been posted in every mining camp, and an army under "Judge" Cox, an ebullient gold commissioner and magistrate, had been built up to over fifty men who set out from Alexandria and, following the Palmer trail, arrived at Puntzi Lake on the 12th of June.

Scouting parties found the Indians armed and prepared for war. One group, caught in an Indian ambush, engaged in a shouting, shooting, running engagement with the Indians, who followed the white soldiery — if such untrained volunteers could be called soldiers — almost into camp. In plain sight of the camp they shouted insults and discharged their muskets.

"Damned saucy, what!" was the comment of one of the volunteers.

Next day, following a decision to penetrate no farther into enemy territory until reinforcements were procured the army, now numbering sixty-five, established itself in a little log fort at Puntzi. From this fort a flag of friendship was flown.

Among Cox's army was Donald McLean, retired chief trader for the Hudson's Bay Company at Kamloops, who came out of retirement to take part in an Indian hunt, which he considered exhilarating sport. His contempt for Indians made him careless, and while out on a scouting trip with only one friendly Indian he was shot through the heart. His killer, Anukatlh, a Chilcotin, was never apprehended. He did not shoot McLean's companion though he had every chance. His object was to avenge the many Indians McLean had mistreated or killed. Some people considered Anukatlh a provident instrument of justice and the search for him was never vigorously pursued.

The concern caused in Cox's camp by McLean's death — a party sent out to recover the body met with no opposition — mounted but was quickly relieved, for that very same evening the army from Bella Coola under Chartres Brew, with Governor Seymour in the company, arrived at the little fort.

Chasing elusive Indians in their native habitat is unrewarding for anyone except skilled fellow-residents of the same place, and this did not include the now powerful army at Puntzi. Sorties into the Cascades were made by Chartres Brew following rumors that the wanted men were there.

Judge Cox stayed in the fort.

Gradually the Indians became accustomed to the presence of the armed force, contact was made with Alexis, a friendly Chilcotin chief, and Indian women came to the fort to trade. Then word came via the moccasin telegraph that Tellot and Klattasine and some of the other wanted men were in Alexis' camp. Cox sent a messenger loaded with gifts to say that he wanted to make friends with the wanted men. The Indians, in turn, sent a messenger back with gifts asking what were the terms of surrender, and Cox replied that since they had acted without knowledge of the white man's laws, he would on his word of honor guarantee to spare their lives if they would surrender.

What Cox did *not* tell the Indians was that he was merely a magistrate and that Chief Justice Begbie frequently altered his, Cox's, decisions; that he was not in a position to promise amnesty; that the expedition was costing a huge sum; and that it had almost been decided they would never be able to capture the men by force in any event, and therefore some guile was necessary.

By agreement, Cox had his men encamped at the old fort of the Hudson's Bay Company on the Chuzko River, and on August 11 Klattasine and Tellot and six others, bearing gifts, came with their families, and surrendered.

The Indians were greatly surprised to find themselves surrounded by armed men and told to lay down their arms. All did as commanded except Tellot, who seized his musket by the barrel and smashed it across a tree. Then, lifting himself to his full height, he said, "Shoot me now. King George's men are great liars."

Tellot's assessment of the promised amnesty was correct.

Cox and his men took the prisoners to Quesnel, where the little army was disbanded and the Chilcotins surrendered for regular trial under Chief Justice Matthew Begbie. Of the eight involved, two were retained as witnesses, one was sentenced to life imprisonment but escaped as he was being taken to Westminster to serve his time, and the remaining five, including Tellot and Klattasine, were hanged in the presence of a great crowd of Indians. A story that many of the Indians were paid to come and see 'the show' was never convincingly denied.

To all intents and purposes the Chilcotin War was over. The majority of the murderers were still at liberty and unpunished, and there were persistent stories that some of the men hanged were not guilty but merely convenient pawns turned over by the chiefs so the white man and his army would be satisfied and go home.

Nevertheless, the government officials felt the justice of the white man had been impartially imposed.

As one Chilcotin father put it, trying to impress some of the facts of life on his son, "Times are changing. No longer may you go around killing indiscriminately. From now on, if you must kill someone, just make sure it isn't a white man."

Chartres Brew, who had pursued the campaign vigorously, now marched his men along the trail back to Bella Coola still hoping to find some of the other murderers on the way. In this he was unsuccessful, but he did meet with Anahiem, another chief of the Chilcotins, and obtained from him the horses and much of the loot from McDonald's pack train. Anahiem convinced Brew that he had had nothing to do with the massacres, and promised to capture the rest of the murderers next spring. At the present time they were reported to be hiding in the vastness of the western mountains, the Cascades.

In Bella Coola life had failed to return to normal. Some of the settlers, who had faced the several fearful fortnights of barricaded homes in fear of imminent attack, had departed on the *Labouchère*. Now the ship was again in harbor, southbound.

Peter White, who had bought the Bella Coola end of Barron's business, had decided to leave. "The Cariboo Road is taking most of our traffic," he said. "Now this business is going to spoil local trade. And the Bella Coolas are killing themselves off, and will likely try to kill us off, too. I'm going."

When he announced his decision to Rosabelle, she said she wanted to go with him. "Civilization is no place for an Indian woman," Peter told her. "People in towns turn up their noses at Indian women."

"Governor Douglas's woman is a half breed," Rosabelle argued. Arguing with their men was something Indian women seldom did, but Rosabelle was doing it, much to Peter's surprise. "And Judge Cox has an Indian woman. Are these women lonely?"

Peter had become adept at the Bella Coola language, and the argument was carried on in that tongue.

"Likely they are lonely," he said. "Anyway, you would be better off here with your own people. All this that I am leaving here will be yours," and he indicated the trade goods around them. "You will be the richest woman in Bella Coola."

"I don't want to live with an Indian man," Rosabelle thrust. "You've spoiled me." "I'll send you a white man," Peter White

114

promised, feeling he was regaining control of the situation, "a young white man with a broad chest and bushy beard."

"And our child, when he is born?" Rosabelle asked, touching her thickening waist. "Even an Indian woman's child needs a father."

"The Indian village will produce a father for the child, even if I don't," Peter countered, feeling he was losing ground. "Yours is not the first unborn child left by a departing white man in the Bella Coola village, nor will it be the last."

Rosabelle had to accept the state of affairs and recovered her good humor almost effortlessly. "Just be sure he is a lively young man," she demanded laughingly as she waved him goodbye.

When Peter White reached New Westminster he negotiated the sale of his business in Bella Coola. Because of the lurid tales of Indian massacre carried by the newspapers he had some difficulty in finding a buyer. When he did and the papers were drawn up, an eight thousand dollar inventory changed hands for eight hundred. All these business details were put on paper, but Rosabelle and her unborn child were not listed among either the assets, or the liabilities.

At Quesnel where the Indian murderers were hanged the last body had scarcely ceased its convulsive twitching when a lithe young Indian, who had stayed well at the edge of the crowd, departed unobtrusively from the scene and, while the rest were watching with hypnotized gaze the five swaying bodies on their gibbets, moved cautiously to where a number of saddled horses were tied among the cottonwoods. Nearby was an Indian encampment, entirely deserted while the occupants were at the hanging. Taking the saddle from his own mount he put it on a big bay, the strongest looking animal of the group and, mounting swiftly, trotted briskly to the nearby Fraser River. Urging the animal into the water, he directed it to the farther bank and, slipping from the saddle, clung to the horse's tail and was towed across the grey turbulent river. The current washed them downstream and onto a gravel bar, and the dripping horse had barely gained the shallows at the edge of the stream before the Indian was again in the saddle. Before plunging into the bushes he stopped long enough to look back across the Fraser. There was no sign of pursuit. He shook his fist in a gesture of hatred toward the settlement; then, unaware of bodily cold, urged his horse westward.

The big bay responded readily, and that evening the Indian camped fifty miles to the west, dining sparsely on the body of a grouse which a well aimed rock had killed. Next day he rode on and that evening came across a small Indian village. He avoided being seen as he studied the dozen or so people there and the horses picketed in the meadow a short distance away. Next morning at dawn it was discovered that the strongest horse had gone and the bay left in its place. Except for the one grouse the rider had not eaten for two days, but he did not dare risk detection by stealing food, or killing a dog to eat. Thus when, toward noon, a porcupine waddled into view, a halt was called, the porcupine was despatched with a club, and its meatiest parts were soon roasting over a small, hot fire.

Late that afternoon, when the sun was sliding rapidly toward the high mountains now not far distant, the horse was abandoned after the saddle and bridle were removed; the saddle was stripped of its leather, and the iron parts placed in a little pack along with the saddle leather and bridle. The saddletree was burned, and the remainder of the porcupine meat heated and eaten. Then, shouldering his small pack and satisfied that no sign remained in the brief camp to indicate either his activity or the direction he was taking, the Indian trotted purposefully towards the setting sun.

To anyone less skilled it would not have appeared that he was following any trail, but at rare intervals bent grass or a broken twig indicated the passage of animals, and once a child's foot print showed up clearly in the mud by a forest stream. When the man saw this he carefully leveled the mud and scattered a handful of dried pine needles around. Then he went on his way.

Deep dusk was thickening into blackness when the short, staccato opening notes of a coyote's call stopped him in his tracks. His arms went aloft and were deliberately lowered before he went forward at a slow walk.

Another human form stepped from a black shadow. The two exchanged greetings and then the young Indian followed the other to a nearby stream-side glade in which burned several small fires. There were several brush shelters at the edge of the glade, and between these and the fires some women and children moved. As the young Indian and his guide stepped into the firelight six other Indians with muskets appeared from the shadows.

"You are not followed?" When the Indian shook his head, wood was heaped on the fires and roast venison brought to him. The women and children retreated into the brush shelters, and the men sat around the fires waiting for him to satisfy his hunger. Presently he began his story.

"We are hunted men," he said. "Three days ago I, Stelles, saw five of our people dancing themselves to death in the air, their bodies twisting and doubling like snakes with a sharp stick through their necks. There was a great gathering of our people there, for white men made it a potlatch and gave rewards of flour to many so they would come to see our people die. The white men did not kill suddenly in a rage. Rather they had many talks. Our people were kept shut up in buildings, and when the most powerful of the white chiefs decided that five of our men should die he said they should hang by the neck until dead. The white men were very proud of what they had done and were very proud of their chief with the forked tongue who had told our people they would be pardoned if they surrendered.

"We are hunted men," he repeated. "Alexis, who has become the friend of the white man and took his food and money for leading our people to captivity and death, has promised to make us captives to the white men next spring so we, too, may do the death dance. Anahiem too, who wishes to escape unnoticed with the white man's horses we took at Nankootloon, has said there will be another potlatch next summer when he captures us and takes us before the great white chief who kills his prisoners with the death dance. "We are hunted men," he continued. "If we are not as wily as the wolverine we will die. Our children will starve, fighting over food scraps that the white men throw to their dogs."

He stopped and his companions sat in silence for a few moments.

"Who of our people died?" asked the chief, Sorrence.

"Klattasine, Tellot, and Tappet — and Neel and Tcheness."

There was a sharp intake of breath at the recital of the last two names.

"We know that Neel and Tcheness were not with any of the war parties," Sorrence stated.

"You are correct, Chief," replied the young Indian, "but the white man was not the only one there with a forked tongue. Two of our people, Cusheen and Lowwa, told stories. For this they were given their freedom. They told stories that were true and they told stories that were false, and because of this two men, who did not kill but who were not able to think very quickly, died. Another man, Chiddaki, is to spend the rest of his life in the white man's prison. He will not live long."

A session of heavy council followed.

117

"We are dead men, yet we live," Chief Sorrence finally summarized. "We fought against the white men who became our enemies and wished to take our land. Our own people prefer the food of the white men to freedom and have turned against us. We will go to a new land. We will go to that land south of the Bella Coola where no man has ever before been, and we will live as free men, beyond the reach of the killing rope of the white man or the forked tongues of our own people."

The next morning at dawn the camp was deserted and eight men, three women and six children followed the morning shadows westward, facing toward country so mountainous that the people of the plateaus and river valleys feared and avoided it. In this country mountain peaks reared high, and clouds spawned glaciers which in turn spawned rivers that plunged down in cataracts. All guarded this area and hid its secrets. Into this unknown land Chief Sorrence's small band hoped to thrust themselves and leave behind the inimical white men as well as those of their own people who had failed to rally in the strike for freedom.

Aware that there was no immediate pursuit, the small party gave their energy to swift progress rather than to subtly concealing the telltale signs of their passage. From early morning to late night they travelled, stopping only when they killed a deer or caribou, and then only to dry and carry the meat with them. They dropped off the plateau country, crossed a valley above a long lake and climbed the almost perpendicular wall west of this lake to reach a bench half a mile above on which they found a chain of lakes leading them across a wide massif that nurtured glaciers and a thousand streams. Off the west side of this massif they dropped down into a valley through which ran a broad and milky glacier stream, and they camped on its banks. In the mornings the stream was slightly lower than in the afternoons or evenings but at all times it was too big and tumultuous for wading or swimming. They travelled up and down its banks for several miles hoping to find a quiet spot which would allow passage with a raft, but none showed.

Finally Stelles suggested a plan. "If you will tie a rope to me I will try to guide a log across the current. If I reach the other side we will have a bridge of buckskin."

"You are the fearless one," Chief Sorrence commented. "We gamble a man for a rope bridge." "We gamble the life of one man for the lives of us all," Stelles replied.

So they prepared a rope as long as all their packs would provide and tied it to the smaller end of a dried snag about twelve feet long. This they put in the water just below a projecting point of land and Stelles, astride it, pushed out into the current. With a rudely fashioned paddle in his hands he attempted to keep the log at an angle against the current so that the force of the water and the holding power of the rope would carry him across the stream.

It was a dangerous task. The log rolled and he dipped under water. The log submerged several times, but rose again. The temperature was numbing. Then the watchers saw him leap from the log and, waist deep in water, push it ashore on the far side of the river.

They now released towards him enough rope to span the river twice and on it he sent back the log. The rest was easy though very wet going. A second log was lashed to the first and on this small raft the entire party and their supplies reached the west bank of the river. The last to cross was Sorrence and, as he untied the rope from the logs, he pointed northward down the river.

"Those are the mountains of the Bella Coola down there," he said, "where live the salmon eaters. Some day it might be safe for us to visit among them." With that he pushed the logs into the river knowing, that unless they lodged in a log jamb, they would eventually reach the sea at Bella Coola.

Turning towards the forest the party started into the mouth of a tributary valley and as they climbed they came on a path made by grizzly bears. Giant footprints twenty to twenty-four inches apart had been impressed six inches deep through the mossy carpet of conifer needles. This pleased the Indians for they reasoned that an old bear trail would surely lead through a pass into other valleys.

That evening they came to the edge of the forest. Above them a stream was born from an icy cavern at the snout of a glacier and over this the ice, white and crystalline and cut with bottle green crevasses, offered a slippery pathway to the horizon. A little to one side a lateral moraine splashed down the white skyway over a slender streak of boulders. Near the other side a giant icefall dominated the scene and as the Indians watched a lofty pinnacle of ice plunged down with terrifying thunder in the rarified air.

"Do we have to cross over there?" one of the Indians asked. "Could we not return to the river valley behind us and live?"

"And be coyotes howling at the camps of the white men who are hunting us?" Chief Sorrence replied scornfully. "We go over the ice."

There were murmurs of fear and dissent. For the first time in the journey the chief's authority was threatened. By blind chance, however, a showdown and possible disastrous division of the party was avoided.

Stelles, studying the terrain in front of them, cautioned them to be quiet. "There's a bear coming across the rocks." He cautiously pointed and his companions saw the huge ursine nonchalantly picking its way over the terminal moraines. "It's the bad bear, the one the white men call the grizzly," he said.

"Let us flee," a woman cried softly. "It will kill us."

"Women and children go back down the trail. The men will stay. We will kill the bear," the chief said, and at his command the women and children deserted their packs and hurried back into the forest.

The chief then divided his men into two groups of four and stationed each group about twenty feet on either side of the trail. Six of them had muskets while two had hunting bows and arrows.

"When the bear is passing yonder boulder," — and the chief pointed to a rock about forty feet away past which went the faint trail and along which they expected the bear to come, — "I will shout. The bear will rise up, and when he is on his hind feet like a man, shoot him. Shoot to break his shoulders, you men with muskets. The bow and arrow men will then pierce his throat." They crouched down among the stunted trees at the edge of the forest.

The bear, unchallenged king in his realm, unaware of enemies or fear, was only desirous of descending from this land of ice to the region of fish and berries. The cold evening air flowing in from the glacier was unfavorable for the beast — though it might have carried a warning scent of the Indians it did not. When the chief's shout rang out the bear stopped — more in curiosity than alarm — tried to catch the scent, then rose up on its hind feet its long snout swinging back and forth as it strained for the smell of the enemy. A shot rang out, followed by a close volley. Two arrows embedded themselves in the animal's throat. The impact of the shots knocked the bear off its feet, and when it tried to rise two broken shoulders prevented it doing so. Roaring with rage and frothing blood it threshed around in a vain effort to rise and close with its enemies.

Stelles seized a boulder as big as his chest and within feet of the bear, heaved it onto the animal's thrashing head. Others were right behind him and in minutes the animal lay still.

Chief Sorrence leaped on the bear with his knife, sliced open the hide and chest cavity, and ripped out the still quivering heart. "Eat of this, my men," he cried, holding out the heart to them, "and you will know as little fear as the grizzly bear."

He smote his bloody hand on his chest, as did his men, and they ate the heart and did a victory dance around the prostrate body of the bear.

Shortly, when the women and children returned they carried their packs back into the shelter of the forest and dragged the body of the bear with them. There they built brush bivouacs to protect themselves from the cold downflow of air which penetrated even the forest, and built a huge fire. As the women skinned the bear and cut up the meat the men reminded each other that they were mighty hunters. Throughout their history the Indians, armed only with bows and arrows, had been afraid of the grizzly bear which because he was never challenged, had never been other than fearless. Therefore the killing of one of these great beasts — healthy and untrapped — was a major event commemorated in stories among the Indians of the Chilcotin.

Objections to crossing the icy horizon were forgotten for now within them was the heart of the mighty bear which knew no fear. And Chief Sorrence felt the rising power of command. His leadership had been good. This successful killing of the much feared grizzly had been well done, not bungled like the attack on the pack train where most of their intended victims had escaped. He had thought clearly and his men had obeyed him; now they were more willing than ever to follow him. Tomorrow they would go into the unknown, but he was not afraid for within him, too, was the heart of the mighty bear which knew no fear.

Next morning, in the fierce enveloping cold from the glacier, the women cut the bear hide into pieces to wrap around their feet. Their chief had commanded; their chief had said that when they got onto the ice of the white world above their buckskin moccasins even the caribou hide moccasins would be cut to pieces by the ice and snow. The thick hair of the bear would protect their feet and keep them from freezing. The chief was wise.

At the point where they had to leave the rocks for the ice, they laced on their snowboots, hair side out, and tried them — they were as good as anticipated. The chief was wise.

They struggled upward over the glacier to an unknown and alien world. The river of ice flowed and curved between high walls of sombre rock to which adhered great patches of snow and green ice. The surface of the glacier was, for a short distance, crystallized ice cut laterally with great green crevasses. Most of these did not extend all the way across the glacier and they stepped over them where they narrowed, but one giant crack went from a rock wall on one side which they could not surmount to a giant icefall on the other where the frigid stream tumbled over a huge rocky ledge and tall columns seemed ready to topple. The Indians were forced to go, one foot ahead of the other, along the wedge bottoms of the defiles between these almost trembling blocks. In two places they scrambled over mounds of fresh ice, the ruins of pillars or seracs which had been forced off balance by the pressure of the icefield above. The groaning and cracking beneath the ice increased the eeriness of the terrain. A child started to wail its fears and its mother, already tensed to the breaking point, cuffed it so hard it fell and lay sobbing until a man jerked it to its feet and propelled it onward. When a pillar fell with a thunderous roar a few yards behind them and sprayed them with splinters of ice they stood transfixed, aware that their lives were indeed in great danger amidst delicately balanced multi-ton ice structures which could all tumble crushingly as the glacier moved. The Indians went on more rapidly after this escape and shortly onto the solid snow-covered ice beyond.

In comparison with what they had been through the gently sloping ice field was a pleasure but there were greater trials ahead. A storm rolling across the ice field blotted out the sun and enveloped them in a fog which cut off every geographical feature, even the craggy peaks and green glaciers, the sight of which an hour before had repelled them but which they would now have welcomed. The fog turned to snow; they lost track of time and direction. At Sorrence's command they tied themselves to each other so that none could get lost. The snow deepened and blew about in the wind so that they lived in a sighing, whirling, grey world without depth, breadth or substance. They wandered blindly.

Then they bumped into the solid wall of a mountain and, feeling this with their hands, came to a spot where an outjutting ridge created some shelter. The blackness of the mountain wall comforted them by its presence; instead of blowing in their faces the snow eddied down, peacefully, upon them.

They huddled together to get warmth from each other's bodies. The remainder of the bear hide plus a caribou hide afforded some protection. They dug into their packs and each had a piece of bear meat to chew upon. Here darkness overtook them.

"We are dead people, and we are in the world of the spirits," one woman said to another. Others heard her and mulled the thought over in their minds as they passed hour after hour of misery. It offered an explanation for these unknown things like huge mountains and groaning rivers of ice. "If we are dead people and in the spirit world, then no one can kill us," another stated, and the group took courage from these words.

"Maybe there are stars in this afterworld," exclaimed Stelles presently. "Look up." Those still awake did look up, and saw stars; the storm had abated and the skies had partially cleared.

They suffered in their icy discomfort until dawn filtered in from the east, when gradually they aroused themselves to stiff and pained activity. The sun finally picked them out and they left their sheltering rock, each chewing a piece of raw bear meat. Now they had eighteen inches of snow to plough through.

When they had gone a few rods beyond the sheltering ridge they turned away from the slanting rays of the sun and, following their shadows, looked down into a distant deep valley where there were trees and a lake. They stared and cried out in joy, for if they were to live in a spirit world they preferred one better than that in which they had spent the night.

With courage they began the descent of the glacier toward this promised land and nature, seeming content with the punishment already meted out to her children, tortured them no further. The snow hindered them and there were crevasses to be bypassed, but a growing medial moraine and, as they descended, a decreasing depth of snow, encouraged them. The sun had little more than passed the zenith when they stepped from the ice and picked their way over a moraine to gain a grassy valley close to the timberline.

The most amazing thing about this new haven into which they had dropped was the herds of goats which pastured or lay at ease there. The bewhiskered animals showed no fear of the Indians, not even fleeing after two of them were shot with arrows. The goats were dressed and added to the packs, and the Indians continued to lower levels where were firewood, dry earth and meat. They made camp on the edge of the lake they had seen from the white snow world, now gleaming high against the blue sky above. That afternoon they spent in eating and resting. They knew that no human enemies would follow them through the icy hell they had recently travelled. They had made their way to a world of abundant game. Mutton could well replace venison as their staple diet, and wool from the goat hides promised warm blankets and warm mats on which to sleep. Marmots whistled their shrill warnings and scurried for cover only at the last moment, and several porcupines waddled out of their way. It was obvious that the wild animals were totally unafraid of man, and from this the Indians reasoned that no man had ever trod here before.

Next day the chief and several of the men reconnoitered down the valley and found much to make them happy. There were beaver working everywhere, plenty of berries and, in an open fir forest under a face of overhanging rock, they found a dry ledge where with little effort they could construct shelters of small logs chinked with moss and mud. There were some huge fallen cedar trees which, even with their limited tools, would provide bark and slabs for roofing.

That evening, encamped near the goat pasture, Sorrence divided his followers into two groups. The two men with bows and arrows were to stay in this high camp and shoot goats and groundhogs, and help the women and children smoke the meat and cure the hides. As soon as loads of these were ready they were to be packed down to the lower camp, which would be their winter home. The others were to prepare this camp.

"And it might be our permanent home," Sorrence said. But he did not add that in this new world they might grow strong in numbers and at some future time go and thrust the white man from the homeland they had just fled. Right now he did not want his people thinking of their homeland.

Everything might have gone as planned had it not been for a few handfuls of pebbles the forces of creation, in capricious mood, had scattered in various parts of the world and which men would drive themselves to torturing lengths to collect.

Three weeks later, with three rough but tight shelters built under the overhanging rock, and meat and hides accumulating from the upper camp, one of the hunters showed Sorrence two shiny globules of metal. "Is that white man's chickamin rock?" he asked, using the Chinook word for gold.

Sorrence took the pebbles. They were heavy. He bit one and his teeth marks showed plainly in the soft surface.

"Where did you get them?" he asked.

"Around our cooking fires when we use hot wood. Lots come out of the gravel. Some big. Some small. You think it is chickamin rock?"

"Yes," Sorrence thought it was.

"Then crazy white man comes," the other said.

"Not unless he finds out," Sorrence stated. "We won't go and tell him."

"And if his god tells him it is here?"

"We will kill every white man that comes," Sorrence averred. "This country is only for us and our children. Before white men and his greed came, Indians did not know chickamin rock. When white men showed it, it brought smallpox and death. It brought more white men, and it starved the Indian, took his meat and land away. Chickamin rock is the white man's god. Let us forget it."

They went back to their work, but the shiny pebbles in the ashes of their fires intrigued the Indians and they collected some of them, for they were distinctive, as well as useful in their games. Before snow blanketed the upper camp they had collected enough food to last through a very long winter, a stack of wooly hides, and two fistfuls of the shining yellow pebbles.

They considered their lot here much better than out on the level land of the lodgepole pine where perhaps even now blizzards were whirling and food was hard to get.

Snow came to their lower camp, but not so deeply that they could not take beaver and marten and, with enough meat, they feasted and played games on the stormy days. A child was born to one of the women, and a fight occurred over the favors of another. Because of the predominance in number of males over females a ratio of eight to three, it had been decided that a woman should not belong to one man only but, if she agreed, be the comforter of more than one. This arrangement worked well for months before one of the men suddenly became jealous of another and a fierce fight occurred, during which one man died of knife wounds and the other of infection four days later.

But the inactivity told on them. In their homeland of the Chilcotin, winter was as active as summer with the pursuit of furs for trade with the white man, and the securing of meat and cutting of fire wood. Here, although they did a little exploratory trapping, there was no need for strenuous hunting for there was no white man to buy their furs, besides which fur-bearing animals here were abundant and easily taken. The meat stored up in the first month or so of their stay was much more than they had ever laid away for a winter in their homeland and this, added to the frequent beavers taken, kept them well in food for the winter. They spent their time in eating and gaming, and in their games the little globules of gold became more important. Along with this, developed cases of cabin fever — that peculiar mental malady that makes man hate his associate when kept in close quarters with him for long periods. The chief, Sorrence, was wise enough to recognize the evils casting their shadows upon them and, when occasion offered, sent his men on trips to explore more of this new world into which they had come. When snow was too deep for travel without snowshoes, and too wet to allow their use, tension increased.

One day the sun peered over the mountain to the south and picked out their shelter under the overhanging ledge. It was only a thin shaft of light from the upper edge of the disc, but it was a glimmer of coming spring. Children laughed and made animated shadows on the long walls and adults smiled at each other.

"Tomorrow," Sorrence stated, "we will see if this stream below us leads to the Stinking Lake."

Next morning six men on snowshoes, with packs on their backs, commenced a three day journey which, indeed, did bring them to tidewater. At the end of the first day they were below the snow area and cached their snowshoes. On the second day they found skunk cabbages showing yellow growth in the swampy places, and on the afternoon of the third day they smelled wood smoke. Pushing on, they came to a small fortified village on the edge of the tide flats, astride one of the tidal sloughs. A scout challenged them, and when he saw they were obviously not from the sea allowed them into the village.

This was one of the villages of the Talio people; they called it Noick. It was one day's paddle to Bella Coola, they told the Chilcotins. The villagers were short in stature compared with the six-foot Chilcotins. They said they were expecting a marine attack from the Kwakiutls, from down coast, by whom they were frequently harried. But they showed their visitors every hospitality and traded dried eulachons, salmon, and eulachon grease for the dried goat meat and a few furs. The Chilcotins also managed to replenish their supplies of powder and shot.

Relating that they were men of the mountains but not revealing their identity, the Chilcotins stayed overnight and next morning started back to their camp. The expected Kwakiutl attack on the Talio Village did not materialize at that time. A war party was indeed on its way but was intercepted by a boat load of white men looking for an escaped murderer.

On May 6 John D.B. Ogilvy, Deputy Collector of Customs and Indian Agent at Bella Coola, in pursuit of one Antoine Lucanage, a smuggler and whisky peddler, was killed on board the schooner *Langley,* anchored at Bella Coola. Having killed his pursuer, the culprit leaped into a small boat and escaped down channel. Three weeks later a reward of one thousand dollars was offered by Chartres Brew for the capture of the ill-reputed Antoine. The chase was taken up by white-skinned adventurers who searched Indian villages and cross-questioned travelers. One such boat, a cannon mounted on its foredeck and muskets thrust from several port holes, intercepted the Kwakiutl war party.

In reply to all the questions, complicated by the language barrier, from the captain of the armed boat, the Kwakiutl warriors answered only one word "Belaxula", thereby indicating that Antoine, the wanted criminal, was probably in hiding in Bella Coola, the scene of the crime. And this led eventually to a Bella Coola village being shelled.

The Kwakiutls, however, not fully understanding what information was wanted, nor even some of the questions, had told only of their intended destination. When the white captain fired his cannon over their heads — "just to see the red devils jump," — they decided that Bella Coola, with white men's boats ready to shoot, was *not* their destination. Instead, they again crossed Queen Charlotte Sound and many months later, when the "Cultus white man" was hunted down and shot in their own territory, they did not connect the incident with their white interceptors.

Sorrence and his men returned to their wintering place but their restlessness returned with them. After a few days they climbed to the goat pasture, which was still covered by deep snow. The goats were not there, but they found the snow would support them and from this plateau they got on to the glacier and climbed to the skyline.

On the snowfield above the glacier they found themselves in a white world to which they were almost total strangers. Far above and dwarfing them towered huge peaks, sending down thundering avalanches which reverberated from wall to wall of this icy world. They had been here before, but then they had been blinded and buffeted by cloud and blizzard. Now they could see that beside the white route by which they had just ascended was the pass up which they had come last fall from the big river. The memory of the cascading icefalls was still so vivid and terrifying that they abandoned any thought of retracing their steps. A third route showed itself, dropping away from the noonday sun across long glaciers and snowfields to a dark green forest. Beyond the forest a white mountain thrust a slender cone into the air.

"That is Nooskultz," Sorrence told his men. "It's the god-mountain of the Bella Coola people. At the foot of that mountain is the Big Village."

Only then did one of the men put into words the thought in the minds of all of them: "Do you think we can get home that way?"

They made a sortie down the glacier and found no difficulty. But it was a long distance and Sorrence, whose leadership had grown with time, made a suggestion new to Indian psychology. "We will bring a heavy load of our food as far as we can come in one day and make a cache of it. That will hasten our progress when we bring the young ones. Maybe only one camp on the snow will be necessary."

Thus was a decision made to leave their refuge, to go back to the land of their people. They had found that security in isolation was worse than danger in the midst of their own people.

Two days later six Indians with heavy packs, and footgear made of woolly bear's hide, wound across the snow and, as the sun was leaving even the highest peaks, they made a pyramid of supplies where it could be seen for miles. Then they hurriedly retraced their steps to their winter shelters which they reached about the middle of the star-lit spring night. After a day of resting and final preparation, they left their winter camp and in the evening, according to plan, reached the pile of supplies.

This time they did not experience near death in their camp on the snow. Goatskins provided warmth and dried goat meat, sustenance. Next night they camped in the forest alongside the Noosatsum River and the following evening were in the village at the foot of Mount Nooskultz.

To the people there they told of spending not one but several summers beyond the big ice. They told of the abundant goats, of the terrible passage through the icefalls, and they showed the globules of gold. But they did not say that they had fled from the white man. Nor, in fact, was there more than casual mention of the white man's army which marched through last year; other problems, such as smallpox and food, were of more immediate importance.

The next day the Chilcotins, inwardly proud of their accomplishments in escaping the pursuing white men and in conquering the big snows, borrowed a canoe from the villagers. It was their intention to paddle down to the mouth of the Bella Coola River where there were three white traders. But the dugout canoe was not for the dry-country Indian. After three of them had been dumped into the stream, much to the glee of the villagers, Sorrence and his men cautiously poled the canoe back to the landing, whereupon two of the villagers leaped into it and seized the poles. In their skilled hands the craft skimmed downstream with the grace and assurance of a waterbird.

Two hours later as they went around the last bend in the river, the Bella Coola Indians called excitedly to each other in their own language and, pointing down river to the bay where a large ship lay at anchor, told their Chilcotin guests that it was a white man's ship with big guns and maybe it would blow an Indian village right out of the forest. The Bella Coolas talked to the Chilcotins in Chinook, and described the ship as 'cultus" because it might bring trouble to the Indians. "They think a man is hiding here who killed a white man."

It was the policy of the government of the colony of British Columbia and of the Hudson's Bay Company not to let a major crime like murder escape unpunished. If the culprits were found to be residents of an Indian village the authorities, whether government or Hudson's Bay Company, would demand that the villagers produce the criminals. If they failed to comply a warning was given to evacuate and, after a certain number of hours, the ship's cannons would shell the village, razing it to the ground. This form of punishment — for the most part bloodless — and the vigorous prosecution of murderers, eventually and firmly established the fact that the white man's law must be obeyed.

When the Chilcotins and their hosts landed at the trading establishment, an air of excitement was as evident as the tension before a thunder storm. They learned that officers from the gunboat in the bay had come ashore in the morning in search of the man who had killed Mr. Ogilvie. Since the villagers could not produce the culprits, an ultimatum was issued — "Have the murderers at the ship at sunrise tomorrow or we will destroy your village in one hour thereafter."

It seemed the Bella Coola villages were fresh out of murderers, or at least any which could be induced or coerced into surrendering and thus save the village from destruction. Nor was the village — or rather villages, for there were four different ones at the mouth of the valley — sufficiently organized or policed to seize hostages.

There were three white men, all traders, in the trading compound, which was a barricaded building within a small stockaded clearing. It had been built with the idea of defence against an attack. When the gate was closed and chained at night, and the four large dogs (now fastened to the side of the buildings) turned loose within the enclosure, a solid protection against surprise attack was ensured. The three white men had joined forces, creating a triumvirate which made it their policy to get as much trade and wealth from the Indians as possible, regardless of consequences. Two of the men, Angus Macleod and Jim Taylor had, several years earlier, taken blankets from the graves of Indian smallpox victims and thus caused the deadly smallpox epidemic of 1864 — and perhaps even the Chilcotin War.

Macleod and Taylor had made a profit on the blankets, but a thousand Indians had died of smallpox, and the Chilcotin War had been precipitated in which twenty white men lost their lives. The Waddington Road effort was wiped out and the military endeavour to bring peace cost the new colony $80,000.00. In spite of the fact that the Chilcotin War and its indirect results had reduced the traffic of white men to almost nil on the Bella Coola trade route, they still managed to make a good deal from their dealings with the Indians.

As a common defence against possible Indian attacks they formed a trading and domestic triumvirate with Ian Black, the man who had bought out the interests of Peter White. When he arrived on the *Labouchère,* the Indians were at first puzzled by a white man called Black, then quickly decided to refer to Peter White as Peter the Whiteman and to call Ian Black simply "The Blackman." And so, into the lore of the Bella Coola Indians were woven stories of The Blackman — which had nothing to do with those of Negro origin.

Macleod, Taylor and Black had met the officials who were searching for Ogilvie's murderer and had tried to convince them that the man had fled Bella Coola immediately following his crime.

"Look here," the top official told them. "We are told he is in Bella Coola; we have it on our records. Therefore, if Bella Coola doesn't surrender the culprit, it will have to take the consequences. We have no time for further investigation."

"But there are a half dozen villages in the mouth of the Bella Coola Valley," Ian Black expostulated. "Are you going to level all of them?"

"Our records just say the culprit is in Bella Coola; therefore, any or all of the villages might be shelled."

"We are three white men here, with investments and business," Black countered. "You realize that if any damage is done to our property, and particularly if one of us is killed, your job might come to a sudden end; you would probably be court-martialed."

The official hesitated before bombastically replying, "Of course we have no plans to threaten the life and property of *our* citizens; we will not shell the main village."

"I have heard stories of some bad ones from that village at the foot of the mountain over there," Macleod interposed, pointing southward. "It's the only one you can see from the bay."

"That's the one," the official stated. "I'll enter it in our records that evidence supports our suspicion that the murderers came from that village." He drew himself up with satisfaction. "Will you tell the villagers that if they don't deliver their criminals by sunrise tomorrow we shall destroy their village." His voice rose with the importance of his proclamation. "If any people get killed, we will not be responsible."

So it was.

When the Indians of that little village — the only one you could see from the bay, thus making shelling easier — were told that their village was to be destroyed on the morrow, consternation reigned.

"Better get your stuff out of the houses," the white men told the Indians, "and go live in some of the other villages until it's over. Unless, that is, you have a good stock of murderers who would like to be hanged."

Into this atmosphere came the six Chilcotins with small packs of last winter's furs and a need for some of the things a white man's trade could give them.

Trading their furs for goods was done in an hour or so, Black and Taylor attending to the transaction while Macleod worked at the rear of the room. When the trading was finished one of the Chilcotins drew from his belt a small bag, from which he poured half a dozen yellow pebbles.

"You think chickamin rock?" he asked Black, who was nearest.

Black picked up several of the pebbles without much interest. Many times Indians had brought rocks to him with the idea that they might be precious metal. Then the weight of these impressed him, and he bit one. His teeth left faint marks on the surface. Suddenly he became extremely interested.

"Jim! Mack!" he called to his companions, "I think we have some big gold nuggets here."

"It's gold, alright," Macleod said, with a deep intake of breath. And to the Indian he said, "Where did you get this?"

"We go across the river that flows white water and climb over big ice to summer pasture of many goats. We find chickamin rock in our camp-fire."

"You go back that way and take me. I give you all the blankets, all the horses, all the guns you want." To the chief he said, "You will be the most powerful chief between here and Alexandria!"

Sorrence had been studying the white men. He saw their excitement when they recognized the gold, and suddenly remembered where he had seen two of them before. They had come into his camp with pack horses loaded with blankets, and these blankets had been stolen from the graves of Indians who had died from smallpox.

"We go to make camp now," he said, picking up the pieces of gold. "That is not white man's land. We will not take you." Whereupon he walked out, his men following, and disappeared into the forest.

The three white men stared after the Indians. Curtness from an Indian was an unusual thing, and not to accept a white man's offer of sudden wealth was almost totally unprecedented.

Taylor was for following the Indians and getting more information from them, maybe a map so they could find this gold deposit, but the others held him back.

"There's something different about those fellows," Macleod said. "That chief has those fellows under control. That whole bunch isn't easy to push around."

Despite the fact that they were more than usually busy with people rushing around vacating the Indian village against the foot of the southern mountain, the thought of the gold, coupled with the Indians' refusal to show them to its source, was constantly in their minds and they made frequent reference to the matter in their conversation.

Over their evening meal the talk was again of the Indians and their gold. "I think," Macleod suddenly burst out, "those are some of the bastards that killed McDonald and the others at Nankootloon. You know the story was that a bunch of them had run into the mountains when Brew and Cox were trying to round up the murderers. This could be that bunch!"

"If they are, they'd be a bad bunch to fool with," Black said.

"They're still Indians," Macleod said. "Treat them rough and they'll lie down for you. I'm going to see them and get them to take us up there whether they like it or not. You fellows coming?"

Taylor agreed to go, with Black staying at the trading post to let them into the stockade when they returned.

The two white men thrust revolvers into their belts, a bottle of liquor into their pocket and, going in the direction taken by the Chilcotins in the afternoon, soon saw a little fire flickering through the deepening shadows. There was only one man in the light of the fire, and he rose to his feet as the two white men stepped out of the shadows into the small circle of light given by the camp fire.

"Where are your men?" Macleod asked the man, whom he recognized as the chief. He spoke to him in the Chilcotin language, for he had recognized that these men were from the interior, and in speaking Chilcotin to them hoped to establish clearly that they were from that area.

"My men are away," Sorrence replied in Chilcotin. "Why do you come to my camp?"

"We came to be your friends," Macleod replied, bringing the bottle of liquor from his pocket. Pulling the cork, he offered the bottle to Sorrence.

The chief looked at the bottle, then fixedly at the white men. "White man's fire-water make slaves of Indians," he said. "I do not wish to become a slave. Why do you wish our friendship? You already have our furs."

Macleod and Taylor realized the meeting was not going well. This Indian had turned away their liquor, the first weapon with which they had hoped to win him, and was questioning the motives of their profferred friendship. One now stood on either side of the chief, so that when he faced one his back was to the other.

"We want you to go with us to where you found the chickamin rock," Taylor said. "We will give you half the gold we find, enough to make you the biggest chief west of the Fraser River."

"We already have found the gold," the Indian levelly replied. "You have not any gold from which to give half."

Thus far, Taylor had allowed Macleod to do the talking but now he realized, as did Macleod, that here was a type of Indian they had never before had to deal with. They could not know the conditions which had brought out in Sorrence the dispassionate ability to appraise a situation and the reasoning power to suggest a way out of difficulties. Nor could they see from his calm exterior the deep current of distrust for all white men, and the hatred of themselves in particular. The Indians among whom they moved had for the most part been good-natured creatures who were putty in their hands. Here was a different breed.

"You know Indians are not allowed to stake claims and dig gold from the earth," Taylor told Sorrence pointedly. "White man has never seen this land," Sorrence countered. "He does not know where it is. His law cannot go to land that he does not know."

The white men then made a mistake; they allowed their frustration to change to irritation. Macleod spoke sharply: "You are Chilcotin. Some of your people are wanted for the murder of white men. If you do not agree to take us to where you found the gold, we will give you to the captain of the ship out there," pointing to the bay, "and tell him you are the men that the white man's army were looking for last summer."

Not a muscle of Sorrence's face moved to indicate that the thrust had gone home. He knew that white men might put chains on him, keep him in prison, or hang him. Then a faint smile played disdainfully around his lips.

"If the white men with forked tongues went into the mountains with us, would they not be afraid that we would kill them also?"

"That is easy," Macleod said. "We will keep you a prisoner here, while your men take two of us to where the gold is. When they come safely back with the gold, we will set you free."

Sorrence laughed scornfully.

"You would keep me tied up like a dog for maybe one moon. If there are summertime snows, maybe two moons. Then you give us all to the captain of the ship and tell him to hang us. If all of the white man's army could not take us prisoner, only two white men cannot."

"We'll show you," Macleod snarled in anger. He snatched his revolver from his belt and aimed it at the Indian's chest. On Sorrence's other side Taylor did the same. "Put up your hands!"

Sorrence wore a faint, taunting smile as his hands started to rise from his side. At first they rose slowly as if in indecision, then suddenly shot straight up. Almost immediately, five arrows hissed out of the forest and found their targets in the throats of the white men. As their revolvers dropped to the ground the white men's hands groped upwards as they tried in vain to scream through throats cut by razor-sharp arrowheads.

Sorrence watched their dying struggles impassively. When they lay still, he signalled his men to come from behind the bushes where they had stationed themselves when the sound of the white men's boots had announced the coming of visitors. From the moment the white men had stepped into the firelight, arrows had been set against bow-strings. Sorrence's slow lifting of his arms had signalled his men to draw the strings tight and aim, while the last thrust upward had been a command to release the arrows.

"No dance," he commanded his men, as they surrounded the two dead traders. "No shouting. We are in danger. Let us put these men where the ship's captain will bury them tomorrow morning."

So they carried the two bodies into one of the big houses of the condemned village, now deserted and awaiting its destruction on the morrow. A fire still smoldered in some logs in the fireplace as the bodies were laid inside.

Next morning, an hour after the sun had risen over the eastern mountains, the cannons of the ship roared and a salvo of 10-pound shot followed by another heavier round tumbled the several large dwellings to the ground. The cedar logs and hewn slabs caught fire from the still hot coals in the fireplace and the ruins burned briskly for an hour or two. When the officials from the ship made a cursory inspection of their work, they did not even guess they had cremated the bodies of two men whose killing might well have been an act of retributive justice.

Ian Black at first felt no concern when his two trading companions failed to return. Frequently in their association either or both men had departed suddenly to trade with the Indians. When the excitement created by the shelling of the village had somewhat abated, he inquired regarding the Chilcotins as well as the missing white men but could gain no information. After several weeks he learned that the women and children of the Chilcotins, encamped at the Great Village under Mount Noosgultz, had disappeared as completely as had their men. He considered the possibility of his companions having convinced the Indians to take them to their gold deposits, and let the matter go for a month or so.

In his enquiries regarding their whereabouts he told of the visit of the gold-bearing Chilcotins, and from these stories grew the oft-repeated tale of the Whitewater gold, a tale that has haunted generations. Is there a gold deposit of almost unimaginable wealth back of those fierce crags south of the Bella Coola Valley? The streams indicate there is, as fine powdered gold comes down the Whitewater River, and in 1912 an already rich man gambled his life in an attempt to reach the forbidden area, but lost; whether he was murdered by his Indian guide or lost his life in some other way is still frequently debated. One stream born in the general area referred to in the saga of the Chilcotins carried enough gold yearly to induce Frank Render, who later bought a ranch in the Anahim Lake area, to leave his job at the Namu salmon canneries. Yearly Render washed gold in a stream which flows into Owakena Lake and the Indians called this stream Wash-Wash Creek because of his activity.

When the Chilcotins left the bodies of their victims in the deserted Indian house, they returned immediately to camp where, under their chief's urging, they rapidly arranged packs, shouldered them and, circumventing the traders' compound and the Indian village near it, trotted rapidly up the river-side trail. Those men were hardened travellers. In their native Chilcotin, when horses were first introduced, their ancestors could outrun them. While they had lost this power to some extent, their experiences of the last year had hardened their bodies and disciplined their minds.

The people of the Great Village were still slumbering when the Chilcotins silently awakened their women and children and, after they had arranged and donned packs, drew them onto the trail. Fortune favored them, for when the thunder of the ship's cannons roared from peak to peak the residents of the villages in the upper valley took to their canoes and raced downriver to see the excitement. The trail was deserted. In the agony of excitement and suspense caused by the repeated bombardment it was not noticed that the camp of the Chilcotin women and children was deserted.

Several days later, encamped for the night at the edge of the Chilcotins' territory, the chief addressed his followers: "Tomorrow we will scatter as the leaves before the wind. We will be returning to our own people. We do not know whether we will be greeted with friendship or with spears. If white men are still searching for us, they

136

will be looking for many people, not just one man or a family. We will scatter; but we will remember that we have been where no man ever walked before, and we have come back again. We have been the dead, and now we live again. If trouble comes to one, we must all go and fight for that man."

The next few weeks, in various parts of the country, strangers appeared in strange lands. In Ulkatcho, at Tetachuck, at Nazko, strangers came who spoke the tongue of the Chilcotins, but said nothing of the immediate past; and they were accepted.

Sorrence, realizing his people could not live happily without others of their kind, settled with his family near Nimpo Lake, across which he could see the snowy crags of the Cascades rising into the western skies. Then he approached, in succession, to Alexis and Anahiem, the chiefs who had promised the white authorities they would capture and turn in Sorrence and his men.

"You who have sold your fellowmen to the white soldiers shall listen. I am Sorrence, whom you were to give to the white chiefs for some money and food. I am Sorrence, who was as dead and has returned to live among people again. We wish to live in peace, my men and I. I tell you now that you know not how many we are nor where we live. I tell you that if any man tries to harm any of us, or to capture him for the white chiefs to hang, then that man will die. But before he dies his horses will die; his children will die; his wife will have to beg at the camps of white men and finally, when fear has chilled his blood, that man will die also, with an arrow in his throat. You are a wise man. Live at peace with your neighbors."

Sorrence was right. The chiefs did not know how many men Sorrence had, nor where they were. A legend grew up and peace reigned in the Chilcotin, and from distant places some of Sorrence's men returned and several small villages grew anew on sites left deserted through smallpox and war.

Again fortune smiled on Sorrence. When he returned to the land of his people white men were no longer offering rewards for the capture of suspected Indian murderers; in fact, they had written off the Chilcotin war as concluded. When the government of British Columbia in the spring of 1865 imported two silver tea services at a cost of $2,000 for presentation to Chartres Brew and Judge Cox, it put an end to the whole matter. Besides which, Governor Seymour went to England to get married, and officials in New Westminster were struggling with such financial problems that the thought of another $80,000 for a second punitive expedition would not have been entertained. Sorrence was never sought.

One of the party, a girl who at the time of the flight into the mountains was only ten years old, grew up to become known by the name of Kwut. She, in full womanhood, took her son Tulkay (The Swan) up the Whitewater River and clambered up onto the ice from which she pointed to the distant upland green valley.

"There is where we dried the meat of many goats, and found golden pebbles by the ashes of our fires," she told Tulkay.

But they didn't descend from the icefield, which would have necessitated cutting steps in a long steep face of ice. They had ventured farther into this strange land than Indians customarily did, and though buoyed by an adventurous spirit were nervous of their unusual surroundings.

"Some day you come back with more men," Kwut told her young son, "with axes to cut steps in the ice, and poles to put across the cracks, and maybe you will get a bag of chickamin rocks and become rich and be the biggest chief in the land." They then returned to the green world of the forests and to the land of their people.

Kwut passed away; Tulkay became a man, then a middle-aged man. He became known as Old Tulkay, and visited much with the family of Macks in Bella Coola. Due to an eye infection he lost the sight of one eye and was threatened with loss of sight in the other. He told the story of the gold of the Whitewater to the young boys of the Mack family — Clayton, Ordon and Sampson — and promised to guide them to it when they were big enough to make the journey.

Then, one day when he was in the ranching country around Anahim Lake, and his remaining functional eye started to pain him, he poured strong horse linament into it, thinking to effect a cure. He suffered an agony of pain and became totally blind. He had to surrender his dream of guiding the young Macks to the gold fields.

Instead, he became a living legend. His sense of touch became so well developed that with the aid of a stick he could feel his way along a forest path with amazing speed. He walked from Bella Coola to Ulkatcho, a distance of about 120 miles, over rough and swampy trails. His sense of smell became so acute that he could name the family of a person who entered a room where he was, and if someone had been hunting Old Tulkay's nostrils told him so as well as what kind of game had been taken.

But he never attempted to smell or feel his way to the gold field.

6 The Hudson's Bay Co. in Bella Coola

White men first met traders from Bella Bella in 1793 when Alexander Mackenzie encountered the Malevolent One in the channels en route. Less than forty years later Hudson's Bay Company traders were following that route from Bella Bella to Bella Coola. In May, 1833 they established their trading post at Fort McLoughlin, only a few miles from present Bella Bella, and used this as a midcoast base to visit other nearby Indian villages.

In 1843 the post was abandoned and partly torn down in order to use the materials for building Fort Victoria. The Indians burned what was left to get the metal used in the construction. For ten years there was no trading post at Bella Bella until, in 1853, a new post was erected, and from it expeditions were again made to surrounding villages for trading.

From the southern and headquarters post of Fort Victoria ships were dispatched which frequently found their way to Bella Coola. There was the *Beaver,* the *Labouchère,* the *Otter* and others, with instructions to stop at Bella Coola, Bela Kula, Billhoola, or even New Aberdeen — all meaning the same place.

The instructions from Chief Factor W.F. Tolmie (who had served as factor at the Bella Bella post 1833-1834) to Captain H.G. Lewis of the Hudson's Bay Company Steamer *Otter* Victoria, January 6, 1867: "You will also call at Billhoola, and any other places to the southward where prospects of trade might appear."

In the summer of 1867, during a period in which the Indians were recurringly troublesome and white people were moving out of the district, the Hudson's Bay Company established their post ashore at Bella Coola. Just above high tide mark, by the river that whispered stories of lost gold mines, and told of rich salmon runs and of Indian glories that were past, they established their fort. The record they had earned across the continent of fair and just dealings with the Indians was enhanced here. Besides this, the Company, frequently the only authority for hundreds of miles, maintained a firm disciplinary hand. Its reward in Bella Coola was peaceful coexistence and trade with the Indians.

For the first two years the post was directly under the command of the *Otter*. Commencing in 1869 the servants of the Company at Bella Coola were as follows:

1869	Matthew Feak.
1870	Matthew Feak, Temporary Postmaster.
1871-1873	George Clayton, Postmaster.
1874	Archibald Napier.
1875-1876	John Clayton, Postmaster.
1877	F. Kennedy, Postmaster.
1878-1882	William Sinclair, Postmaster.

In November 1882 the Bella Coola post was closed, the goods being taken aboard the *Otter* and transferred to Fort Simpson.

Shortly after this the property was sold to John Clayton of Bella Bella, who came thereupon to Bella Coola and was the last of the Bella Bella traders to do so.

In 1869 Governor Frederick Seymour died at Bella Coola. Governor Seymour prided himself on his ability to settle Indian troubles, and when an outbreak of hostilities occurred between the Nass and the Tsimshian Indians in 1869, a series of murders took place, one in retaliation for another, all resulting from the accidental killing of a man in a drunken orgy at an Indian wedding feast. Governor Seymour had for some time suffered from ill health but, eager to settle the Indian trouble, sailed north on *H.M.S. Sparrow - hawk* on May 17. He spent three weeks of intensive investigation and questioning, and re-established peace. But he paid for the effort with his life, for the illness which had weakened him — dysentery — finally killed him when at anchor in the Bella Coola bay on June 10. The *Sparrowhawk* proceeded immediately to Victoria and Frederick Seymour was buried in the Esquimalt naval cemetery on June 16, 1869.

It fell to the lot of the Hudson's Bay Company to patch the rent in the relations between white man and Indian in Bella Coola, and to arrange for peace between the two races. At a time when the people of the southern part of British Columbia were beginning to take an almost fierce interest in elections and the position of the capital of the colony (whether it should be in Victoria or New Westminster), matters of public debt and the prospect of joining the rest of Canada, Bella Coola was still a territory where Indians were looked upon as a threat to one's very life. They had learned that it was still permissible to kill other Indians, and on occasional forays with such a purpose they either died, or returned with scalps, slaves or the heads of their enemies.

The chain of circumstances that was ultimately to change the whole face of British Columbia was in process of being forged as far back as 1865 when a publication appeared advocating a railway from Halifax by way of Chicago, St. Paul, Fort Garry, Edmonton and the Yellowhead Pass to the Pacific at either Bute Inlet or Dean Channel. In the years that followed Yellowhead Pass was used as the most favorable railway pass through the Rockies, but neither the Bute Inlet nor Dean Channel passes through the Coast Range had been used by railways. Yet parallel lines of steel brought to an end the old way of life, for they carried on them the multitudes of settlers who knew and cared little about dying cultures.

When serious consideration was given the finding of a suitable railroad route through the mountains of British Columbia — the union of this western colony with Canada was dependent upon the building of a railway link from Canada to the Pacific Coast — the territory from the International Boundary northward was given thorough inspection. In the summer of 1874 seven exploratory parties were in the field. Engineers in charge of the parties were E. W. Jarvis, H. P. Bell, C. H. Gamsby, H. J. Cambie, John Trutch, Charles Horetzky and Marcus Smith. Their crews consisted of more than three hundred men.

All possible routes from the Fraser River northward were investigated. Charles Horetzky explored and recommended the route from Bentinck Arm through the Bella Coola gap to Giscombe Portage, thence by Fort McLeod and the Peace River. This was in 1873. Again in 1874 an exploratory survey was made from the head of Dean Channel on the Dean River to connect with other routes in the Blackwater River Valley. In 1876 harbour possibilities in the Dean Channel were inspected.

The route of the railway was finally decided upon. It was to terminate at Burrard Inlet and the site of the present city of Vancouver.

It was when he was only 14 that Samuel Shields was left stranded in the Indian Village at Bella Coola.

It was really no one's fault, just a quirk of circumstance, that fall day in 1873 when the two men who had adopted him were killed. They had taken care of him when his father died and left him an orphan. When they acquired a thirty-six foot sailing boat and sailed it up the coast on a trading venture, they brought him along. From one village to another they went, trading with varied success, and finally arrived at the mouth of the Bella Coola River.

When they awoke it was a clear morning on the tail of the southeaster that had lifted them up the channel. Smoke arose from the dark spruce trees, but there was no sign of human activity as the two men and the gangling youth stood on the deck of their little ship and looked at the scene around them.

They saw the snowline two-thirds of the way down the high mountains around them.

"Winter's close by up north here," Jim Sheppard, the elder of the two men and nominal captain of the boat, remarked. "When we get through here, we're going back to Victoria." "I'll go ashore and see if I can stir up some trade," the other, Fred Neilson, volunteered, starting to unlash the small rowboat. "You come with me, Sam." Jim stayed with the sailboat.

With the lad in the stern of the small landing craft, Neilson rowed for the river mouth. Breasting the river current, they passed the palisaded establishment of the Hudson's Bay Company and came to an Indian village perched on the side of the river. High totem poles and carved house fronts rose in silhouette against the morning sun, and several ravens in a tree croaked raucously to themselves and the world in general. A dozen or so dugout canoes were tied to posts or trees. Among these some Indians were working, and as the dinghy approached they stopped their work to greet the white men.

One of them pointed at the mountains north of them, waved his arms, cupped his hands to his mouth and blew with an undulating whistling sound through his teeth. He spoke rapidly and emphatically in his own language. Then another spoke up.

"Cultis wind come," he said. "Delate cultis!"

Suddenly the Indians became very excited, seeming almost angry.

Above: The last of the Bella Coola Indian medicine men, Kimsquit Alec, wears his official head-dress.

Right: Billy Jones, last survivor of the group of Bella Coola Indians who went to Germany with B.F. Jacobsen, wears a ceremonial blanket.

Above: A carved sea canoe. Made in the Queen Charlotte Islands, it was probably procured by trade or gift from the northerly Indians. Photo – Iver Fougner

Left: Nuxalk eagle mortuary post. The coffin contains the body of a chief's child. John Clayton's Hudson's Bay Trading Post is in the background. HBC traded in Bella Coola from 1867 until 1882.

Right: An ornately painted chest from Bella Bella, each plank hand-hewn from yellow cedar.

Below: The mask on the right is a Hamesta mask worn by the Man-eaters in their winter ceremonies. These two masks are part of the B.F. Jacobsen collection.

Q'umk'uts (Bella Coola),
1897. Main street in the Old
Village on the south side of
the Bella Coola River. The
distinctive spired Clellamin
House was replicated in
1989 in the Grand Hall at
the Canadian Museum of
Civilization in Hull,
Quebec. Photos – Iver
Fougner.

One held up his hand in a gesture to command silence, and when the other had quieted down held his hands to his ears and pointed northward.

The three turned their faces northward and heard a heavy roar, rapidly growing in volume and intensity.

"Look at the tops of the mountains," Neilson told Samuel. "That noise we hear is wind!"

Samuel followed the direction of his pointing finger and saw snow being torn off the mountain tops and drive out in long plumes that resembled clouds.

"Our boat," he cried, "and Jim . . ."

"We'll get out there right now," Neilson replied, seizing his oars and pulling away from the Indian canoes. "If we can get up an inch of sail we might run before it."

Two hundred yards downstream a dugout canoe darted from the bank below the Hudson's Bay Company post. Four Indians with poles propelled it over the water at top speed. In the centre of the canoe sat a bearded white man, who hailed the other two whites.

"Are you men from the boat out there?" he asked, nodding toward the bay. "The Indians just told me you were there. There is a northwind coming and no small boat will live through it. If you hurry you might have time to work it up into one of the sloughs."

Suddenly Samuel had the feeling this was all a dream, that they were part of a crystalline picture which he, disembodied, was regarding dispassionately.

"You will have to hurry. The Indians say it will hit with terrific force," the bearded man said insistently.

"Can I leave the lad here with you?" he heard Neilson ask, and saw the bearded man nod. "Sam, stay here so I can get out to the boat faster."

He whipped the dinghy over to the canoe and Sam scrambled in behind the elderly white man.

Neilson braced his feet against the bottom of his craft and with long powerful pulls on the oars, into which he put the strength of every muscle, he sent the dinghy leaping almost out of the water. The bearded man spoke a brief command and the dugout canoe followed close behind.

In a few minutes they reached the river mouth.

At the same time the vanguard of the big wind hit them in the shape of buffeting whirlwinds, whipping water into their faces and almost blinding them. The canoe pulled over to the river bank, and the Indians, leaning heavily on their poles, held it tight.

Neilson, still pulling on the oars with every ounce of his strength, drew rapidly away. A mile away the sailboat rode at anchor.

Then, with a bestial scream, the wind hit them. The white man and his youthful guest had to crouch to keep from being bowled out of the canoe, and it swept across the bay picking up a wall of spray that broke into battalions of rapidly advancing water devils. When these hit the sailboat the watchers could see it start to buck and strain against the anchor rope like a frightened horse trying to free itself from a restraining picket. Frequently the flying spume was so dense that neither the straining Neilson nor the plunging sailboat could be seen. As the tortured water mounted into higher waves, the actions of both the dinghy and its mother craft became more violent.

"White man mamaloos," the canoe captain told the white man. "Now he killopie!"

"The Indian says the dinghy has overturned," the white man interpreted.

They watched intently, but the rowboat no longer rose on the crest of the waves. Only the sailboat was still riding, plunging, rearing, bucking. Occasionally a black figure could be seen attempting to work the rigging, but having to spend much of the time hanging on to avoid going overboard.

"How many aboard?" the white man asked Samuel and when he was told that there was only one, he said, "I'm afraid he's trapped. He just hasn't got room to sail out."

He gave a command to the Indians, who pushed the canoe away from the bank. The wind caught the craft and swung it against the lower south bank. Two of the Indians leaped and started running across the tidal flats.

"They are going to go around the bay and be ashore to help in case the anchor loosens and the boat goes up on the rocks," the white man explained to Samuel.

They clambered up on the land to watch. The running Indians had disappeared among the bushes that marked the edge of the forest, but a half mile or so away the sailboat still fought the rising waves and punishing spray.

Then she seemed to calm.

"She's adrift," the white man said. "In five minutes she'll be finished."

Helplessly they watched the craft, now broadside to the wind, rise and fall as she approached the rocky shoreline. All time, all distance seemed to stop as the trim vessel bowed and danced toward her doom. They saw her rise high, as if trying to leap the foam, saw her momentarily stand clear of the water as the wave subsided, and then fall outward as her deep keel caught on a rock. The next wave washed over her completely, then lifted and pounded her on the rocks, and suddenly they saw the figure of a man catapult into the frothing sea.

"I'm sorry, laddie," the white man said to the youth at his side. "He had about ten seconds to jump, and a thousand chances against him. The Indians will be there to help — if there is anyone to help."

They returned to the canoe, the wind buffeting them at every step, and now the white man took a canoe pole and handed one to Samuel.

"We will need your help," he said curtly to the numbed youngster, "to get this canoe back to the post."

The canoe could have been handled by the two remaining Indians without the assistance of even the bearded white man, but the act of balancing himself and pushing in unity with the other three, while at the same time resisting the attack of the screaming wind which threatened to bowl him out of the canoe, kept Samuel from dwelling on the crushing blow dealt him. They crept up against the current, staying close to the heavily forested river bank which offered some vestige of shelter, and eventually thrust the bow of the canoe up on the gravel beneath the post.

"We'll send some more of the men around the bay to see if they can help, or maybe save something," the white man said.

He took Samuel into the trading post, poured coffee and put some food out, then sat down at the table opposite the youth, who had said scarcely a word since leaving the canoe.

"I'm George Clayton," the bearded man said, "in charge of the post for the Hudson's Bay Company. What is your name?" And when he was told he said, "Samuel is too long a name for even a tall fellow like yourself. We'll call you Sam."

When Samuel, in reply to his questioning, told him that the two men who had just drowned were the only friends he had in the world, that his father had just died a few months before and these men, who knew his father, had befriended him and cared for him, Clayton whistled softly.

"You have no near relatives? No friends with whom you could live? Have you any idea how you could live when you go back to Victoria?" to which he received a shake of the head for each question. "Would you like to stay here for the winter?"

Samuel's face lit up. "I would like to stay with you," he said.

And so it was arranged. George Clayton was gruff, kindly and clever. He worked Samuel — making him feel important, and he taught him — humbling him. He fathered him and fed him so that Sam truly increased in wisdom and stature.

Soon, too, the boy's personality began to change.

Apart from Clayton, his sole human contacts were Indians. These people were unable to enunciate some of the white man's words. "G" for instance became "K" when it was near the end of a word — for example, "dogs", became "docks", and "frogs" became "frocks". An even more pronounced difficulty was the pronunciation of the sound "sh" which became "S", and from the word "shoot" grew the Indian version "soot", and from "hush" came "huss". It was natural for the Indians, then, to call Shields "Seelds", and the name was further distorted when the natives ran first and last names together in a sibilant "Samseels". So Sam told his new acquaintances to call him simply "White Sam" and with this they had no difficulty.

So "White Sam" came into being and Samuel Shields disappeared. Samuel Shields' few contacts when he shipped with his two drowned benefactors disappeared with their deaths and the assuming of his new name. When Clayton introduced him to others he used the name White Sam.

White Sam rapidly learned the Chinook dialect but then discovered that this was only a limited trade language, that many of the Indians could not use it, and that they talked to each other in their own tongue when they wished to put a language barrier between them and the white man. So instead of speaking Chinook he started, much to the delight and amazement of the Indians, to talk to them in their own language. At first it was several twisted words which sent the natives into gales of laughter. In a few months he was able to converse intelligently in the difficult language, and before the winter had passed a group of natives who tried to erect a language baffle found him laughingly entering into the conversation.

His knowledge of their language proved the key which opened the door to extraordinary acceptance by the natives. He was invited to their ceremonial dances — as a spectator, of course — on the same basis as visitors from other Indian villages such as Bella Bella and Owakina. Only initiated members of the powerful secret societies could take part in these ceremonials. If by accident or spying someone learned too much of a secret society — which spread its influence through all the Bella Coola tribes of the Bella Coola Valley, South Bentinck Arm villages and the villages of Dean Channel and Kimsquit valley — that person was either taken into the society or killed. Sam saw the village terrorized by the Cannibal Dancers; saw men, seemingly disembowelled, return to life and health before the coming of dawn; saw a man's head torn off and blood dripping from the severed parts, later saw the head returned to the body and the man return to life.

George Clayton was pleased that his protégé had learned the language of the natives and observed their dances.

"There's a lot of real art and a lot of hoodwinkery in what those fellows show us," Clayton told Sam. "All this is harmless enough. No one seems to get killed. But they have some real black magic which results in death. Last year it was rumoured that a strapping big fellow had had a curse put on him for some reason and that he would die in four months. And sure enough, he started to wither away and in less than four months they had doubled his dead body into a sitting position and put him in his coffin! Most white men would ridicule the idea and say it was only mind over matter. It might be but it works. Sometimes things happen that you can't just shrug away."

Sam found many things in the psychology of the Indian village that contradicted the thinking of white men. An Indian's greatness was measured by the amount of goods he gave away rather than by the amount he accumulated. If he were successful enough in fishing or trapping; or if his family or his wife's family could gather together enough goods to give one or more large potlatches at which the accumulated wealth was given away, he could become a great chief. The potlatch system was one in which guests were invited to a feast and each received a gift. Many thousand dollars worth of goods were given away and the man's fame and prestige spread in direct ratio to his giving. It was expected of the recipients of such gifts that they would later return the present with considerable interest added.

Meanwhile the work of the trading post went on. Records of business with incoming trappers were kept. Credit was given to trappers to equip them, and the bill was paid scrupulously on their return from the traplines. It was part of Sam's work to record receipts and expenditures. His entries for a week read thus:

	Jan. 1st.		Trade Value	Cost
Returns:	1 mink	1/6 lb. Tobacco	18	10
	1 bro. martin 1¼ lbs	do	2.50	62-1/2
		1 lb yel. soap		10
	order for $1.00			
	2 mink	½ lb. leaf tobacco.	.50	26
Post expense	Letter to Bella Bella			
	½ lb. leaf tobacco.		.25	
	Jan 2nd.			
Returns	1 deer skin 1/8lb tobacco		12½	07
	1 mink	1 lb aaa shot	25	
Meps.	1 sk.	50 lbs. flour		
	Boat left for Bella Bella.			
	Jan. 3rd.			
Returns	1 mink	¼ lb. tobacco	25	13
	Amspatseiwalls (John) died 6 P.M.			
	of general debility			
	Jan. 4th.			
	No Trade.			

Rec'd information that there are 4 or 5 men lurking in this neighborhood, name, nation, color and intentions unknown.

Will not speak.

Jan. 5th.

No Trade.

Meps.	2 lbs sugar
	2 lbs ground coffee.
C. J.	1 lb tobacco.

January 7th was a Sunday, during which the trading post was closed and no work other than domestic was done.

The man who died, Amspatseiwalls, was a man-of-all-work around the post, and when he had become chronically ill Clayton kept him at the post and cared for him until his death.

"Their native remedies and witch doctors aren't for half-civilized members of the tribe," he told Sam.

During the course of helping with the record-keeping Sam learned that a land otter was worth $1.25 for which the Indian received 6 lbs. biscuits, 1 box caps, ¼ dz. cuts cotton, and 5/8 lbs. sugar.

A beaver was worth 50 maybe 25 cents, while a beaver pup brought 12½ cents. Hair seals varied from 12½ to 25 cents. A mink was sometimes worth 25 cents, while a black bear pup brought 2 lbs. of biscuits or 25 cents. A fur seal, wet, was purchased for 12½ cents, while a dry fur seal might bring one dollar. A deer hide was worth 1/8 lb. of tobacco or 12½ cents and a lynx would realize $1.25.

On some days no furs were received; on others as many as a hundred pelts might come in and the care of these, particularly if some were not dried, involved a great deal of work. The wet pelts had to be stretched for drying, and all furs had to be graded, tabulated and made ready for storage and eventual shipment.

When native hunters offered game it was bought to supplement the larder. A deer paid for 2 lbs. aaa shot, ½ lb. tobacco, 1 box of caps and some powdered vermilion, the trade value of which was $1.50. On another occasion 3 quarts of rice, valued at seventy-five cents, were traded for some venison. Twenty-five dried salmon were bought for 1 lb. tobacco, valued at $1.00. The salmon were used for dog food. A goose was worth a quarter pound of tobacco, a halibut three-eighths of a pound of the same. A duck was worth 12½ cents, while seal oil was 25 cents per gallon. Dog fish oil was the same price.

Besides having a few regular Indian workers around, others were frequently hired for some particular job, such as cleaning and drying skins and piling wood (for which they received 35 cents a cord for carrying it from the river bank to the woodshed and piling it there). For carrying a letter to Bella Coola, eighty miles away, the carrier received a reward of 25 cents. Wood was bought for $1.50 a cord. When it was necessary to bring a canoe load of freight from Bella Bella, the canoe men received $2.00 each and the canoe owner received an extra $1.50. In the spring, when women were hired to work in the garden, they were paid at the rate of 25 cents per day.

A strict accounting was kept of the prices of goods sold or traded. A pound of tobacco was worth $1.00 as was a gallon of molasses.

Rice brought 17½ cents a pound and was sometimes sold by the quart which brought 25 cents. A pound of shot (S.S.G.) sold for 25 cents, gunpowder for $1.00 a pound and a box of caps for 25 cents. A pound of soap was worth $1.50, and soda biscuits were two pounds for 25 cents. Bottles of hair oil sold for $1.00 each, a common briar pipe for 25 cents and a better pipe for $1.00. A mink skin was traded for a cotton handkerchief plus one-eighth of a pound of tobacco, and two mink skins for 3 yards of cotton.

Cost records for all these articles were entered in the ledgers. Sometimes the selling price was three and sometimes even five times the cost of the article.

"Our real profit is by no means that high," Clayton explained. "Out of that comes the cost of getting the articles here, and of operating the post."

Eulachon grease was also an article of trade at $1.00 a gallon. There were no dealings in butter as eulachon grease was used in preference.

The busy life of the trading post and his interest in these new people gradually erased from Sam's mind any thoughts of wanting to return to Victoria, and when Clayton brought up the story of the loss of the sailboat and his two guardians the boy found he could discuss the matter as if it had no bearing on his life.

"A wind like that hits only once in many years," Clayton explained. "North winds are always bad, but these killers have built up an evil reputation. The Indians' term for winter is simply 'the whistling of the wind'." Sam remembered the sound "s-p-s" which the Indians made like a shrill piercing of the wind. "The Indians knew a half day before it struck; there was a feeling of floating lightness about things. Very few white men could have predicted a blow like that!"

While no trace of the two men was ever found, the wrecked hulk of the sailboat was hauled up at a low tide, and some axes and knives retrieved. When these were given to Sam he gave them to the Indians who had hauled the smashed boat up where it could be searched.

"Potlatch!" one of them cried. "One day maybe you Indian chief!"

In the spring White Sam went on small fur-collecting trips to the nearby villages of Talio and Kimsquit. Clayton sent him with a canoe team of four men he considered to be the most trusted of the Bella Coola. One of them, Chief Qowi, — captain of the canoe and a man of powerful physique — had with him on the team his son Qwinoa, who was several years older than White Sam and about the same size. The chief's son found the young white man, who could converse freely with him in the Indian tongue, very entertaining and receptive to knowledge. Qwinoa told stories of the bays and headlands they encountered. When they passed around Mesatchi Nose where strong tides and sudden winds kick up murderous seas, food was spread upon the water and eagle-down blown into the air while Qowi made a prayer to the god. "If we don't do this, we will have trouble when we come here again." Qwinoa said.

But despite these precautions, trouble did overtake them just a few miles beyond Mesatchi Nose when a school of whales rose around them. One of these creatures came up under the canoe containing White Sam and his Indian associates, lifting the craft from the water and, when it dived, it flipped its immense tail and smashed the canoe. All the occupants were able swimmers, and they were only a few hundred yards from a point with a shelving beach. White Sam saw Qwinoa motionless, blood welling from his nose and mouth. When he called to him and received no answer, he seized Qwinoa by the hair and towed him to the rocky beach. The others had reached shore moments before and hauled Sam and Qwinoa out of the water as soon as they came within reach.

Qwinoa died there. As he was pulled from the water they could hear the grating of broken bones in his chest, and while others kindled a fire Sam cradled the unfortunate youth's head in his lap. A part of the broken canoe impelled by the force of a tail strong enough to smash two-inch thick wood had been driven into his body.

Though still breathing, Qwinoa only regained consciousness long enough to look into the face of his father, who was crouched over him, and into Sam's face.

"My brother," he said, and his head rolled sideways as with a gasp he died.

White Sam looked up at Qowi. "Chief," he said simply, laying his hand on Qowi's shoulder, "Your son is dead."

"White Sam, you are my son," the chief replied. "You are Qwinoa."

(It was as simple as that to begin with, but the burial of the dead youth and the full adoption of White Sam into the family of Qowi and the tribe was, the following winter, the subject of many ritualistic performances. Not only did he become recognised as the chief's son, but in several years, by virtue of holding many potlatches, he became a chief and a member of the powerful secret society — the Kusiut.)

They carried the dead Qwinoa and laid him on the moss above high tide mark. Then, leaving Qowi and one of the canoe men, White Sam and the fourth crew member made a difficult ten-mile hike back to a little village at Green Bay where they borrowed a large canoe and returned to pick up the body and the other canoe men.

They arrived back in the Bella Coola village about midnight, where many willing hands helped carry Qwinoa to his father's house. Boards were torn off the side of the building so that the body would not have to be taken through the door. If this had happened, others who followed through the doorway might be called by the supernatural and suffer an early death.

George Clayton was among those who met the returning canoe, and he went with White Sam to conduct Qwinoa's body to Qowi's house.

Back at the trading post Clayton and White Sam sat down to a midnight meal while the latter told of his experiences of the day.

"So Qowi wants to adopt you," Clayton said, and when Sam looked at him in amazement he explained, "That is what he meant when he said that you are his son Qwinoa. Qwinoa's spirit entered your body and in a few days Qowi will be thinking you look and act like him. There's a lot of mind-over-matter demonstrations in these villages, and it's uncanny what sometimes does happen. There's black magic and sorcery and deaths by the evil eye — enough to keep story writers busy for a hundred years. This death today will most likely be interpreted by a medicine man as murder."

"This sounds more like Africa, not British Columbia in 1874," Sam said.

"It's here, and it's real enough. Maybe it is acceptable as some phases of our white man's philosophy. I will be going to Victoria when the *Otter* calls. Do you want to go with me? I'll pay your way — or do you want to stay here?"

"I have nobody in Victoria," Sam said simply. "I think I will stay here and see what it is like to be a chief's son."

Clayton paid Sam for his services, gave him a repeating rifle and enough ammunition to last him until the next winter, and when the Hudson's Bay ship, the *Otter,* blew its whistle, Sam was left with the family that adopted him and the tribe that was happy to accept him.

Almost immediately he was asked to interpret the white man's ideas to the Indians, which he did, always to their intense interest and sometimes to their amusement. Steamships they had become acquainted with, but when Sam told them that "back east" there were steam locomotives that rushed at thirty miles an hour and could haul five hundred head of horses on cars, their astonishment knew no bounds.

"But it must have tracks laid first," he explained.

"You mean this locomotive makes its tracks before it travels somewhere?" the Indians asked, and roared with laughter at such a ridiculous idea!

In this new environment life was interesting and time flowed swiftly. During the winters few strangers were seen but summer visitors were many from other coastal villages and the plateau country. George Clayton as Hudson's Bay Company trader was replaced by Archibald Napier and he by John Clayton. There were prospectors looking for gold and surveyors looking for railway routes and sometimes just wanderers . . . tourists.

White Sam, living almost constantly out-of-doors, darkened to a color as brown as his foster-folk. His youthful beard compared with the scant facial growth of the Indians while his body filled out with foods of the sea and thickened with muscles developed by many hours of poling or paddling canoes.

"You look like a young chief," Clayton said on the eve of his departure to Victoria in the early summer of 1876. "You are part of the tribe."

When, several weeks after Clayton left, word came from the Kimsquit tribes that a small army of men was camped on the land that juts out into Dean Channel to create the landlocked bay between the Dean and Kimsquit River mouths, a flotilla of Bella Coola canoes traveled to the head of Dean Channel.

Two dozen of the Indians silently watched the white men at work surveying the land and sounding the channel and bays and continued to stare throughout the evening, when twenty tired white men washed noisily before sitting to eat in a tent with the sides rolled up.

"These damned savages give me the shivers," one of the men said to another. "I don't relish the idea of waking up in the morning without a scalp."

"Maybe we won't wake up," replied the other. "Better say your prayers and be prepared."

"We didn't come for your scalps," White Sam spoke clearly in English from the group of Bella Coola.

The white men jumped as if stabbed, and gazed intently at the Indian group. "Who said that?" one of them asked. And when Sam stepped forth he looked him up and down intently. "Are you a white man?" he asked.

"I am White Sam, born to white parents and adopted by Chief Qowi of the Bella Coola."

"Damned if I would take you for a white man, except from your tongue," the white man said. "Sit in and have a meal with us." Sam shook his head. "Not unless the others eat too."

"We'll feed them too as soon as the men are through," the white man said. "Tell the men to stack their muskets and sit down." And when White Sam told the Indians there would be food for them, they quietly stacked their guns and sat down on the ground watching their white companion, who had risen in their opinion because he was eating with white chiefs.

White Sam learned that this group was making a survey of the head of Dean Channel as to its suitability as a western terminus of a transcontinental railway.

"It's not even at the definite planning stage as yet," the engineer said to White Sam, "and this country may never see a railway. But if Canada is going to stretch from sea to sea a western port is necessary. If it turns out to be this Dean Channel, a great city will grow up here."

"It will be the death of my people," White Sam said.

"Your people? Oh, you mean the Indians," the surveyor remarked, and White Sam realized he had unconsciously identified himself as a native. "Well, it might not happen at all, and your people will be able to continue their free and easy life of trapping and hunting."

When they had finished eating the surveyor said: "We have to have a funeral now. One of our men died the other night after horrible stomach cramps. Would you like to come?"

And so White Sam and his Indian companions went with the white men to where a grave had been dug back off the beach. A cedar tree had been cut off about four feet from the ground, and the stump split to reveal the light red heart of the wood. The clean flat surface had been neatly inscribed with the words: In memory of Isaac Hough, died, July 20th, 1876.

The surveyor stood by the open grave, a Bible in his hand. He removed his hat, and the men around him followed suit.

"Men," he addressed the small gathering, "it is our sad duty to lay in their final resting place the earthly remains of one who has forever gone from us. Isaac Hough, whom we knew as Ike, has gone to meet his Maker. From him we receive a legacy of memories of his kindliness, cheerfulness and courage. Our sorrow is not for the one who has gone but for those who remain, for the wife who will never more know his greeting, for the children who will no longer have his guidance. Ike's influence among us was for good, and we can pay our debt to his memory by copying his virtues.

"I am going to read from the Bible a brief passage from the Psalmist David: 'The earth is the Lord's, and the fullness thereof; the world and they that dwell therein: For He hath founded it upon the seas, and established it upon the floods. Who shall ascend into the hill of the Lord? Or who shall stand in his holy place? He that hath clean hands and a pure heart; who hath not lifted his soul unto vanity, nor sworn deceitfully. He shall receive the blessing from the Lord, and righteousness from the God of his salvation.' "

The reading finished, the surveyor knelt by the coffin and, lifting a loose board from the top, put the Bible on the body's crossed hands.

"With this, this becomes hallowed ground," he said. "Let no one disturb it."

There were murmurs of approbation, and as he rose to his feet the coffin was lowered into the grave. Six strong men with shovels poured in the earth, mounded it, and returned to camp.

(Thus came into tradition the C.P.R. Grave at the head of Dean Channel. It was never disturbed and the wooden marker, preserved by the natural oils of cedar, still gave its message to visitors seventy years later.)

That evening the Bella Coola Indians suddenly decided to return to their village.

"There are bad things happening there," one of the chiefs said when he announced his decision. "Bad medicine is being prepared."

For several reasons it was practical to return by night from the head of Dean Channel to Bella Coola. They were less likely to be waylaid by marauding parties of Haidas, Tsimshians, Kitkatlas from the north or Kwakiutls to the south. During the day west winds frequently blew up channel with such velocity that canoes would have to lay to in a bay.

But the real reason for the Indians' sudden decision to depart homeward was that in the evening clouds an eagle was seen pursued by many song birds. While during the day such an event would have been without significance, its occurrence against evening clouds, at an hour when birds are habitually seeking a place of rest for the night, was interpreted by the Indians as an evil omen. This was explained to White Sam by his canoe companions as they paddled through the night. "Maybe when we get home we will find big trouble," they told him.

"What for did the Tyee white man put the little black book in with dead man?" one of the Indians asked Sam, referring to the funeral they had just seen.

"That is the white man's Bible," Sam explained. "It is a paper that talks. It tells about white man's god."

"Then dead man can read about his god. That is good," one man said.

"Has white man got only one god?" one of the Indians asked. "We have many gods." When White Sam assured him that for the white man there was only one god, the Indian expressed wonderment. "One god look after everything? He's delate busy."

"That god-book the white man put in with the dead man," another said, "that must be real skookum medicine book. Maybe some day a sorcerer dig that man up and steal his book. Then sorcerer be so strong, maybe he kill everybody in the tribe."

"The book is written in white man's language and would be no good unless the sorcerer could read white man's writing," White Sam explained.

A sorcerer, White Sam had learned, was a person who had gained knowledge of black magic and could kill by such means. Sorcerers had tremendous powers, and were deeply feared. When their identity was disclosed they were violently killed, along with their relatives. Chief Qowi had come to believe that the death of his son Qwinoa was due to the machinations of a sorcerer.

Since sorcerers were held in such fear and loathing they did their work in the deepest secrecy to avoid being discovered.

"If Indian learned read white man's words and took his god as well as kept all his own, he would have more power than anyone else," one of the paddlers suggested.

160

"If you take upon yourself white man's god, then you can't keep your old gods," White Sam explained.

"Will white man's god fight our gods?" the Indian asked.

The canoe captain interrupted: "You are talking like a bunch of old women and we have fallen behind the others. Set to and overtake them."

Through the night the skies clouded over and, as they went around Mesatchi Nose in a flat calm, rain fell. Dawn was slow in coming and heavy streamers swept down from the low cloud ceiling like strips torn loose from the heavens. In the east a bit of silver showed where the sun was trying to rise. In this beautiful and almost mystical setting the shamans rose to cast food upon the water for the gods, and to utter their short prayers. White Sam realized that these storied beings of the Indians were becoming more real to him than the God he had heard of from his mother.

A few miles past this point he was seized with such violent pain in his stomach that he dropped his paddle and writhed in agony in the bottom of the canoe. When it seemed that he would surely die, the pain suddenly left. For a while he was faint and sweating profusely but after a while he recovered and picked up his paddle.

"I think a bad witch doctor is trying to kill you, White Sam," one of his fellow canoe men said to him. "Maybe you will die soon."

The canoe man's face was wrinkled with concern, and Sam realized he was not joking. He felt a stab of fear, but the pain did not return.

The homecoming of the small flotilla to Bella Coola drew a number of the villagers to the landing beach. Among these was White Sam's foster father, Chief Qowi, who walked with him to their house, carrying with him some of the gear from the canoe.

In the house, as they ate the roast salmon that was placed before them, White Sam received another shock. A week or so previously a young man had been found dead by his canoe; bruises around his throat indicated that he might have been strangled to death.

"Yesterday it was discovered that he had been taken from his grave," Qowi said. "Maybe there is a sorcerer at work."

White Sam felt again the fear which had stabbed through him following his canoe mate's remark that he might be marked for death. When he told his foster father of the sudden stomach pains which had assailed him the elder man became so excited he literally shook with emotion.

"We must do something at once," he said vehemently. "You must not die!" Then he calmed himself, remembering that a chief should not act in an undignified manner.

At the same moment another chief, Skuna, came through the door.

"Do we talk before your son?" he asked Qowi, and when the latter nodded an affirmative he went on to say, "Today something of great importance may have been discovered. My sister's boy, who you know is a mere youth, was hunting for an eagle's nest on the mountain two days ago when he heard someone coming through the woods. He hid and watched and saw two men carrying what appeared to be a new coffin. When they passed close to him he saw the men were Qwinso and Kwallit. They didn't know he was watching them and when they had passed he followed them into a shallow cave. He saw them light a small fire of dry wood — because it didn't make any smoke — and when they started to open the coffin he became frightened and ran away. He was afraid to tell anyone until today, when he told my sister."

"Qwinso and Kwallit!" Qowi exclaimed. "They are an evil pair." He again became so agitated that he trembled. "Maybe they killed Qwinoa, and now they want to kill Qwinoa again!"

He told Skuna about White Sam's pain.

"Your belly," he cried. "Let us see your belly."

White Sam pulled up his shirt. To his amazement, directly beneath his navel was an abrasion showing traces of darkened blood. He might have scratched it on a thwart when writhing with agony in the canoe, but when his foster father cried out, "Somebody is sticking a knife into your belly, somebody with supernatural powers! He is killing you!", this seemed the more plausible explanation.

Qowi and Skuna looked at each other with a meaning beyond White Sam's comprehension.

"We will have a feast," Qowi said softly. "Qwinoa," — he called White Sam by the name of the son White Sam had replaced — "we must go hunting. I wish to have a feast of seals."

White Sam and his foster father and another son of Qowi prepared immediately for the hunt. Word was passed around that if they were successful there would be a seal feast that night. As the three of them prepared their canoe, White Sam saw that the villagers gathered around were watching him in an unusual fashion. He said as much to Qowi.

"My son," his foster father replied quietly, so no one else would hear, "it has been told about already that you are marked for death by someone who has power from the supernatural to kill."

"They watch me as if already I were a dead man," said Sam and he felt a tugging pain in his insides.

When the canoe was equipped with long poles furnished with hooks to which were attached ropes with weights and long pronged anchors, thin stalking paddles and a camouflage of hemlock branches were also loaded and the three of them embarked. This time White Sam crouched in the prow, his repeating rifle within easy reach. The canoe floated out to the river mouth, skirting the tidal flats to the northern side of the inlet. In this distance not a seal showed. They paddled and then drifted with the outgoing tide to a little bay on the lip of a much larger bay. On a reef in the mouth of the former they could see seals slipping into the water.

"We will go past them," Chief Qowi instructed quietly, "past the point, and you, Qwinoa, will climb over the land to where you can shoot the seals as they return to their rest on the reef."

This was done. Sam climbed over the low point to a spot within reasonable rifle shot. He could see a dozen seals which had returned to the reef after the canoe had disappeared. Now, as he watched, he saw them become alert. But they were not peering at him; they were peering at the canoe which had reappeared, but at a distance that caused the seals no concern.

Sam's first shot was followed rapidly by a second, and two seals lay dead on the reef as the others splashed to comparative safety in the water. One, trying to discover from whence came the death-dealing shots, rose high out of the water and Sam's third bullet took off the top of its head. The canoe came leaping across the water, and with a long pole with a metal hook on the end the occupants pulled the sinking animal aboard, then quickly retrieved the two dead seals from the reef.

As they picked up White Sam, Chief Qowi said, "My son, you are a great shot. You will bring honor to our tribe."

That night the Feast of the Seals began when the tide reached its height. The house of Chief Qowi was full of steam, smoke and invited guests. A strong odor of cooking seals came from the bubbling contents of six large iron pots. Previously, wooden cooking vessels into which hot rocks from the fire were dumped had been, apart from broiling, the only means of cooking, and much of the fat had been lost. Now, however, white man's large iron pots, as supplied by the Hudson's Bay Company, provided a cleaner, faster, easier method. Every guest was an invited one and every guest who was invited appeared. A feast of seals was unusual, for the animals were clever and wary, and their capture by the means at the Indians' disposal was an extraordinary accomplishment. The taking of three seals by one hunting party in an afternoon was an almost unprecedented event. Seal meat was a delicacy, so that no one refused an invitation; besides, to refuse would have been considered an insult.

In the heat and smoke of the fires, and in the noise of sticks being beaten on planks and the singing, the tempo of the dance built up until the marshal who was conducting the dance announced that the Kusiuts, or members of the powerful secret society which staged the winter ceremonials, would retire to consult with the supernatural spirits. The initiated members retired to a room behind one of the stages, and the uninitiated were asked to take positions as remote as possible from the fires. The fires were smothered with piles of green foliage, and in near darkness figures were detected moving about by the fireplace. The sounds of shrill whistles seemingly in the air around them, of large creatures landing on the roof, were explained by the marshal who was acting as interpreter. "The supernatural ones are arriving."

With much whistling and calling, and the sound of the wings flapping, the piles of green leaves were raked from the fires. The audience saw in the light of the freed flames that two parallel walls of planks about five feet high with kelp along their tops had been placed beside the fires. Between these walls seals were travelling, only their heads showing — as if they were swimming in the waters of the channel. Then, between protecting lines of marshals, appeared a seal fully twice as large as any seen before. The marshals helped it into the lane between the two parallel walls, where it apparently swam along without help. Midway of the passage it stopped, rose high and barked and snorted, to the intense amazement of the uninitiated. At the far end of the passage the seal disappeared into a group of initiated members.

A marshal, the interpreter, announced: "Tonight we are going to do something unusual. We are going to let two uninitiated guests see how we communicate with the supernatural. Any two."

"Let Qwinso and Kwallit be the two," a chief cried out.

There were shouts of approbation, tinged with relief, for the Kusiut organization was very powerful but also feared, and while most wished to be a member, almost all feared the initiation process, for it was known that if the initiate made a mistake he was sometimes killed for his error.

If Qwinso and Kwallit feared the position in which they found themselves, they did not show it, for as four marshals came to accompany them to the centre of the ceremony they arose with alacrity. In a few bounds they had disappeared into the group of Kusiuts.

Again the fires were subdued by a steaming mat of greenery. When they were allowed to flame up again, seals were to be seen floating along the simulated stream between the parallel walls, and the huge seal made a triumphant, barking, snorting return.

As this seal, assumed to be supernatural, was about to be accepted by the group of Kusiuts, a heavy club wielded by a stalwart marshal flashed down in the firelight with crushing force on one of the other seals. The seal skin fell off revealing the head of Qwinso crushed by the cudgel.

A few feet behind Qwinso moved Kwallit. When he saw his fellow initiate clubbed down, he tore off his seal-head mask and emitted a scream of rage. Seizing a man near him he raised him over his head as if he were but a faggot of wood and threw him at the marshal who already had his club ready to bludgeon him down. Confusion among the Kusiut delayed them momentarily, and bewilderment reigned in the audience for they were not sure but that this was part of the show arranged for them by the Kusiut society. They were not even sure when Kwallit, with surprising agility and a look of demoniacal fury on his face, seized a burning log and rushed toward the door. When the blazing battering ram knocked two men over who did not get out of Kwallit's way in time, at least those men knew that here was a maniac turned murderer. Pandemonium raged and screaming burst like thunder. One of the marshals appointed by the Kusiut to guard the door knocked the burning brand from his hands, but Kwallit was at once at the marshal's throat with crazed strength. Almost breaking the man's neck, Kwallit forced him against the other marshal, then turned and leaped to the centre of the room. By this time the Kusiut had recovered from their confusion and in the next thirty fierce seconds had surrounded him and beaten him to the floor, dead.

Chief Skuna leaped upon a stage. "Brothers," he cried, "you have looked upon the just execution of two men who have been killing by supernatural means. They have been robbing graves. If you come with me, I will show you their Mesatchi Box."

The audience, who had subsided into silence to listen to Skuna, recoiled visibly at the mention of the dread Mesatchi Box. "Mesatchi" was a word taken from the Chinook dialect, because it was intertribal in use, and this dreaded box was not confined to Bella Coola alone. In fact, Bella Bella sorcerers sometimes combined with those of Bella Coola to accomplish their machinations. Hence the Indians found it more convenient to use the Chinook word. As well as meaning bad or evil, it carried a connotation of the supernatural, just as "Mesatchi Nose" meant the dwelling place of evil spirits whose presence caused violent waves and tides. Sorcerers who used the Mesatchi Box were in league with demons, were feared and loathed and, when discovered, were hunted out and killed. At Skuna's revelation that these dead men were sorcerers of this nature there was a general movement away from their bodies.

"Come," Chief Skuna urged them, "come and we will see their instruments of death."

The Mesatchi Box, the very mention of which caused a wave of fear among the Indians, was a box containing, among other devilish accoutrements, a potion of fat rendered from flesh taken from the insides of the thighs of a corpse. This potion was the very essence of death, for when something from the intended victim — such as a fingernail cutting, some hair, or carefully preserved spittle, or even urine-soaked earth, — was immersed in it, illness resulted. The deeper the immersion, the more intense the illness and the more sudden the death. If the sorcerer changed his mind or, in cat-and-mouse fashion, pulled from the potion the various bits of the intended victim, the victim would recover until further immersion took place. It hastened the death of the victim if word was passed among the villagers that he was a condemned man, that "his time" had indeed come.

"Come!" and when Chief Qowi and White Sam stepped forward, Skuna called by name upon a dozen others who could not refuse lest they reveal their fear. In all a band of twenty men, carrying burning faggots to light the way, followed Skuna.

In the forest no light at all filtered through the tree tops, so that the lights from the burning faggots flickered in a black void. No words were spoken, for though Skuna had to feel his way along with his feet he was, like most of his fellow-tribesmen, skilled in remembering his way through the woods. After about fifteen minutes parading through the leaning, towering, moving shapes of the forest trees, the party stopped behind its leader.

"We are almost there," Skuna said. "Listen!"

By straining their ears they could hear the hiss and splash of a small stream falling over rocks.

"That stream is our guide," Skuna said, and as he resumed the way his followers realized that they were following a stream bed, one which would be full of water after a heavy rain or in the wet season. In a few minutes they came to where the stream cascaded like a veil over a rim twenty feet above them before disappearing among the boulders at their feet.

"We go behind the curtain of water," Skuna told them. "You will have to rush through lest your lights be extinguished."

They followed him along a narrow ledge and through the edge of the spraying waterfall. Inside a cave opened up, deep enough for its extremity to be almost beyond the reach of their burning torches, and high enough for them to walk upright. All was silence except for the hiss and chatter of the waterfall.

Into a world of spectral unreality the men cautiously proceeded. They were in the presence of death and the supernatural was at hand.

As they neared the far end of the cave the smell of old smoke was detected. Then they saw a cube-shaped box, and recognised it as a coffin in which they had recently buried one of their young men. Behind it was a longer box, thrice the length of the coffin and as high. But their horrified gaze was drawn by the sight of a body, nude except for a piece of cedar bark blanket wound round its head, lying in front of the boxes. As they came closer they saw with mounting horror and disgust that the flesh had been cut from inside the thighs, stripped therefrom so that the thigh bones gleamed white in the light of their torches. To the smell of death which pervaded the place was added a sickening smell of decay from two other partly decomposed bodies.

Skuna stepped forward and lifted the lid of the big box. Holding his flaming torch high to show the interior of the box, he invited his followers to look inside.

They saw the deep tray containing the dark, thick fluid — the death potion. They saw, besides, a collection of sticks, cloth and dolls of deadly portent.

Chief Qowi, with a deep intake of breath, bent quickly and picked up a piece of broken cedar showing adze marks.

"This is why my son's canoe was smashed and my son Qwinoa killed!" he cried softly. "And look, there is prepared the death of Qwinoa once again."

White Sam, following his pointing finger, recognised a crude effigy of himself, clad in a discarded shirt. In the belly of the effigy was the mark of a knife-thrust and beside it a hunting knife with bloodstained blade.

"Qwinoa, my son," Chief Qowi said to him, "next time he thrust the blade into the belly he might have left it there!"

Others recognised clothing or other belongings of relatives who had died, and suddenly fear turned to rage.

"Let us destroy it all, lest some other evil being uses it to destroy us," a man cried.

"Let us burn it all!" another cried.

And they broke up the lid of the Mesatchi Box, and also the coffin, using wood the sorcerers had collected. They then searched outside the cave and found some dry fallen trunks. After carefully removing all the dolls and effigies and anything else identified with actual people, they piled everything else in a heap. Then the bodies and several skulls also there, and a big iron kettle with a broth of human flesh in it, were placed in around the Mesatchi Box, and the grisly lot piled high with wood and lighted. As the smoke filled the cavern they retreated through the veil of water back into the forest and watched the mouth of the cave become a red throat of fire behind a gossamer scarf of spray.

Then, in the first dim light of approaching day, they returned to the village and went to the house of Qwinso and Kwallit, which their two families jointly occupied and, in spite of screams of fear and cries for mercy, they clubbed to death the families of the two dead sorcerers, their wives, children and even a babe at its mother's breast, and a sister resident with them — the fear of sorcerers was such that they must be plucked from their society, root, stem, flower and fruit.

They dumped the dead in a swamp where animals could eat them, but where the remains could never get into the streams and offend the salmon gods.

White Sam went to sleep in his adopted father's house, and dreamt of the cavern of death so cunningly hidden that tracks up the dry stream bed could not be followed, so cunningly hidden that a veil of water would hide the light of an ordinary fire at night and diffuse any smoke by day. He dreamt of a boy following the sorcerers to discover the cave, of showing his find to his uncle, and then almost dying of fear — not so much fear of the bad men, but of the supernatural. He dreamt of children being clubbed to death so they could not carry on the fearful work of the two evil men. When he awoke and looked at his belly in the full light of day, there was no mark there. When he slept again his sleep was dreamless, and he did not waken for many hours.

Nor did he recall that when he and his companions were returning from Dean Channel they had called into a little bay in Labouchère Channel where a snowslide reached down to tidewater even late in the summer, and from that icy water had drunk deeply when he was hot from paddling, which could indeed have caused the stomach cramps.

Nor, when he met any white men, the few travelling through the valley to the interior, or the Hudson's Bay man aboard a trading ship that came a few months later, did he tell them of these events, for he knew they would surely ridicule the story and perhaps call him a simple superstitious Siwash.

Intertribal Politics and War

The story of the Bella Coola Indian might have been vastly different had not the valley that formed their home been endowed by nature with defensive surroundings. The high mountain walls to the north and south prohibited attack from those directions while from the east only narrow mountainous trails afforded entry. And since these led down into a lush, jungled valley where the river was the only practical avenue of travel necessitating the canoes and skill of the native Bella Coola, any major attack, then, was from the west.

Here, indeed, the river-mouth villages faced an occasional enemy but the more remote villages of Kimsquit and Talio suffered at times from raiders intent on pillage, prisoners and sanguinary pleasures. With their nearest neighbors to the west, the Bella Bellas, the Bella Coolas had much of the time a trading alliance that amounted to friendship; for with a tremendously rich salmon stream the Bella Coolas had much to offer. So, even though the Bella Bellas were Kwakiutls whose territory spread down to the lower part of the coastal islands to Knight Inlet, Bute Inlet and some of Vancouver Island, they preferred a loose alliance with the Bella Coolas.

The southerly Kwakiutls did frequently covet the possessions of the wealthy Bella Coola district and made sporadic raids. In defence, the besieged Talio people built fortifications that made an attack on them highly unprofitable; and in rebuttal the Kimsquit people became physically the largest and most war-like of the Bella Coola group. The Kwakiutls eventually had to be satisfied with ambushing a lone fisherman or a group of women berry-pickers who had wandered beyond the realms of safety.

Northward the more warlike and better organized tribes of Kitkatlas and Tsimshians were constantly ready to foray along the coast, and the huge canoes of the Haidas, completely seaworthy and manned by expert seamen, swept as far south as the California coast in quest of warlike adventure.

Had it not been for the coast Indian's complete neglect to acknowledge prowess in war as an attribute to chieftainship the white man's acquisition of the British Pacific Coast would have been more effectively contested. Under the potlatch system fame, prestige and power were gained, not by military achievement, nor by sagacious advice in council but by the number of potlatches given and the amount of wealth given away. A man or a woman might make himself or herself a chief by accumulating food, blankets, etc., and giving potlatches; and he or she might assist a son, brother or friend to become a chief. A chief was shown great respect, had extensive privileges within the tribe but had no great authority. If he decided to go to war his subjects were not obliged to follow him and, if they did, no penalty was meted out if they decided at any time, even in the heat of battle, to leave him and go home.

This resulted in lack of leadership in war and lack of anything but the most primary of planning in their expeditions. Shamans were essential on every expedition to interpret the supernatural and their interpretation of signs and portents might cause an expedition to be abandoned at the most crucial moment.

"Tcibisa is out there!"

With the speed white men could never understand, word swept through the village at the lower end of the valley that the most famous and feared chief of the Kitkatla was only fifteen minutes' paddling away from the mouth of the river. A lone canoe had been detected coming up the channel and the scouts sent to check on it had rushed back with the news that had flashed as by mental telepathy through the villages and had roused a feverish excitement.

"Now is our chance! Let us kill him!" some of the men urged. Generations of warfare between the Bella Coola and the Kitkatla had resulted in many deaths to be mourned among the Bella Coola. A summer-long sortie against the Kitkatla a few summers previously had all but wiped out the invading Bella Coola and the remnants had drifted back with nothing but a terrible defeat to report. The Kitkatla had made retaliatory raids and in one of these, Qotxweliotl, one of the most famous of the Bella Coola chiefs, had been slain. Qotxweliotl had given many potlatches and was therefore a very powerful chief. As such he carried with him an immunity to death in battle. He could have been captured for ransom but his death, except an accidental one in the heat of battle, was considered a contravention of the etiquette of coastal warfare.

"Let us kill every one of them!"

"No, we should see what they want," others counseled.

While these discussions were being held some of the villagers stole along the beach and fired on the Kitkatla from a distance.

Had the visiting Indians fired back they would have declared war. But their reply was to hold aloft, four times in succession, a large deer hide signifying that their errand was a friendly one.

The following day a messenger from Tcibisa, unarmed and carrying a wand which had two pliant limbs close together to denote friendship, walked into Qomots, the principal village near the mouth of the Bella Coola River, and asked to see Potles, the outstanding chief of the Bella Coolas.

Surrounded by excited and inimical Bella Coola the position of the stranger could have been a hazardous one. However, the curiosity of the villagers as well as the two-branched wand of friendship protected him until Potles appeared at the door of his house.

The Kitkatla messenger held his two hands aloft grasping the two-limbed wand until the Bella Coola chief, watching with expressionless face from the doorway, spoke. "You have a message," he said simply. "You may speak."

The messenger slowly lowered his arms until the wand he clutched was in front of his waist. "Great Chief Potles, mightiest of the Bella Coola, Tcibisa, the Chief of the Kitkatla People wishes it to be known to you that he regrets the death of your brother Qotxweliotl. He has many nights been denied the blessing of sleep in reviewing the circumstances of the tragedy. Now he has come to make peace. His people have told him that to come along the Bella Coola without a large following might lead to his death. But he is such a great man that he will let no thoughts of danger dissuade him from following the course he has decided is his duty.

"He wishes that there be peace between the Bella Coola and the Kitkatla. He has come with a canoe heavy with gifts and manned only by chiefs to try to bring about a feeling of trust and friendship."

Potles did not change his expression. "Who are you?" he asked. "If your chief uses chiefs for paddlers, whom does he use for messengers?"

"I am Exwillis," the messenger replied, and at the mention of his name hoarse cries escaped from the bystanders. Exwillis was as famous as Tcibisa or Potles, and stories told the length of the coast credited him with being the wiliest of strategists. When clamor from the surrounding throng grew loud and threatening he raised his wand of peace again and repeated simply "I am Chief Exwillis."

Potles raised his hand in a gesture which calmed the crowd. "You may return to your brother chiefs in peace," he said. "Tell Chief Tcibisa that we will listen to his story."

Potles turned on his heel and stepped into his house and Exwillis likewise turned and, ignoring the crowd around him, strode in swift dignity out of the village. Several minutes later two young men carrying bows and arrows followed. Potles had dispatched them. He had said that the messenger could go in peace but he was not so sure some of his tribesmen would refuse themselves the opportunity to sip on a cup of vengeance. The two young men carried the guarantee that Potles' statement would be honored.

For the next two days the villages at the mouth of the Bella Coola valley seethed with excitement, an excitement that reached fever pitch on the afternoon of the second day when the large, intricately carved canoe of the Kitkatla chiefs entered the mouth of the river. All the occupants were elaborately dressed, and in the bow stood the brother of Tcibisa dressed in full ceremonial Sisoak Society regalia, even to mask. This was a departure from practice but he expected he might be killed and wished to be identified with his supernatural myth.

The canoe beached opposite the house of Potles and the Kitkatla blew eagle down into the air as a demonstration of peaceful intentions.

Above them on the bank gathered most of the population of the villages of the lower valley and among the crowd were some who would disregard promises of safe conduct and slay their erstwhile enemies.

Some of these hurled insults at the Kitkatla hoping to incite them to some untoward act so that a fight might be started. But the Kitkatla ignored the insults, continuing to blow handfuls of eagle down into the air.

Then Chief Potles appeared at the door of his house. "Silence!" he commanded. "These men come to make peace. They shall not be harmed!"

A few more determined ones continued to raise a clangor. "They are our ancestoral enemies!" they shouted. "They have killed our fathers and our brothers!"

"They now come in peace. They shall not be harmed," the chief commanded.

When the belligerent ones persisted in demanding war on their visitors Chief Potles, his face an expressionless mask, cried, "Look here, you who would have bloodshed this afternoon."

Whereupon he lifted a horizontal plank some ten feet long which was part of the wall of his house. Only momentarily was the plank up, but it was enough for the assembly to look into the muzzles of eight muskets trained upon them by as many young men in the chief's house. Then it was lowered.

With his face now a picture of welcoming goodwill the chief raised his arms.

"When the shade of that tree crosses the floor of this house, you are all to be the guests of Chief Potles. Every one of you — chiefs, visitors, commoners, slaves, men, women and children!"

Shouts of approval went up from the crowd.

"We will now welcome our visitors to our house."

He leaped down to the beach where he was met by a small cloud of eagle down blown upon him by the Kitkatla. Six stalwart men immediately behind him carried a large deer hide, which they spread by the bow of the beached canoe so that Chief Tcibisa could be carried to the host chief's house without walking on the ground; it was an honor accorded only the very highest of chiefs.

"You honor me," the visiting chief stated, standing proudly erect in the bow of the ornate canoe. "But I would tell you that I am so heavy from giving so many potlatches that there is no animal cloak in the world strong enough to hold me!"

He leaped onto the outstretched hide which the six young men, appearing to strain hopelessly to hold up the tremendous weight, let slowly and reluctantly to the ground. Then Potles called for help and four more men seized the hide and the ten men staggered with their burden into the house of Chief Potles and carried Chief Tcibisa to the most honored spot, a seat in the right corner of the huge house.

Although he was a tall, stalwart man, Chief Tcibisa could have been carried to his position by any one of the muscular canoe men of the Bella Coola, but the play on the great weight of the visiting chief was necessary to show him the highest honor.

White Sam, in the crowd at the river bank, saw the remaining Kitkatla chiefs accept offers of help to unload the canoe and carry its load of gifts into the Potles house.

"Our chief is a wily one," he heard someone say softly. "He has lured all the Kitkatla into his house. He will kill them all this afternoon."

White Sam did not know who said it, but he remembered the killing of the sorcerers. His blood ran cold. Could Chief Potles have murder in his mind?

He noted that the Kitkatla carried their muskets with them. That was not unusual, however, for carrying their weapons was almost as normal as wearing a cloak or any other garment. But before he went into Chief Potles' house, he got his rifle.

The time set for the start of the potlatch was only several hours away from the arrival of the Kitkatla, and in that time several hundred people entered the big house of Chief Potles. When the shadow of a huge cottonwood tree commenced to darken the door of the house, a hush fell upon the assembly. The starting hour had arrived.

White Sam, seated behind his foster father, felt a strangling excitement growing within him. Suddenly at the door there appeared a screaming young man, carrying a musket, his face smeared with ashes and his hair tied in a topknot with weasel skins, signifying that he was in a war frenzy. Sam struggled to keep from shouting.

It was Nexwinkai, nephew of Chief Potles. His father, Potles' brother, was the chief who had been killed, contrary to rules of war, by the Kitkatla. When White Sam recognised the impassioned young man, he felt his mouth go dry with fear.

Nexwinkai, screaming unintelligibly, danced around the fire, stopped in front of Tcibisa and, not ten feet away, pointed his musket at the visiting chief's face. His face was livid with fury. A sudden deep hush fell on the assembly, so deep that the crackling of a limb in the fire seemed as loud as a pistol shot. For seconds everything in the building, except the sparkling fire, was as still as a carving. With his face a mask of fury and his musket muzzle a few feet from Tcibisa, Nexwinkai stood for many seconds threatening immediate death to the visiting chief.

All the while Tcibisa sat, showing the same deep detached interest he might feel in the launching of a new canoe. There was no evidence that he might be experiencing fear. When Nexwinkai broke his pose and resumed his screaming dance around the fire, Tcibisa watched with the same impersonal interest and, when he again had the musket thrust almost in his face, turned casually to Potles, seated at his side.

"This is an interesting dance," he remarked. "What do you call it?"

"It is the Vengeance Dance," Potles answered. "It is the special dance of Nexwinkai, whose father was killed in battle."

"I wonder if his father was your brother, Chief Qotxweliotl," Tcibisa volunteered.

By this time Nexwinkai was in front of Tcibisa again, his demeanor more threatening, if possible, than before.

Again the crowded house became so quiet that the crackling fire sounded like muskets being discharged. Tension through the building reached the snapping point; had any of the Kitkatla made a move to defend their chief, there would have been an immediate reaction.

Still speaking casually Tcibisa turned to Potles. "If I am the honored guest at this dance it will increase my reputation for fearlessness. As a great chief I do not know fear."

Nexwinkai moved away.

"His father was Chief Qotweliotl," Potles said. "And you are the guest of honor."

When Nexwinkai was on the point of returning from the far side of the fire Potles raised his hand in a signal. The young man stopped, raised his musket to his shoulder, pointed it momentarily at Tcibisa, then raised the muzzle and pulled the trigger. The gun roared, and out of it blew a cloud of eagle down, which settled in a white mantle over the visiting chief. It was the ultimate sign of peaceful intent.

A roar of relief and approval swept through the crowded building.

Chief Potles leaped to his feet. His upheld arm commanded silence.

"Chief Tcibisa is a fearless man, a great chief. He has come here to make peace between the Kitkatla people and the Bella Coola people. He remained without fear while death pointed a finger at him. We shall honor this great chief with a potlatch!"

He had scarcely ceased speaking when Tcibisa, as though in reply to this speech, performed his Sisoak dance. Singers the Kitkatla had brought with them beat time. The dance completed, the Kitkatla chief had his retainers carry in the huge mound of presents they had brought with them and these were presented to the principal Bella

177

Coola chiefs. Among the gifts given to Potles was a sea otter robe worth at least ten slaves.

Then Potles performed a Sisoak dance and likewise presented lavish gifts to the Kitkatla. Chief Tcibisa received a miniature canoe with ten carved figures in it, which represented a canoe and ten slaves to be taken when the northern chief wished to collect them.

Huge trays of food were then passed around and everyone ate to repletion.

Then Tcibisa spoke:

"People of Bella Coola, I am glad that now the two great peoples of Bella Coola and Kitkatla may live together in peace. I, Tcibisa, a warrior whose reputation for strategy and courage reaches from the turbulent seas of the north to where there are no more islands, wish this. I am determined to carry my message directly to your people, even though my followers told me that it would be highly dangerous to go among people who had cause to wish my death. But as a great chief I know no fear. I came, and now I am happy to know that your great chief, Potles, also desires peace. Now our people will increase in numbers and wealth and happiness will be like sunshine where before were the damp mists of morning."

Tcibisa returned shortly to his home in the north, and peace did come to the two tribes but it was an uneasy peace at first because it was difficult to cast off with one visit and one potlatch memories of many generations of war and death. Major chiefs respected the understanding but, if small parties met in the channels, skirmishes frequently resulted.

As if to verify Tcibisa's words the years that followed his visit were good ones. Summer brought many salmon which were dried and traded in great quantities to the tribes of the islands and the interior. Fur catches in the winter were abundant and were traded for goods with the Hudson's Bay trader.

Potles, energetic and intelligent, accumulated a large supply of goods. He decided to give a potlatch at which he wished to have the northern chief Tcibisa as a guest. But at first he could get no one to go far into the northern waters to carry the invitation.

"Tcibisa and Potles are friends; but there are many Kitkatla who would still like to add a Bella Coola scalp to their war trophies," was one objection raised. Another one was that, "If we could get to Tcibisa's house without being attacked by smaller parties we might be safe." Another reviewed with dismay the many miles of channels but this did not have the ring of conviction since the Bella Coola was as much at home in his canoe on the channels as he was beside the fire in his river-side house.

Finally Potles gave a small potlatch and honored with presents six of his chiefs.

"You are brave chiefs," he told them at the feast, "and I am honored to have you in my house."

Before the evening was out the six chiefs volunteered to carry Chief Potles' invitation to Tcibisa. But in conference they decided they would travel at night to lessen the danger of being attacked by the Kitkatla. And they went by way of Bella Bella where they picked up another who volunteered to act as ambassador since he was well-known among the northern Indians.

When the canoe-load of Indians managed to get within ear-shot of Tcibisa's house they started singing the Sisoak song of Potles so that the Kitkatla chief might know they were messengers from the Bella Coola chief.

This stratagem was successful for Tcibisa heard the singing and asked a slave, who happened to be a Bella Coola, whose song it was.

"It is Potles' Sisoak song," the slave replied.

At this Tcibisa dispatched a chief known to the Bella Coola to invite the messengers to his house. The messengers accepted with a flood of relief for they now knew they would not be attacked by some marauding band.

A cannibal dance was going on in Tcibisa's house and while the Bella Bella envoy, and three from Bella Coola who had Bella Bella rights as well, were allowed to take part fully in the rituals, which included the eating of a corpse, the other Bella Coola were treated as uninitiated; but they studied the ceremony with great interest and compared its finer points with their own man-eating dance.

One of the Bella Coola messengers fell seriously ill and the return to Bella Coola was delayed for some time. Tcibisa delegated one of his wives to look after the sick man, and with her nursing and the use of many herbs and the assistance of a shaman, the ill messenger recovered and the return flotilla with many Kitkatla guests was embarked.

When this fleet arrived at Qomots, Potles' village at the mouth of the river, the crowd that met them was noisily hostile. The delays caused by the visit to Bella Bella and the illness of one of the messengers had made the return so late that the Bella Coola had grown apprehensive that the Kitkatla had done them harm. Excitable ones, inflamed with memories of imagined or real wrongs in the past, rushed to the river bank and threw rocks at the Kitkatla seizing their canoes and attempting to smash them. The Kitkatla held their attackers off with their paddles and the messengers upbraided the hostile Bella Coola. But the attackers grew noisier and it seemed that serious trouble as well as a breach of safe conduct rules would come about.

Then Chief Potles appeared at his door.

His topknot was done up with weasel skins, and he had a musket in his hand.

"Quiet, men of Bella Coola," he commanded, and pointed his musket directly at the noisiest of the trouble-makers. "These people are our invited guests. Tcibisa is my brother chief and when he comes to my potlatch he comes in peace."

"Let us kill them! They are our enemies!" someone shouted.

Potles affected a tremendous rage. Leaping at the speaker, he struck him across the neck with his musket barrel and knocked him in the river. When the man rose spluttering to his feet Potles pointed a finger at him.

"If you want to live, go crawl under Chief Tcibisa's canoe!"

The Chief pointed his musket at the man's head and, when his finger started to tighten on the trigger, the man dove under the canoe and, surfacing on the far side, waded ashore.

Potles glared around the crowd.

"Are there any more who want to be at war with my friends?" he demanded, his musket halfway to his shoulder and his expression indicating that sudden death was near.

When there were no challengers his mien changed.

"Let peace reign then."

Tearing the weasel skins from his topknot and letting his hair drop into its usual position, he strode over to Tcibisa's canoe in which the chief was standing watching the proceedings with the same disinterested air with which he had watched the Dance of Vengeance on his previous visit.

"My brother chief," he addressed Potles, "you do put on the most interesting dances every time we come from the north!"

Potles stood several feet from the northern chief.

"My musket is yours, O Brother Chief," he said and presented it to Tcibisa.

Before he accepted the musket Tcibisa placed his hands on the shoulders of his host, squeezed, then leaped lightly to the gravel.

"All that is Tcibisa's is also Potles'," he said.

The potlatch given that night by Potles at which two of the coast's most famous chiefs attempted to outdo the other was, in truth, a potlatch to end all potlatches. It erased the memory of other potlatches and compared to all that followed, was declared the major potlatch of all time. Potles' house was filled with people and presents. Ceremonial dancing and oratory ceased only to give time for eating the lavish food. And the fires, usually fuelled with wood, were this time fed by a whale which vomited eulachon grease on the flames to make them leap. The uninitiated did not know, or were not supposed to know, that under the black skin of the whale, fabricated of cedar bark and stretched on a frame of willow wands, two of Potles' retainers worked with pails and dippers and gallons of eulachon oil.

It marked the beginning of the winter ceremonials wherein the dramatic artistry of a whole tribe portrayed life, death and birth, and presented the supernatural on stage in such a realistic and terrifying manner that the uninitiated sometimes hid in quivering, abject fear; and even the initiated, the members of the Kusiut and the Sisoak societies, became hypnotized with their own sensual potions and forgot reality in their portrayal of things beyond the natural. The Bella Coola were natural actors and in their periods of relaxation did indeed completely disguise the border between the natural and the supernatural.

Chief Tcibisa sent messengers to his northland village, announcing that he would return when travelling conditions were better — which was only a form of saying that his host-village was so much to his liking that he was going to stay and be entertained. And through the winter, while snowstorms blotted out the towering mountains, or rains slashed in from the west, he taught the Kitkatla ceremonies to the Bella Coola so that by the time Tcibisa went northward in early spring there had been a marriage of the two cultures. And peace had been firmly established between the two peoples. Tcibisa and Potles were great chiefs in more than one respect.

It was hard on the heels of this peace with the Kitkatla that a truce was brought about with traditional enemies to the south, the Kwakiutl.

Linguistically the people of Bella Bella belong to the same group as these people south of Queen Charlotte Sound, in Knight Inlet, Kingcome Inlet and around Blunden Harbor. But distance, and the barrier of Queen Charlotte Sound, had separated the peoples of the districts. In fact, the name Djoldainix had been given collectively to the southern Kwakiutl so that rather than being at war with the Kwakiutl, the Bella Coola participated in a many-generation war with the Djoldainix. Of course this war was not intense. In fact, at times it relaxed sufficiently to allow visiting and trading between the two tribes!

When the Djoldainix felt the urge for warfare they assessed possibilities in the Bella Coola area. The valley itself, heavily peopled and defended by high mountains, was not considered. The villages at the head of Dean Channel were generally stoutly defended and raids on them were expensive. A third point of settlement of the Bella Coola was Talio where there were several comparatively small villages. It was on these that the warriors of the Djoldainix frequently swooped carrying away loot, heads and captives.

Finally, the Talio people built defences around their principal village in the form of a stockade of vertical logs tightly lashed together on the inside of which a platform ran around near the top from which defenders had a vantage point. There was a water gate through which canoes could come at high tide.

During the building of the stockade a hollow tree was used but only after extensive discussion. A Djoldainix visitor who aided in building the stockade helped put this weak timber in the wall and, when he returned to his southern home, he related to his people the strengths and weaknesses of the Talio defences.

It was little more than a year later that a raid was decided upon, the Talio people to be the victims.

"We should not attack them," one of the Djoldainix chiefs argued. "They are now too strongly fortified. We cannot beat them without loss of many warriors."

"But we shall beat them," others replied. "We always have, and because they have built a fence around their village is no reason we cannot beat them now."

The fever of war was in their veins and the marauding canoes started out. A few days later they approached the Talio village.

A better time for the marauders could not have been chosen for all the inhabitants except six were away on hunting and fishing errands. Of the six, three were children.

When the attackers were seen approaching the three adults, men, closed all the openings and prepared to defend themselves.

The attacking fleet, outnumbering the defenders twenty to one, cut a tree and using it as a battering ram attempted to force the canoe gate. But the gate was strongly built, and the manoeuvre forced the attackers into the open and under the fire of the three defenders. These men took such deadly toll that there seemed more corpses than living warriors in the canoes. The attackers withdrew.

Their next objective was the hollow log of which they had been told by one of their number. But again they were met with a withering, deadly fire. It was an incessant fire, though the defenders had been reduced to one man. One had fallen to an enemy bullet; a second had fallen from the fighting-platform and had shot himself when he struck the ground.

The third, Sniniq, an exceptional shot and a clever strategist, found himself running short of powder. He rushed from spot to spot in the wall shouting commands in different tones and by this ruse concealed from the enemy the woeful weakness of the defending garrison. When he was assured of a kill he shot, at the same time shouting a call of victory.

Finally the raiders withdrew carrying their dead with them.

Sniniq, exulting in his own victory and burning with desire for more revenge because Djoldainix raiders in a previous raid had killed his children, followed cautiously in a small canoe and when a collection of crows revealed where the attackers had buried their dead he exhumed one of the corpses, beheaded it, and impaled it in a crouching position on a stake, its head upside down beneath the buttocks.

The big chief of the Djoldainix was Siwid, ranking in stature with Potles and Tcibisa in matters of warfare. The defeat his warriors had suffered at Talio rankled in Siwid's mind, particularly when it became known that one man only had brought about their shame. Two years elapsed, and he led another raid against Talio. This time the stockade was fully manned and the attackers were given an active reception. When they were approaching with a battering ram one of the defenders killed three of the warriors with one shot. The attackers retreated, having lost many men and having killed only two of their intended victims. And on the way down channel two Bella Coola hunters took long shots from the mountain-side and scored hits on the hapless would-be attackers.

After licking their actual and psychological wounds for a year or two the Djoldainix planned to attack Bella Coola itself. However, after an unsuccessful skirmish with a small party of Dean Channel Indians Siwid and his followers decided to return home.

Paddling down channel near Kwatna Bay, about thirty miles from Bella Coola, they were called to by one of the members of a party of Kwatna women who were picking berries. Beneath them, in a bay, some youths were waiting in canoes. If the women, who had thought they were Bella Coola, had not called to them the raiders would have passed without noticing them. Now they paddled into the bay, slew the youths, and started climbing the mountain to capture the women.

The berry-pickers, aware almost as soon as the call had been made that they had attracted enemies, started to flee. Two of them who had fled as soon as they saw the canoes leave mid-channel succeeded in escaping across the mountain to the village in Kwatna Bay. Of the others, one left the group and sought escape by herself. The remainder found a narrow cave and hastily barricaded the mouth with sticks. When the Djoldainix warriors approached there was room for only one at a time to traverse the narrow ledge leading to the cave mouth, and each brave as he appeared was met with a shower of boulders that nearly swept him from the ledge and down the mountainside. A brief council ensued.

"We'll have to starve them out," one volunteered. "We can't get close enough to them to fight."

"We haven't time to starve them out. Before another high tide canoes too numerous to land on a big beach will be here. Not one of us will escape to take the story of our deaths back to our people."

Just then one of them spotted the fleeing figure of the woman who had tried to escape by herself.

"We'll get her!" they shouted and, even without planning, divided into two parties.

Eventually the woman, after running from one side of an enclosed circle to the other, screaming as she saw her enemies closing in upon her, found herself brought to bay on a bare eminence of rock. At least fifteen enemy warriors, armed with spears, surrounded her.

"I am a chief," she screamed at them. "I have no fear of being killed."

"You will be made our slave," one of the warriors taunted her. "You would do well picking clams."

"I am a chief," she retorted. "I will not be made a slave!"

The circle was now less than ten feet across.

"You are cowardly warriors to slay boys and make war upon women," she screamed at them. Stooping swiftly she picked up a rock the size of a big man's fist. "Do not come any closer!"

One young chief stepped out, spear in hand, and she swung the rock at him hard. It caught him a slashing, glancing blow on the cheek, cutting it like a knife so that his comrades saw the white bone by his ear laid bare before the blood started to flow. The force of the blow spun him partly around and, to regain his balance, he dropped his spear and threw his hands in the air. The spear clattered down the mountainside.

In the ensuing confusion the woman tried to escape the closing ring but without avail. The young chief, recovering his balance, rushed in, seized her around the waist and dashed her heavily to the ground. His knees pinioning her arms he mercilessly cut her throat so that her screams ended in a bloody babbling.

Rising, his face almost as bloody as hers, he said to his companions, "This is what happens to Bilixwala!" In his excitement he used the name given by his people in the long past to the people of the Bella Coola area.

For a brief moment they looked down at the still twitching body of the woman.

"She said she was a chief," one said. "Anybody know her?"

"I did," another answered. "She was Bilxwalaks of Kwatna. Some of her ancestors came from Bella Coola and her husband was from Bella Bella."

"This is reason for war," another one spoke.

It was, indeed, for in the coastal book of warfare rules were such that a chief should not be deliberately killed but captured and held for ransom which would certainly be forthcoming. This killing, then, would be interpreted as a crime and as such must be avenged. These warriors could now see avenging flotillas closing in on them from Bella Coola, Bella Bella and Kwatna.

"We'd better go," one spoke for them all.

While the rest started for the canoes the chief whose knife had cut Bilxwalak's throat and another stayed behind and cut off her head.

"Better the head of a chief than the body of a slave," one of them said as he impaled the head on his spear and gave it to the chief. "This is yours to decorate your canoe."

They made haste to their canoes and by the time they had reached their home villages the stories that had grown from the seeds of their adventures were indeed worthy of the telling.

And the wiser of the chiefs waited for reprisals.

Two women escapees reached Kwatna that afternoon, scratched, bruised and exhausted but full of their story, and a half hour later a canoe load of warriors was out on the prowl. But their quarry was now far distant. Instead they went up the mountain and found the decapitated body of Bilxwalaks; and then found and cared for the women still barricaded in the cave.

"Poor Bilxwalaks," one of them said on seeing the headless body. "It was she that called to the Djoldainix. She thought they were Bella Coola. She was too friendly."

In Bella Coola chiefs of the villages in the lower end of the valley met in meetings of fiery indignation. Potles, the leading chief, sent a man to search a warehouse owned by the murdered Bilxwalaks; when a large store of ammunition was found it was moved to Potles' house.

When the news of the attack spread in Bella Coola the excitable tribespeople dashed hither and thither; that is, most of them. Potles, the great chief, stayed indoors out of sight, and would not be seen except by his own messengers.

Then, as the morning sun, rising over the mountain to the east, picked out his doorway the chief appeared, his face grayish white with ashes and his hair tied up in a topknot bound with a weasel skin.

Anyone who had just killed a man, or who planned to do so, could wear such a guise; none other. Potles had decided on war.

He had a cocked musket in either hand and, with these held at the ready, spoke.

"I, Potles, tell you. Let no man pass on the sidewalk before me for he shall surely die of a musket shot through his head."

Then, sinking to the floor of the doorway, he sat cross-legged with a cloak draped about him, the barrels of the muskets sticking out in front. For four days and nights he remained thus and not a man, woman or child but obeyed his edict. Children gazed at him in awe-stricken groups from around the corners of buildings, and members of his household used the refuse hole for ingress and egress during the time.

And neither noonday heat nor midnight chill stirred him, nor people, for he was *numitl*. He was a great chief whose privileges were unbounded and if he wished to demonstrate his grief, even to killing someone who might walk in front of him when he was wrestling with his sorrow, that was indeed within his rights.

Of the fifth morning, when the coming day had scarcely started to tint the eastern rim of mountains, Potles rose and called messengers and dispatched them to nearby villages. Before the day was half born the beating of drums filled the air coming from the tidal flats, the deep forests and the high mountainside, drumming, throbbing, exciting, compelling. By sunrise not a soul in the valley slumbered and a hundred warriors gathered in front of the house of Potles.

This time Potles did not sit down; standing regally straight, he spoke but a few words. "Bilxwalaks has been murdered. She was a chief. We must avenge her. And we must teach the Djoldainix that they cannot commit wrongs in our territory. We are going to war and, that she may go with us, we shall use the powder and shot of Bilxwalaks."

There was a hoarse shout of approval.

"We shall start at once."

He dismissed them with a wave of his hand and each man went about his preparations.

One of the warriors was White Sam. In the years he had been with the Indians he had risen, through potlatches, to the position of chief and because he was an expert shot with his repeating rifle rather than with one of the antique trading muskets, he was most welcome on forays requiring good markmanship. Chiefs' meetings of which he was notified were sometimes held in the dead of night on a narrow ledge of rock above the living cauldron of a waterfall. Here a wall of rock, carved by a people lost to memory and legend, rose and hung over the ledge in such a manner as to shut out the sky and all but the rushing leaping waters. Here he met with other chiefs to discuss situations and make decisions of importance to the tribe that had adopted him. He had acquired the thinking of these people and the insult of the Djoldainix to the tribe was an insult to him. And although he might have considered it otherwise in other circumstances he prepared eagerly for this expedition.

When Potles stated they would start "at once" he possibly took into consideration that people would be gathering from villages within the valley and from Kimsquit and Talio for, because of his fame, many warriors did come from these villages.

Three days later a flotilla of sixteen sea canoes slipped silently from the mouth of the Bella Coola River and paddled in battle formation down channel, their destination the villages of the Djoldainix. Since none of the Bella Coola had anything but fragmentary knowledge of the territory into which they were going they took with them a slave, Siwid, of the same name and tribe but not of the same family as the warrior chief to the south. He had for years been a slave and it was considered he would be loyal to the Bella Coola. Siwid asked that his mother be spared, should they come upon her in the attack, and when this was promised he pledged his faithfulness.

The first night was spent at Kwatna where more recruits were added to the floating army.

On the sheltered beach next morning Kwalsantl, a Bella Coola chief, paraded past the canoes, his face smeared with ashes, his hair tied in a topknot.

"Shoot at my topknot," he commanded. "If you hit it and it falls, so will our foes."

"What will happen if the man who shoots misses the topknot and kills Kwalsantl?" White Sam asked a chief squatting near him.

"We will go home and bury Kwalsantl," was the reply.

"And then go fight the Djoldainix?"

"I don't know. Maybe not. If the topknot were not cut it would be a bad omen, a very bad omen indeed. The expedition might be dropped. That would be a decision for the shamans to make."

Kwalsantl was without fear as a chief should be. He had established that firmly by the distribution of much wealth at potlatches. Now, as everyone hesitated to shoot at his topknot, he made a show of anger.

"Are you all cowards?" he screamed. "See, I, Kwalsantl, am not afraid."

"What happens if no one shoots his topknot?" White Sam asked.

"Many warriors will go home. It will cause a great delay."

"That would be bad for Bella Coola for the Djoldainix would become bold and raid right up to our salmon weirs."

Throwing his rifle to his shoulder White Sam fired, seemingly without aiming. Kwalsantl's mouth had been open in exhortation and the hair from the bullet-severed topknot cascaded down, a wad of it catching on his out-thrust tongue so that his scream cut short.

A roar of approval rose from the throats of the warriors.

"We'll slay them! We'll slay them!"

And the flotilla hastened to get under way. Now, because they were leaving friendly waters and going into territory where they might be attacked, two canoes instead of one went ahead of the main group. And in the prow of one of these canoes was Sniniq who had defended Talio almost single-handed against the Djoldainix and in the other, also in the prow, was White Sam whose marksmanship had been proven before the Kwatna incident.

Down through narrow channels, then out among the coastal islands they advanced, stopping for a night on a big beach, cooking clams in a huge trench which had been fired until the rocks were hot. The hot rocks were then covered with seaweed, the seaweed covered with fresh clams, and so on in alternating layers, and over all sand was laid. When the clams had cooked in this manner for the proper time it was a feast for gods and warrior chiefs.

They breasted the swells of the open ocean as they crossed what white men had already called for almost a hundred years Queen Charlotte Sound. Cautiously they worked their way again into the shelter of the island strip where their foe was their fellow man rather than the force of ocean swells born out in the mid-Pacific.

Now they were in enemy territory and going deeper all the while, for they had decided to strike at the heart of their enemies and to raid the home village of the mighty Siwid himself, in Kingcome Inlet. For many days they had hidden pulling their canoes up into the woods, travelling only by night to avoid detection. In the maze of islands they sent a canoe ahead with their slave-guide, Siwid, to see if they could locate an enemy village.

The smell of smoke warned the scouts an encampment was near. They pulled in under the limbs of some trees which overhung the water and offered concealment. While they were discussing their situation a canoe load of Kingcome Inlet men paddled cautiously by, for they had been told the Bella Coola were on the war-path and, suspecting they might be about, had sent two canoes out to scout. They narrowly missed the Bella Coola and returned to their village to report there were no enemies.

The Bella Coola, profiting by their luck, used the next few hours to scout out the position of the village and to carry the information back to their group. Plans were made for an attack at dawn. The men were divided into two groups, one to go into the woods and attack from the rear and the other to man the canoes and, when they were in position in front of the village, to attack from the beach.

Of the equipment brought along possibly the most specialized were the paddles of which there were three distinct types. The working paddle was stubby and thick, used for the work of propelling the canoe and sometimes shoving it off gravel bars or mud shoals. The second was narrower with a thick, strong centre column and a spear-shaped, spear-sharp point. This was an instrument used when the Indians expected to fight from their canoes. They used it as a paddle to close with the enemy and then as a spear or sword with which to thrust and jab. The third was a stalking paddle with a thin, pliable blade carved to a knife edge. This paddle, lighter than the other two and less durable, dipped into the water noiselessly and came out again without collecting water to drop from the blade, its springiness giving an extra thrust to each stroke. It was this third type the paddlers now used as they paddled toward the village.

The warriors who were to attack from the rear, White Sam among them, were put ashore a hundred yards from the village and the canoes stood off shore a few yards to be on hand in case the warning given by barking dogs would have any effect on their intended victims. But if the villagers heard the dogs they did not heed them for there were visitors and the largest house in the village was bulging with people, noise and smoke. Their scouting party had reported no enemies and they believed it.

Before dawn the party ended and the people dispersed to their houses. Their ring of enemies gathered closer, awaiting the coming of dawn in order to tell friend from foe.

Then, when the trees on the eastern horizon became distinguishable against the graying sky the throbbing hoot of an owl vibrated through the stillness. Not even a dog barked for they were used to the owls hooting; and their masters were in the first deep sleep. Had a barking dog awakened his master he might have been beaten to death for it, even though the master's life might have been saved.

After a discreet waiting interval, the owl's hoots commenced again and a score of savage throats screamed a war-cry from the forest to be answered in kind from the beach. The battle which followed was gloriously one-sided. The victims, awakened from deep sleep, had scarcely time to shout their fear when a club or thrusting spear ended their effort.

Between the beach and the houses White Sam saw a figure sprinting for the water. He raised his rifle to shoot when a flying figure struck him and knocked him over. This assailant, rather than pursuing the advantage, leaped to its feet and ran to escape. But White Sam recovered himself, sprang up and pursued the flying figure. Overtaking it, for it was both slower and smaller than he, he bore it to the ground.

It was only then he noticed that the person was wearing a dress of the long, shapeless type sold by the traders and, as the creature turned to attempt to defend herself, a long tear from the neck of the garment revealed the breasts of a young woman.

Leaping to his feet with an oath of surprise he seized her two long braids close to her head and lifted her to her feet, facing her away from him. She clawed at his arm and he shook her until she stopped.

"Do all Djoldainix women attack warriors?" he asked sarcastically.

When she did not answer he twisted her braids so that she faced the village, then propelled her at arm's length ahead of him.

A group of the Bella Coola were gathered together assessing their victory. A woman was with them. Siwid, the slave, had found his mother and she had been spared. When White Sam approached with his captive Siwid's mother pointed at the young woman.

"That is Chief Siwid's sister," she said. "Siwid has escaped. I saw him run!"

"And he escaped because this fury jumped on me when I was going to shoot him," White Sam said. "She flattened me just when I was going to pull the trigger."

The mother of Siwid, the slave, warned the Bella Coola that there was another village in the bay just a short distance away and, as soon as news of the raid reached there, warriors would come as thick as a run of salmon.

So the Bella Coola hurried their prisoners down to the canoes where they were left in the care of some of the warriors acting as guards. It was understood without saying that if any prisoner tried to escape he would be shot down. Then the remainder of the men looted the houses, bringing back to the canoes boxes and cans of eulachon grease, stacks of dried fish, armfuls of household effects.

White Sam, appointed as marksman in one of the canoes that was to bring up the rear and engage first with any pursuing enemy craft which might overtake them, tied his captive by her long braids to one of the thwarts in his canoe in such a manner that she had to remain lying down. And he tied her hands together so that she would not be able to undo the other fastenings.

"You might just try to escape and get yourself killed," he chided her, "or, worse still, you might find occasion to thrust me overboard when I would least like it."

His captive remained mute but glared at him in defiance.

When their canoes were loaded and they were beginning to take up their travel positions, a shout was raised.

"There's a bunch of them in a canoe!" Sneaking along the shore was a canoe load of villagers attempting to escape. They had only two paddles but some had taken short boards as substitutes. Two of the Bella Coola canoes hastily overtook them; the villagers were not armed and could offer no resistance.

A shout came from one of the other Bella Coola canoes.

"It's Dxilis," it was stated. "Wait for him."

Dxilis was an able Bella Coola warrior whose parents had been killed in a raid by the Djoldainix and was still thirsting for blood in revenge.

While the canoes of Bella Coola held the Djoldainix captive, Dxilis leaped into their canoe. He was so excited he screamed instead of talked.

"You murderers! You coyotes! You have killed my people! Now I will kill you."

His first victim was a youth not yet grown to sufficient maturity to go on a raid, and now never to do so. Momentarily calming his frenzy to a cold fury Dxilis placed his spear against the youth's throat and thrust with such power that the head almost left the body. Leaping over the twitching body Dxilis aimed for the throat of his second victim. However, in an attempt to avoid the thrust, the person lifted up but only sufficiently for the spearhead to stick in his ribcage rather than his throat. Dxilis' efforts to remove the spear were in vain and suddenly the victim ceased struggling but the spear remained in his body. The frustration enraged Dxilis and, seizing a war-club handed out by one of the Bella Coola, he leaped screaming from one victim to another, smashing their skulls in a frenzy of passion. Eight people lay dead in the canoe when he finished.

"Sink the canoe, so the crabs will eat them," someone called, and two men with hatchets leaped aboard the death craft and chopped holes in the cedar bottom, then leaped back to their own vessel as the canoe started to fill with water.

While this interruption was one of satisfaction to the enraged Dxilis, it almost spelt disaster for the Bella Coola invaders. Around a point of land to the east six canoes darted with the speed provided by fresh paddlers and warriors out for vengeance. Rapidly the Bella Coola started their flight westward and northward. Purposely the canoe carrying White Sam and the canoe carrying Sniniq dropped behind while the others sprinted away as fast as they could. It was the duty of White Sam and Sniniq to hold the Djoldainix at bay. Sniniq had two men immediately behind him in his canoe prepared to load muskets for him so that he could continue firing if the enemy closed in. White Sam, with his repeating rifle, did not need assistance in loading.

And more canoes came pouring out from behind the point so that the Bella Coola truly had to fight or run.

When the enemy came within rifle range White Sam commanded his paddlers to stop momentarily. His shot went through two of the approaching canoe men and crippled the third. The canoe swung round and was rammed so hard by the craft immediately behind that it upset and spilled its occupants, dead or alive, into the water. The third canoe swept round this tangle and ran into the combined fire of Sniniq and White Sam and, when four of its occupants were either killed or wounded, it fell back.

Then Siwid the slave unwittingly helped in the flight. He had been given the task of guarding a woman captive whom he recognized as a chief in the Djoldainix villages. Wishing to help her escape, he picked a time when excitement was high.

"Slip overboard, now," he said, "and swim underwater until the Bella Coola canoes have swept over you. Then your canoes can pick you up."

He turned his back on her and then appeared to attempt to catch her as she dropped overboard.

"She will drown," he screamed. "Stop!" he called to the canoe captain.

"She'll have to drown," the captain replied and the canoe sped away.

The woman, an excellent swimmer, remained underwater and when the canoes of White Sam and Sniniq passed over her she was too deep to allow a shot to be expended on her. She surfaced, and the leading canoe of her people stopped to pick her up. The delay allowed the Bella Coola to put considerable distance between them and their pursuers.

Two more attempts on the part of the Djoldainix to overtake the

Bella Coola were thrown off by the marksmanship of the two always-ready rear guards. Finally the chase was given up. By this time the Bella Coola had broken out of the islands and into a strong tidal stream which took them up coast at an accelerated rate.

The flotilla, after several hours of strenuous paddling, pulled into a little bay. Much talk occurred, some of the men wishing to stop and have a feast, others desirous of going to a spot farther from enemy territory. They checked over their number and found that while a few had wounds, only one man had been killed. How many of the enemy they had killed they could only guess. Their first guess was twenty-five but before the talk ended this number had been doubled. Besides which they had with them twelve captives who would either remain as slaves or be ransomed by their people. In several of the canoes rolled heads of the slain enemy, and scalps decorated the belts of several of the warriors. Loot filled the vessels, and the careful ones were anxious to escape with their riches.

Finally this group won, and it was decided to go to a sheltered harbor adjacent to Cape Caution. If there were no signs of current visitors they would spend the night there.

And so it was. Pursuit had seemingly ceased; weather was good. Outside the protective fringe of islands there was only a gentle ground swell and no wind. When they paddled cautiously through an opening in the surf into the mirror-calm of the bay, there was no sign on the sand, no smell of smoke, to indicate that there were humans anywhere around.

Relieved, they pulled their canoes up on the sandy beach, unloaded them and, after a long evening of feasting and bragging, slept for a few hours. Slaves were then unbound and put to work and shortly, with some of them handling the paddles to give the Bella Coola a rest, they pulled out of their snug harbor.

Again two canoes took positions slightly in the rear and again in the stern of one was White Sam and in the other Sniniq with their weapons ready to hold at bay a whole Indian nation.

In the harbor a canopy of fog had dropped so that even the tree-tops were lost in it. When they left the harbor mouth the flotilla travelled in a gray void. Nothing but the canoe immediately ahead of them was real and it floated on a gray cloud. The ground swell had increased overnight, and the Indians directed their craft by keeping the sound of the surf on their right and guiding the canoes so that they rolled almost broadside to swells heaving in from the left.

White Sam, crouched in the stern of his canoe, his rifle over his knees, scanned the heaving wastes but saw no enemy craft; scanned it until he decided there could be no possibility of a nearby enemy.

Then out of the fog slowly appeared the great black masts and hull of a ship. From the viewpoint of the men in the canoe the phantom appeared to fill the whole world. White Sam recognised it as one of the warships the government of the white man used to impose its will, and run errands, along the coast.

"Have they heard already about our expedition," he thought, "and come to shell our village?"

But the big black vessel, steam propelled, with its sail rigging kept only as a salute to tradition, crept slowly past, either ignoring them or not seeing them in the fog. Truly, out of the fog to the south a new day was being born. That huge vessel carried white man's authority and it was more powerful than all the Indian fleets along the coast. While Victoria was seemingly too far away for white men to interfere in Indian wars — unless a white man happened to be killed — the turning of the tide might come at any time when an Indian's death would be as worthy of attention as that of a white man.

There were scalps, along with the several heads, which would be dropped overboard if the white men stopped to investigate. This might even be the last warring expedition. But the ship disappeared into the fog again.

White Sam remembered the first time he had seen heads without bodies, four of them impaled on spears, one at each corner of a burial box. The heads now being carried home would probably grace the grave-house of the departed Bilxwalak as evidence that her death had been avenged.

And he remembered once taking a young man about his own age, who had come with two partners in a small sloop to trade, to show him a similar sight. He had not told the young trader where he was taking him and when, in the last mysterious light of day, they had come upon the grave site and his companion had almost walked into one of the heads before recognizing what it was, he had recoiled in horror.

"My gawd! You bastards are head-hunters," he had gasped, and turning, had plunged down to the beach and rowed like a man possessed out to the sloop. In the morning the sloop had disappeared and had never appeared again off the river mouth at Bella Coola.

White Sam wondered why white men showed such distaste for cutting off an enemy's head. They didn't mind killing — and a dead enemy had no more use for a head.

His attention was caught by his woman captive stirring to a new position. She had been asleep and was awakening. Her long black hair, which she wore in two neat, tight braids, curled around her forehead and was festooned with a thousand globules of mist. She had a pretty face and her body was trim and shapely and full of the promise of womanhood.

She was a prisoner. As the sister of a chief, maybe a chief in her own right, she might be ransomed. But if her people had suffered too badly in the raid she might not be. Then she would be a slave, the absolute property of her owner. Generally slaves were treated well but they were subject to the will of their owners. They might be buried alive when a totem pole was erected, being placed alive in the hole and crushed when the pole was dropped in upon them. A female slave could become the plaything of her owner and could be sold or given away — as also could her male counterpart — or she could be sold to a northern tribe who might eat her in one of their cannibal dances.

The woman, as if aware he was watching her, opened her eyes and smiled up at him, then shivered. Sam tossed her his robe which she donned gratefully.

"What is your name?" he asked.

She gave a name of about ten syllables, then laughed.

"White man who talked about god tells me my name is Ma-ree," she said, emphasising the last syllable.

"And you're Siwid's sister?" She nodded.

"Do you think he will send ransom for you?"

She looked at him. "I am your captive," she said. "How much are you going to ask for me?"

He looked at her appraisingly, mockingly. "Maybe I will ask too much and have to keep you," he said, "or maybe I'll give you away. I could give you to Dxilis."

She recoiled in horror. "You mean the man who goes crazy with killing?" And when he nodded, "No! No! I will go crazy and kill many people and run away and be a mad creature."

"And if I keep you and make you my woman?" he asked.

"I will cook for you," she said earnestly, "and bear your children and fight for you. I will be your woman."

"Then you shall not be offered for ransom nor given away. Tonight you shall cook my food and share my blanket."

Thus ended the brief courtship of White Sam. And while the union was never blessed by clergy nor entered in government records, it produced many fine youngsters and lasted a full four decades. White Sam kept her, honored her and Ma-ree, whose name eventually became Mary, cooked for him, bore and cared for his children and, on several occasions, indeed fought for him.

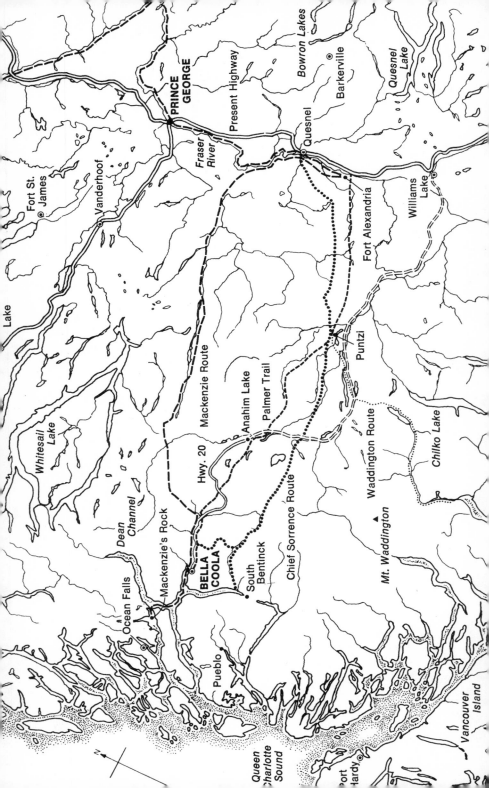

The Coming of
the Missionaries

For a hundred years following the coming of Mackenzie and Vancouver the coast of British Columbia was visited regularly for the purposes of exploration and trade. Curiosity prompted exploration and cupidity prompted much of the trade. And, whereas in the interior of the continent, extensive trading operations were costly enough to keep unwealthy operators from participating, the sheltered coastal waters and permanent Indian villages made it easy for enterprising adventurers to make a trip up coast and return with a fortune. Boats, which constituted a place of business and a home as well as a medium of travel, could be built or were available in the southerly ports of Victoria, New Westminster and Seattle, as were merchants who on a profit-sharing deal would finance the expedition and fill the hull with trade goods.

To some of these traders, the native people were fit subjects to be stripped of their goods, their furs, fish or oil at any cost — to the Indians. With their goods, traders, good men and bad, visited the Indian villages. It was common practice for a trading period to be preceded by a drinking period during which the Indian was given enough "free" liquor to prime his thirst. It was against the law to supply Indians with liquor, but for any crime less serious than murder (of a white man) the upper coast was too remote for serious attention. Undoubtedly many violent deaths did follow the visits of the whisky-sellers, but these were considered as natural as birth and mating and not any more statistical.

To some observers, also, the terrifying fervor of the winter ceremonials was closely akin to liquor debauchery. The drinking of liquor by Indians became totally lawless but survived. Many winter ceremonials, catalogued as "potlatches," were declared illegal by section 114 of the Indian Act in 1886 and eventually met extinction. With them went an artistic and complex culture. No activity was substituted.

In the latter part of the nineteenth century several of the churches became aware of a field of service along the British Columbian Coast.

The first recorded visit of a missionary to Bella Coola was by the Rev. W. H. Collison, who, en route to his mission field among the northern Indians, came ashore from the Hudson's Bay Company boat in which he was traveling. A medicine dance was being conducted by the Bella Coola Indians, and after watching for awhile, the missionary turned away in helpless distress.

"How these people need the word of God!" he said. "A mission should be set up here."

For a decade his words were interpreted to convey the message that the Anglican Church was on the verge of starting a mission at Bella Coola.

In the summer of 1883 the Methodist Church established a mission at Bella Coola, and that same fall Rev. Thomas Crosby and Rev. Wm. Pierce visited Bella Coola.

"Only a few days ago," they were told, "a white man came with his trade goods. He told us before many moons a man called an Anglican will come to tell us how to follow the white man's god."

The next morning as the two missionaries were about to leave in their canoe two chiefs approached.

"I am Tactulus," one of the men said, "but white man who can't say our Indian names call me Chief Tom. And he (pointing to his companion) is also of a name white man cannot say. We have come to tell you," and he spoke in Chinook, "that if the Anglican god-men have not come by the time the sun has stopped going lower behind the mountains to the south, then you may come and tell us about your god."

Two shots pounding out into the dark January night brought White Sam to startled wakefulness. He had been asleep for several hours and the fire had died down until there was only a glowing bed of coals giving a faint light on the walls and ceiling of the house.

What could this be? No Indian war party ever raided in the dead of winter. Maybe a fight among some of the tribesmen, resulting in shooting.

In the seconds that it took for these thoughts to race through his mind, pandemonium broke loose throughout the village. Men shouted, women screamed. Dogs barked.

Then from the river came the repeated call, "Don't shoot. I am Tactulus. Don't shoot. I am Tactulus. I am Tactulus."

White Sam reached for his rifle, grabbed a branch from the fireplace, and waving it to active flame, stepped out the door and joined the half-dozen others who were running toward the canoe-landing.

There was a knot of torch-bearing men there by the time White Sam and the others reached the gravel beach where canoes were pulled up.

In the centre of the throng a Bella Coola man kept calling in a loud voice, "Don't shoot. I am Tactulus. Don't shoot."

Then he changed his chant. "Don't shoot! I am with the god-man of the white people. I am with the god-man of the white people!"

As suddenly as the excitement had flared, it died down. White Sam saw a man of slight stature standing beside Tactulus smiling gently as the crowd boiled in excitement, then quieted.

"Why did Tactulus shoot?" White Sam asked the man nearest him. "He could have well have been shot, getting the village all excited like this."

"When he went out to Bella Bella to see the missionary," the man explained, and White Sam saw that he was not armed, "Tactulus said he would fire two shots if he came back with him. If he had failed he would have returned in silence."

Tactulus stopped calling, and four or five of the men who had gathered picked up the parcels and bundles in the canoe. Chief Tactulus gathered his family from the canoe and, with the missionary beside him, led the way to his house, the others following.

Friends had started the fire and heaped wood on it so that the house was full of light and smoke. Not many moments elapsed before enough villagers had arrived to see the stranger that the house was full almost to capacity.

The missionary's bundles had been piled in a corner, on the elevated sleeping platform. He was going to be the guest of Tactulus, and this corner, later to be partitioned off by split cedar, would be his home for many months.

As the crowd stood around watching the missionary, his host spoke to him.

"Talk to them," he said in Chinook. "They want to hear you talk."

So, in Chinook, the missionary said:

"Friends, I was happy when your Chief, whom we shall call Chief Tom, said that you wanted me to come to you with the message of the Lord. We left Bella Bella early this morning, and the Lord blessed us with good weather, so that in one day we came over here. Tonight I saw your roof tops against the sky and I was happy the journey was done and I was where there was Lord's work to be done."

He bowed his head and lifting his arms intoned a brief prayer: "May the Lord give me guidance and bring these people soon into His fold. Amen."

During the prayer the Indians gazed in wide-eyed amazement.

"What does he say?" one of them asked Chief Tom. "You talk?"

"He says he will tell you more about white man's God after everybody has had a sleep. You go home now and come back tomorrow."

The crowd laughed good-naturedly and filed out.

White Sam went home, lay down, but did not sleep. All his life in Bella Coola he had known that these people who had adopted him, whom he had adopted and become a part of, were soon to face the problem of how to meet the white flood. He remembered when, on the return from the land of the Kwakiutls, the gunboat of the white man had materialized out of the fog. He remembered knowing then that had the white man decided, he could have blown the victorious flotilla out of the water in the matter of moments. The cannons of the white man could destroy a village in a roar of thunder. Could the Indian run away?

So far, the white man had not asked the Indian to change his manner of life. He had brought to him trade goods, and supplemented cedar bark blankets with cloth, taking the fish oil and furs of the Indian in exchange. Smallpox, brought by the white man, had all but wiped out sections of the Indian population, so that where once had been many thousands of Indians in the Bella Coola Valley, now there were not more than two hundred. Through it the white man had not tried to impose his thinking or his religion on the Indian. The winter dances, potlatches, feasts had gone on without interference.

Now here was a man, the god-man of the white man, here to tell the Indians about the God of the white man. Up north, on the

Skeena and the Nass, the god-men of the whites had started schools in their churches, so that some of the Indians could read and write. They had caused the Indian to desert the warpath, and liquor feasts, and to build houses after the style of the white man.

Was it good? Would it help the Indian to meet the incoming tide of white men to be able to talk like one? White Sam had become so thoroughly like an Indian that he thought like one most of the time, enough to realize what a confusing trail led from this one house of thought.

"Will I help build a bridge for them?" he pondered, "or will I just let things drift?" and before he had crystallized an answer, he dropped to sleep.

Next day he went to the house of Chief Tom and found a score of the others there. The missionary had arranged a high desk (which to White Sam looked like the pulpit in the church he had attended long ago in eastern Canada before his father and mother had died) and was standing beside it. He greeted Sam as he entered.

"I am going to talk to you about the Supreme Being," he told his assembly in Chinook. "He wants me to teach you about Him. He wants me to teach you His holy word. He wants me to teach you to read His Book," and he held aloft a Bible.

His audience listened with impassive faces as he talked on.

"This is the God of the white man I am going to tell you about. He is a God of love and mercy. To know Him you must give up your potlatches, your dances, and your beliefs in the supernatural beings of your fathers and forefathers."

When the significance of these utterances struck his audience, one of the chiefs challenged him.

"Your white man's God wants us to cast off all the gods of our fathers and take only him."

"There is only one God, the Supreme Being of the white man."

"Is this Supreme Being the god of all white men?"

"He is the God of all Christians. He is ultimately the God of everyone because He is the only one God."

"If Christians have a god like you talk, why do they come here and kill us, make us drunk and rob us of our furs, take our women away and make them as rotten as old salmon? Will white man's god make us creatures like these white men?"

"These men are not acting as God wishes them," the missionary countered.

"Then they are not Christians, and their god is not good."

At this the chief and most of the others swept out of the building.

White Sam, watching the missionary close his eyes and mutter a word of prayer, realized the opposition this man was faced with. His path, like that of the Christ of whom he talked, would be one of rocks and thorns.

The missionary had completed his prayer and, opening his eyes, saw White Sam looking at him.

"You are a white man?" he asked.

"No," answered White Sam, then corrected himself. "Yes."

"What do you mean 'no, yes'?" the missionary queried.

"I was born a white person but I became an Indian," White Sam explained.

"You mean you abandoned your race and became as these people of-of-of darkness?"

Sam felt his anger rising at this suggestion that his chosen people, the Bella Coola Indians, were creatures of darkness.

"These people gave me a home," he said slowly. "I have been happy with them. I do not think they are creatures of darkness."

"But they have not had an opportunity to see the light. They worship their false gods and they live together without knowledge of the Supreme Being!"

"They have a very real belief in the supernatural. Maybe their window into the next world is just as clear as yours!"

"It has led them to near extinction," the missionary replied.

"Not their traditions," White Sam argued. "These people were as simple as children and they have been visited by white people who debauched them, robbed them, prostituted their women. You should carry your Bible to these white people!"

"We aim to help these people, your people, so that they need not be victims of unscrupulous white people." The missionary looked at White Sam shrewdly. "If you love these people who, as you say, adopted you, you will help me help them!"

At this moment two young chiefs came in through the door, each with a partly grown boy in tow. The disturbance broke the tension between White Sam and the missionary, and White Sam strode out.

Several hours later he left on a trip along his trap line, a trip that kept him away for most of a week.

When he returned, his wife put food in front of him and as he ate she told him of the village happenings.

"That white man's god-man is going to be killed," she said. "He says that potlatches are bad, and that they must go. He says that all our supernatural beings are like the deep shadows before the sun comes up and we must forget them. He says that everything our fathers believed in is not right. He says if we are going to be happy after we are dead, we must believe in the god of the white man!"

She became more excited as she talked, her voice rising and her words in the Bella Coola tongue tumbling faster.

"Did he say all this in one week?" White Sam asked with a show of incredulity.

"He said it all in one day. I went to hear him talk," his wife affirmed.

"Do you know what I think?" White Sam looked hard at his wife.

"What?"

"That you are eating too much salmon and getting fat."

"When I tell you things you do not listen," his wife objected. "But it is not salmon fat. It is just another of your babies."

White Sam slapped her playfully on the buttocks as she turned away, seized his coat and strode out into the street. As he walked along he saw marks on the buildings, in snow, and where the wind had blown the snow off the gravel, in the ground. Marks done with the end of a charred stick on the hewn planks of the buildings, and by a blunt stick in the snow or gravel, looked like a simple "x". Then he noted that one of the stems was constantly longer, so that it had the form of the Christian's cross.

He had not yet decided on the significance of this when a boy of about ten danced past him, swinging a stick and chanting.

White Sam stopped up short.

"Jesus, I can write Jesus," the boy was chanting.

Sam stopped the boy.

"Where'd you learn that?" he asked.

"White man's god-man showed us."

"You show me," whereupon the boy willingly drew a Christian cross in the gravel, grinned "you see," and went on.

White Sam went into the house of one of the older chiefs.

Four of the tribesmen were squatted around the fire, and Sam could tell that serious discussion was taking place. He squatted beside them as they greeted him.

"This white man god-man is not good. He will make us all as slaves, without wealth to give away. Without potlatches."

"He will teach our sons to be different than we are."

"We must kill him before the division in our people grows too large," growled another.

"We can't kill him, for if we do the white men will come with their gunboats and blow us from the valley," one more elderly than the others remarked. "And he is a smart man. If we make him as one of us, we will change him and use him."

"And if he does not change?"

"Then we might talk of killing him in such a way that the guns of the white man will not roar at our houses."

"And how will you attempt to change him?"

"All white men like women, and maybe we should start by letting him have a woman of our tribe," the wily old chief explained. "Women are like earth. According to the kind of woman a man chooses, that is the kind of children he has. If we give this man our women, then he will grow our kind of children."

"But what if he goes away and takes our women with him?"

"If he goes away, then is no more a threat to us. If he takes the women with him, it will be not a very great price to pay for removing him."

White Sam left the chiefs with their discussion of how to get the missionary to take unto himself one or several of the women of the Bella Coola tribe.

His next stop was at Tactulus' big house, where the missionary lived.

The missionary was working with two boys of the village, drawing figures on the earth beside the fire. He was talking to them in English and to White Sam's astonishment the boys answered in the same language.

"This is a house," the missionary stressed, drawing a simple house. "House, house. People live in a house."

He drew a column of smoke from the roof.

"That is smoke," he said. "Smoke from the house. What comes from the house?" he asked one of the boys.

The boy hung his head for a minute, then answered "Boys."

"That was yesterday," the missionary corrected, and when the other boy gave the right answer he patted him on the back. "Yes, smoke comes from the house."

He saw White Sam watching him.

"You may go now, boys," he said. "Come back at daylight."

"I have not seen you for some time," he said to White Sam when the boys had run outside. "I have wanted your help in doing God's work here."

"I am not sure yet whether it would be good to have your god replace the many supernatural beings of these people. It would destroy everything they believed in. They would be lost."

"They will be lost unless they do forsake their old superstitions and accept the one true God," the missionary replied with the appearance of conviction.

White Sam curbed a rising feeling of anger. Why, he thought, does every contact with this man irritate me? Yet the missionary would be of little force if he did not have the courage of his convictions. Instead of retorting in anger he said quietly, "I am glad you are teaching the boys to speak English."

"I have only the two pupils so far," the missionary said. "I could do as much for a dozen. Have you any children?"

"Three," replied White Sam. And when the missionary asked him when he was married, he replied, "I have never married in the way you probably suggest. But this woman is true to me, and I to her, and we intend to live together for the rest of our lives."

"But it is not sanctified by God, this— this union of yours!"

"Such unions created families for many generations before missionaries ever heard of the British Columbia coast. They have been good."

"But there is no reason now to keep living in sin."

"Living in sin? These people are not living in sin. You will never make them believe they live in sin. They live in the same manner as their ancestors since the beginning of time!"

"But if they are told better, if they are shown the light, then they should accept. Will you set an example and marry your woman?"

"I married her according to the customs and beliefs of these, my people. That is enough. I will not marry the way you suggest."

And he never did.

If anything, winter ceremonials went on with more vigor than they had in previous years. Several big potlatches were given, and the several secret societies vied with each other to put on more spectacular shows than they had heretofore. It looked as if there was an unconscious fear that this might be the last big display of such theatricals. To some of these shows the missionary was invited, but he did not accept.

The tension that gradually built up between the large faction of chiefs who opposed the missionary and the handful who showed willingness to accept the white man god-man and his teachings was lessened by an unusually severe stretch of weather that blanketed the valley and its surrounding peaks in whirling blizzard and fierce draughts of winds that made cruel sport of blowing through the cracks of the large but not tightly constructed homes of the Indians. Keeping fuel on hand for the fires in the open hearths became work of deadly earnest, for it was impossible to bring drift logs in from the beaches, while deep snow in the forest made the task of gathering fuel there a wearisome one. Added to this, reserves of food became depleted. Some families faced actual starvation.

"Can your white man god-man bring us food, now?" some of the chiefs snarled at Chief Tom. "If his god is stronger than ours, get him to send us food."

One morning during this crisis Chief Tom found a hibernating black bear bedded down under the root of a large Cedar tree, and, fearing that if he tried to kill it alone, the large beast might escape, he hurried to the village and got several other men to come and capture the bear. This was successfully done, and to the starving village three or four hundred pounds of meat were delivered.

"Why didn't the white man god-man help kill the bear?" one of the chiefs asked Chief Tom.

"He prayed, and maybe his God sent me to where the bear was sleeping," Chief Tom replied.

The weather moderated, and the men got out along the beaches and secured more firewood and took an abundance of beaver and muskrats. A venturesome boat-load of traders anchored off the mouth of the river, and brisk trading for the winter catch of furs resulted in enough food and trade goods being bought by the Indians to enable one of the chiefs to stage a potlatch.

"White Sam," the chief told him, "you speak the same tongue as the white man god-man. You ask him to come to the potlatch."

When White Sam went to the missionary with this errand, he was met with a refusal.

"It is ungodly, and I could not go," the missionary said.

"If you are going to carry your message to all people, you must take it into the camp of the enemy."

"It is heathen, and I cannot attend," the missionary reiterated.

"Months ago you asked me to help you in spreading the word of your God," White Sam said. "There is talk of opposing you and your teaching. If you do not come to this potlatch, I cannot guard against the stories that you are afraid to go, that you have not enough faith in the strength of your God to protect you. Soon you may be laughed at in this village."

The missionary looked at him levelly.

"If it is God's will that I die, or suffer harm at the hands of these people, then it shall be so. I am not afraid. I will go."

On the appointed night White Sam called for the missionary and walked with him along the hewn-plank walk to the large house of the chief. People were gathering, chiefs in their regalia, and as they stepped through the mouth of the large curved whale that formed the doorway of the house, a slave showed the missionary to a place beside the host. Sam found his place a few feet away from the missionary and behind him. He did not expect trouble, for a potlatch was not a time of killing. But he knew that the chief who was giving this one was one of the fiercest of those in opposition to the missionary. He had not brought his rifle with him, and he noted with relief that none of the others was armed.

As if the missionary's arrival was the signal for commencement, the party began. The fire, which had been burning brightly, was smothered with earth until there were only a few feeble flames. Then, amidst the sound of much whistling and stamping and crashing on the roof, a large black creature in the guise of a bird hopped into the room and around the feeble fire. It was a bird as big as a crouched man. One side of the bird-like creature was painted white, and the other side a reddish brown. White Sam's apprehension rose as he realized this was a dramatization of the coming of the missionary, who was a half-breed, his mother being Indian and his father a white trader. With fascination he watched the effigy of the missionary pluck dried plumes of cedar and spruce from his vari-colored cloak and feed them into the fire. The result of this was a sparkling array of various colors of fire, which rose and then dropped to give darkness, denoting, White Sam interpreted, the confusion that was caused by the missionary's teaching.

Then another large bird, this time brown only in color, hopped in, with enough regalia about him to denote that he was a chief. Under his wing he carried a load of dried twigs, which, when put on the fire, quite overcame the mixed light from the twigs of the other creature.

When the light from the second bird's twigs was still strong and that of the two-toned bird non-existent, a further commotion was heard and from behind a curtain of cedar-bark at one end of the room a canoe came into view, riding on the shoulders of six young tribesmen. (It was a shell only, for the real dug-out canoes of either river or ocean-going varieties were very heavy.) Seated in it was a comely young girl, dressed as a chief's daughter, and accompanied by two young female slaves. They circled the fire twice, and then set the canoe down in front of the bird representing the missionary. Following this, another shell bearing blankets and furs and some of the accoutrements of the chief status followed the same path and was set down beside the shell bearing the young woman and her slaves.

During the arrival of the two canoe-shells the uni-colored bird had disappeared. By some magic the white part of the other bird had become darker, so that it was now of the same color as its erstwhile competitor, except for its head, which still remained half white. Also as by magic the fire flared up again and burned as brightly as when the missionary first came into the building.

Then, mysteriously the fire died. There was again much whistling and stomping on the roof, and the sound of rustling of wings. The audience did not move, for it knew, as White Sam realized, that this was no ordinary potlatch to enhance the weight or fame of the chief, but a picture painted with skillful strokes of living brushes illustrating the confusion caused by the teaching of the missionary, and what could be his if he accepted the invitation and became one of the tribe — women, wealth, a chieftainship, products of the old order of things. Like the others, White Sam waited, tense, for the enactment of the next act of the drama.

After a few moments of darkness the fire burned brightly again.

The birds were gone, but in front of the missionary now sat the two canoes, the one still piled with trade goods, the other still occupied by the chief's daughter and her two slaves. All eyes were on the missionary. If he accepted, he would become part of the tribe. If he refused . . .

The missionary rose to his feet.

"I cannot accept the gifts which you have placed before me. When I accepted the call to come here and tell you of the God of love and of His son Jesus Christ, it was not that I should take from you your earthly treasures. Rather it was that I should obey God's will and tell you of His Holy Word. I could not take for my wife this young woman you have placed in front of me unless we were united in holy wedlock. The Supreme Being says that there shall be no slaves. The law of the white men says that there shall be no slaves, so that if I were to accept the gift of these slaves, I would immediately free them.

"If you will accept the Holy Word of the white man's god you will free your slaves and you will yourselves be freed from your burdens of sin."

He lifted his arms, closed his eyes. "Father in heaven," he prayed aloud, "give these people the hunger for Your word that they may become Your Creatures. Amen."

Facing the chief who was his host, he said, "Bring your people to me that I may teach them a better way of life."

He bowed, then turning, strode out of the building.

No one attempted to follow him, but his departure was the signal for pandemonium to break loose. The chief-host let this run for a few moments, then effectually stopped it by having the fire dampened. For a few moments silence and waiting again reigned.

There was the sound of whistling and the beating of wings, and the thud as of heavy birds landing on the roof. Shortly the fire began to burn, increasing gradually as with the coming of day. When dark had turned to gray and the gray brightened to where things were visible, the two-colored bird representing the missionary was seen asleep beside a log. To the almost hysterical tension of the audience was added another source of excitement and one of apprehension when two dreaded Hao-Hao birds thrust their long slender beaks over the log. Even small children knew of the Hao-Hao, that supernatural being who lived in deep forests and dark canyons most of the time, but came out occasionally, and when he found a victim asleep or helpless, sucked the entrails therefrom. Since the appetite of these creatures was known to be voracious, it was feared that they might sometimes pick another victim, maybe from the audience.

In front of the hypnotized assembly the two Hao-Hao birds scrambled silently over the log, and as silently approached the two-colored bird. Stopping for a moment, as if gloating over their victim, one inserted its long beak in the rectum of the victim and snatched therefrom a portion of the creature's entrails. While this one was gobbling its tid-bit up, the other did likewise. Then the first had its turn again, followed by the second. At the fifth or sixth turn the two-colored bird awakened, saw the two Hao-Hao birds flipping portions of its entrails in the air in order to get them into their beaks. The unfortunate victim gave a squawk, tried to jump away, collapsed, and after a few weak flutterings of its wings died.

Each Hao-Hao tried to find more entrails in the fallen bird, but failed. Without further hesitation, they clambered over the log and hid.

Again the fire fell away, and when it grew up and lightened the room again the two Hao-Hao had disappeared, as had the remains of the victim.

And then the handing out of gifts of great value took place, and clowns and mimics repeated the performance in lighter vein, not so much to relieve the audience, but to impress again that the missionary had rejected a woman of the tribe, had rejected chieftainship, and when he was found dead, it would not be because of an act of man but because Hao-Hao had visited him.

And about two weeks later it was told about that the finger-nail parings of the missionary had been picked up by a village sorcerer, that these had been attached to an effigy of the missionary, which had been placed in a dreaded Mesatchi box. In a short time, as long as it would take some flesh of the salmon, which had been used for the chest of the effigy, to decompose, the missionary would be dead.

White men would think that the missionary had died of the coughing disease that carried away so many of the Indians. But the Indians would know better.

Not all, however, for the missionary had added several more to his class. And when he started teaching an adult class to sing, he gathered more followers. When he started serving tea (liberally sweetened with sugar) and biscuits at the Sunday evening classes, he made more friends. But he had to admonish them against calling the social gifts "missionary potlatches."

"It is because I care about you and want to share with you good fellowship. Potlatches put you in debt and enslave you."

One day White Sam asked the missionary if he knew of the story of his coming death.

"I have heard the ridiculous story that I shall die by a witch doctor's curse. That is what I am here to destroy. This black, ignorant fear that is of Satan. It is terrible."

"Yet it is powerful," White Sam warned. "It has killed several people I know."

"Surely you do not believe in it?" the missionary challenged him.

212

"I believe in it enough to warn you to be careful," Sam replied.

The missionary refused to be impressed.

It was about three weeks later that, returning from another trip along his trap line, White Sam was putting pelts on drying boards when his wife broke in upon him, panting. She had taken to attending the missionary's classes.

"Sam, Sam," she called to him in a horrified whisper. "They are going to kill him. Stop them! Stop him!"

Sam tried to calm her enough for her to tell her story.

"We were singing," she said, "when Denomix came and said they wanted to meet him at the Chief's Ledge. And he promised he would go just at the time when the light begins to fade. Stop him! Stop him! You know that no one but chiefs can go on that ledge and live! And he refused to become a chief. He will die for it."

She was speaking of the most secret meeting place of the chiefs, the three-foot wide ledge clinging to the side of a darksome canyon a quarter of a mile from the village. A stream, the Taxquan, born in the glaciers high above plunged down through canyons and in its final leap roared over a waterfall by the ledge. A hundred feet down, the waters of a great cauldron boiled and growled as the plunging stream fed into it. The roar was so great that it created an effective screen of sound. No eavesdropper could listen in on discussions. No one could see from the top, nor gain access to the ledge except by walking along the poles that had been fastened by ropes to trees high upon the mountain-side.

From one hidden spot on the opposite mountainside White Sam had discovered, a man could get a restricted view of the ledge. It was too distant for a spear or an arrow — but for a good rifle it might be close enough.

On the face of the canyon, people long past had carved likenesses of men and of their gods in the hard rock. It had been a place of worship of powerful dieties.

White Sam leaped through the door and strode rapidly down the street to the home of Chief Tom, where he found the missionary putting on a cloak in preparation to go to the Chief's Ledge.

"I have warned you before that you are in danger," White Sam told him abruptly. "No one but Chiefs go on this ledge and live. This is just an invitation to your death."

"I am not afraid," the missionary replied. "Chief Denomix is going to take me up there. I promised to go."

"Don't you want to stay alive and continue your work? A dead missionary can't do much teaching!"

"On the contrary," the missionary protested. "The lessons brought to earth by Christ Jesus travelled around the world after he was killed on the cross."

"But, man, you are not Christ!" White Sam expostulated. "And you won't be hoisted on a cross. You will disappear in a whirlpool at the foot of a waterfall. If you are not a fool you will stay away from there."

"I am not a fool. I am going, for there might be an opportunity to teach God's word there." He emphasized the word 'there'. "Go into 'all the world' the Book stresses."

"I'm wasting my time?" White Sam asked, frustration fighting with rage within him.

"I am going at the bidding of the Lord," the missionary replied.

Sam departed as rapidly as he came. Striding swiftly homeward, he noticed that it was snowing, heavily. Snow was coming in large blobs an inch across rather than in flakes. He could see the tracks that he had left a few minutes before and realized it had been snowing then, too.

At his home he seized his rifle, checked it for shells, told his wife he was going. She did not ask where, merely nodded wide-eyed approval. "Be careful," she prayed aloud.

And then he was out and running swiftly along a path through the forest, with a gait he used when he was hunting and in haste to get ahead of his quarry. The path led to Taxquan Stream and to a large fallen log over which he hurried. On the other side of the stream, he left the path and started climbing the almost vertical mountainside. Snow slipped under his feet and carried him down, but, with difficulty he climbed on and came to a spot, where, peering between two large rocks, he was able to command a view of the Chief's Ledge.

What he saw there convinced him that he had not been wrong in trying to dissuade the missionary from coming here. Four chiefs were there, and with them that sinister figure Dxilis. From the time of the successful raid against the Kwakiutls when Dxilis had killed for straight blood-lust the canoe load of prisoners, he had developed into the professional executioner of the village. If a group wanted some one killed, they called upon Dxilis — and because of the position he held, he was under obligation to act. And while his fellow tribesmen came to fear and hate him, his position protected him. His was a sanctified job by ancient tradition; when blame fell on anyone it was upon those who had commissioned him. Throughout the years, however, Dxilis had grown wary and tense, and deadly. Sometimes it was suggested very quietly that a killing performed by Dxilis had not been commissioned at all, but none had the courage to say it loudly, for the next killing might be the talkative one's son or brother.

Now Dxilis was painted as for war, and he carried a heavy war-club made from a caribou antler, a fierce weapon capable of slicing a man's head in two with one blow. As he listened to the chiefs he jerked and twitched in nervous spasms.

Then White Sam saw him sink to a crouching position, his club hidden under his cloak and his head withdrawn into his shoulders. He looked like a huge boulder poised on the lip of the ledge. Behind him and beside him stood the four chiefs.

A movement caught Sam's eyes, and around the rock twenty feet from the crouching Dxilis came the missionary, followed a few feet behind by Denomix. Not a sound could be heard through the curtain of sound of the waterfall, and even the roar of this was dulled by the heavy snow falling.

Sam swiftly and smoothly brought his rifle around and pointing it out through the parapet-like opening, cocked it and trained the sights carefully on Dxilis.

The missionary stepped from the logs to the ledge, saw the chiefs, hesitated a moment, then stepped forward, seemingly unaware of the crouching Dxilis.

Suddenly, the executioner leaped to his feet. Sam from his distance could see the demoniacal expression on the man's face and gathered from the wide open mouth that Dxilis was screaming. The missionary scarcely stepped back.

Then Dxilis' arm rose up high over his head and was starting to sweep back, to give full force to his war club.

As the club reached its apex and Dxilis was balanced on his toes, Sam pressed the trigger. The bullet caught him under the arm-pit and as he crumbled he fell over the brink into oblivion in the cauldron below.

He did not know what hit him, nor did the observers, for the report of the shot had not penetrated the screen of sound and the muffle of heavy snow-flakes.

The chiefs saw the missionary standing unscathed, saved by the seeming intervention of his god, a god who could strike a man down, a fierce capable deadly man, without instrument or sign. They almost pushed the missionary over the brink as they made haste to leave this spot and the white man god-man.

White Sam cautiously removed the empty cartridge, pocketed it, and slid down the mountain, noting that an hour's snow would cover all the signs of his presence.

The story that Dxilis had been snatched from earth by the missionary's god was told many times in the next few days, and while the missionary himself referred to it only briefly in his prayers, the incident opened a new era of thinking for the Indians. Maybe he was right. Maybe his god was the Supreme Being.

Attendance at his classes and services grew greatly.

One evening White Sam went with Mary to the house of Chief Tom. There were about twenty-five people there, and as they sat down White Sam saw Tom dressed in his chief's regalia, standing a little apart. He had an attitude of waiting.

"Chief Tom," the missionary said, "are you ready?"

Tom nodded that he was, and the missionary asked him to come up to the pulpit.

Speaking in Chinook, and occasionally interjecting a phrase or two of the Bella Coola tongue which he had mastered, the missionary explained that Tom was giving his soul to the Lord, that he was renouncing his heathen ways and heathen gods, that henceforth he would be a follower of Christ only. When he turned to Tom, the Indian nodded his approval.

Stepping down by the fire, he spoke to the assembly.

"I have been a big chief among you," he said, turning slowly as he spoke so that all could see his rich chief's regalia. "I have given many potlatches in the manner of my ancestors. But now this is going to change. I am giving up the ways of our forefathers which this man has shown me to be wrong. I am giving up my seat as chief. I am going to be a follower of the Supreme Being of the white man."

At this he started to disrobe, the fire flamed brightly as he fed to it the collar and the leggings of shredded cedar bark and the rich fur cloak he wore. Chief Tom did not speak as he disrobed, but when the last vestige of his clothing was in the fire he stood up, completely nude, and with his arms held aloft, twirled on his toes as if to emphasize his nakedness.

"I have given up the dress of a savage chief," he said. "Now I come to my new god as naked as the day I was born. Now I will be clothed for my new way of life." He stooped, and picked up a shirt and pair of trousers of white man's manufacture, and donned them. He then uncovered two large cedar boxes, skilfully laced together and carved and painted in the designs of his family legends. The Bella Coola Indians had craftsmen who with short planks of hand split cedar and long spruce roots could create chests of exceeding beauty, waterproof and, if the use required, as sturdy as their dugout canoes, or as light as a drum and with sides and top and bottom almost as thin. The two boxes that Tom now opened had tops and bottoms as thin as skin from several generations of use in carrying tools of ceremonials and potlatches to and from the neighboring villages.

He reached into the box on his left and drew forth a whistle shaped like the wrist, palm and fingers of a human hand. The wrist and each finger had a different toned whistle carved into it. It was a most valuable piece, a secret whistle belonging to the cannibal dance, and one for which Tom's grandfather had refused a slave that had been offered in exchange. It was against the rules of the secret societies to sell at any price.

Now only the fire burned brighter as the tinder-dry cedar whistle was given to it.

More whistles followed, and robes and headdresses and scarves.

When a mask was dropped into the fire, and flames came from its eyes and shot from its nostrils, the piercing shriek of a woman rent the air. Tom stopped for a moment and then went on. It was apparent that the scream had broken the tension, but there was no more noise but that of the hungry and gleeful crackling of the fire as symbols and tokens of great wealth were tossed upon it.

"This is the greatest potlatch of them all," White Sam thought. "A man's wealth, his ancestors, his tradition, all, all fed to the flames." When the boxes were empty and had followed their contents into the flames, he said to himself. "I hope what the god of the white man has to give is payment for all this."

Now Tom was on his knees, praying, and every ear strained to hear his words.

"Chief God," he said, "I come to you as a poor man. I want to be your servant. I want to follow you. I want to be a Christian. Help me, Amen."

Then he walked over and stood with bowed head in front of the missionary, down whose face the tears were streaming.

The missionary prayed, then started to sing one of the simple hymns that he had been teaching his classes.

During the singing White Sam felt his wife nudging him. "Do Christians always undress when they become Christians?" she asked. "No." "Are you a Christian?" "I don't know." "Why don't you know?" "Keep quiet and sing the song."

It was during this time that the remnants of the villages throughout the valley whose population had been almost totally destroyed by smallpox moved to the village near the mouth of the river. This village, Qomots, became Bella Coola, and when Indian reservations were created and, in the Bella Coola district, surveyed in 1888 and 1889, there was only one piece of land recognised as Indian land. Surrounding the Indian Village of Qomots, a comparatively large reserve of 3363 acres athwart the mouth of the valley was struck out. While small village sites in the surrounding bays and channels were reserved, the sites of the old villages in the Bella Coola and tributary valleys were not, and in a few decades even their approximate location was a matter of conjecture.

One family, the Squiness family of Nooskultz valley, instead of moving westward, moved eastward, and became chiefs in the Anahim Lake district.

Christianity, first preached to the tribe by the Rev. William Henry Pierce in 1884, was neglected for several years after that for Mr. Pierce left within the year, and there was no missionary during 1885. In 1886 Edward Nicholas came, and stayed until 1895. With him was his wife Kezia, and rather than live in the large but primitive homes of the Indians, they built their own house, and a church. In 1899 Dr. J. C. Spencer, who was a medical missionary, came for an eight-year period until 1907. He was replaced by the Rev. W. H. Gibson who stayed until 1921 except for a period in 1915 when the Rev. Tom Caldwell served in the Bella Coola Valley. Caldwell went overseas during World War 1 and was reported missing in action.

9. Jacobsen: Norway to Bella Coola

In 1885 there appeared in Bella Coola for the second time B. Fillip Jacobsen, long, lean, learned and loquacious, a young man shortly out of Norway. His first visit to Bella Coola had been the year before, in 1884, as part of a trip, alone, from Victoria to Tungas, Alaska, visiting virtually all the Indian villages for the purpose of collecting curios and artifacts for various museums in Germany. The entire trip took all the good weather portion of 1884 and was resumed again in the spring of 1885. His vessels consisted of rowboats and canoes, which he rowed and paddled, or rigged with sail.

He was well trained for this kind of travel for, born on a small island out in the open ocean 14 English miles from the city of Tromso, boats and water were part of his life from babyhood. The long journey that took him from Norway to New York where he landed July 19, 1884, thence by train to San Francisco and by steamer to Victoria, B.C. presented no particular difficulties to him. He went to Victoria because Vancouver was as yet only a shack town on Burrard Inlet at which the steamers did not call.

To quote one of his letters, in his own picturesque English:

> Although I did not speak English I started of on my jurny up the Coast, took a canoe and one Indian with me on my colecting trip, on the first trip I took in all the Indian villages on the East Coast of Vancouver Island — The Indian I had with me was very dubius in being alone with me as he did not think I could Handel and sail a Cannoe — but he soon found out that I was a good saillor and careful at the same time, we had not been out many days until we had a very strong following breas quit strong to, but by this time the Indian know I know how to stear the Cannoe with a padel and handel the sail soo he was quit satisfied after this

to let me goo on, our sail which was just square was made of Flourer saks this struk me very funny, but the Indian was him self very much pleased with it as it was a regular picture gallery all through in fair wind he would sit and admire the different pictures and writings on the saks.

Our main food was Bacon and Beans and Rice and not to forget the Dry salmon wich we laid in a big supply of in the morning and Evening to prepare a meal was just to roast the skinside on the fire, and there we had a good meal. I got to like them very much although no salt was ever uset.

In my trip up the Coast, I saw very few white men. I was not interested in whitemen it was the Indian villages I wantet to find and to buy all the Indian Currio, especially artickels I know we did not have in the museum. I went as far as to Allert Bay where Mr. Spencer an old timer had a cannery and where I laid in new supplies — now this was as far as the Indian had agreed to goo with me. I may mention on the way from Victoria and up as I had hardly seen any whiteman I had no chance in learning English, but the Indian was talking Chinok all the time and by the time we reached Allert Bay I was fair in Chinok — and therefore when I meet a whiteman and I could not tolk English to him I tolket Chinok. Chinok is an Indian Trading Language consisting of about 400 word and if a man can talk it fluently he can express him self fairly wel, I have heard some of the Indians making spetches in big potlases, as one tribe cannot understanding his neighboring tribe, and it is certainly wonderful with as few words as are how well a good Chinok speaker can exspres him self. In my opinion Chinok aught to be the Universal language of the world, they talk about Wollopuck and Esperanto, neither of this 2 could com up to the Chinok.

Jacobsen at Alert Bay got two Indians to take him in a canoe to several villages to the east. He was among the Kwakiutl tribes and his brother, Captain Adrian Jacobsen who had been up the British Columbia Coast coast two years previous, warned that they were not to be trusted — they had tried to attack him.

However this did not scare me although I was allone — I got to Mam-mellika just before Dusk, of course as a white man was a pretty scors article around this part of the world except Spencer at Allert Bay, when I landet, every soull in the tribe it semet came down on the beach to meet me and Inspect me, the first asket what I wanted there I spoake in Chinok, and told them I had been sent by a big Tahie, King to buy some of their Currio, and wanted to take it back with me, some of the men asket me if I was Captain Jacobsen I told them I was his younger brother.

I went in to a haus with one of the Indians that com with me as his relation lived in this Hause — when I made arrangement to stay for the neight or the next day.

I might mention here to buy Indian Currio is not leike going into a store most of the buing was done in the night and some time ofter most of the Indians had goen to bed, you see no Indian would sel any of his wolluable Dans mask and let any of his neabor know anything obout it as all Danses are more leike a religious ofair, and the greatest secret is keep of every thing, and if a man should be caught in selling some of his secret woden Dans mask, Roteles, or any parapernalia belong to the secret Danses he would be killet by the master of sermonies and the Indian Doctors — now the way'this killing takes place, if a man has been found to have sold some of the obove things — it is sent word to him that in a years time he will be dead, the Indian Doctor will by spiritual force and with witchcraft put the stone, bone or Feader — feader is supose to kill quicker than anything elsh. It is strange that Indians as a rule believe it, and worries soo much over it that they take sick and as in nearly every case when the year is up the condemned man Dies, for this reason I had to be soo very careful, and not let the next fellow know what I bought, any ordinary haus article I could of couce buy in the Day time but when it came Wooden masks Dans Ratels and wissels wich was all uset in the secret dances, I had to be soo careful. I might mention here that the British Columbia Cost Indians has some wonderful traditions. I have made big collections of them but pople here in this contry take no interest in the Indians. They certainly are interesting from a scintefic stand point.

Three days were spent in this village, making some fine collections and nailing them firmly in boxes. After some endeavor he got a crew of two, a full-grown man and a boy of 14 or 15 years to take him into Knight Inlet.

When we were ready to start the older Man Tom with name come and asket me if his woman could go along with us as she wanted to wissit some relations at Knight Inlet, or as Indian name the place Souitte Enock, as we had a big canno and I only had a trunk along an our prowission I tol Tom it was allright and she could goo with us. If I only have had an Inkling of whot a trouble maker she was I would never have taken her along. The weather was fine as generally are in August month with westerly brises in the ofternan — things went along fine the first day.

Although Jacobsen was travelling alone, he was by no means helpless. His trousers were equipped with four double pockets, in which he carried, well concealed but immediately available at any time, two loaded pistols. Not so well concealed, but always taken along were a rifle and two other weapons, a combination of three barrels, two shotgun barrels side by side and a rifle barrel underneath. With these Jacobsen shot tin cans in the water to show the Indians that he could shoot accurately.

Not only did Jacobsen consider he was justified in thus protecting his own skin — and its contents — but he had with him at times as much as two thousand dollars in twenty-dollar gold pieces which he carried (except for amounts which he foresaw using during the day) in a strong leather money belt around his waist. The day's money he carried in one of the recesses in his double pockets, from which it could be taken without his associates suspecting his armaments.

At Mammellika he bought some paddles which were very strongly made of yew wood, and sharply pointed at the end of the blade.

"Why do you make them so sharp?" he asked the Indians.

"We use them in battle," the Indians replied. "We can run one of these pointed paddles right through a man."

Jacobsen recounts:

I had noticed from nearly the wery start of our trip that this old Indian woman was continually talking and naging her son on to something — but as this was the first time I had ever been with the Oa Kjul tribe it was not exspect that I should understand their owen language no chinok was spooken among them self. I could see there was something wrong — but could not make out what it could be — but as my brother had warnet me strongli to be on the lookout for the Indians around this part I was keeping a clos look out.

The latter part of this afternan this 2 men tom exspecialy had been very busy sharpening the end of his paddle — the same with the boy as I was sitting in the stern of the cannoe lieschurling steering the cannoe I notiset a sign made by Tom the boy, they borth got up like lightening and com running back towards me with their paddles — I saw at once what it ment quick as

Right: Reverend Christian Saugstad, who led the Norwegian colonists into Bella Coola in 1894. Photo – courtesy Mrs. C. Nygaard.

Below: The side-wheeler *Princess Louise*, in which the colonists travelled from Victoria to Bella Coola.

Above: Mount Saugstad, the highest peak visible from the part of the valley settled by the Norwegians.

Left: Towed by two tractors, Emmanuel Church crosses the Bella Coola River. The bell tower and steeple were removed to take the church through the forest.

Right: The last load.

Below: The triumphant Board of Trade Directorate on the day the bulldozers met to create a third outlet to the Pacific Ocean, September 1953. L. to r.; Eric Hammer, Bill Wright, Wilfred Christensen, G. (Mike) Christensen, Wally Stiles, Elijah Gurr, the author, Andy Widsten, Norman Saugstad, Curtis Urseth, Ralph Sneyd.

Left: Shaking hands from the blades of their machines, the 'cat' operators celebrate the opening of the new road. L. to r.; Alf Bracewell, Elijah Gurr, Mrs. Louise Mackay (camp cook, and first born child to Norwegian colonists), Melvin Gurr, Alger Brynildsen, Mike Stolar, George Dalshaug.

Below: A rock-cut on the mountain road out of the Bella Coola Valley.

leightening I pullet out my 6 shotter and had the drop on them, they got so scaret they droppet right down in the Canno. I could not swer in Chinok as there is not such a word, but I certainly told them whot I would do to them if they did not behave themself — and I let Tom understand that I was fully aware of it was his mother got the thing started and I told him I would put her ashore on the nexst point we come to if she did not behave herself and I also made them understand I was not afraid if there was a Thousan of them. I told them I had been down in Arrisona among the wart cut tribs on Earth, the Apaces — wich was true. now to put the Indian woman aschore on a point around here where there would not leikly to be a cannoe come around in one or 2 months time and no fod — this knoket the wind out of the old lady, and trough Tom she promiset to be as good as gold, however I fealt rother dubious about it did not know if I should turn back or goo on, but I did not want to show the white Feders and desidet to goo right on.

That night, after supper, Jacobsen left the Indians in camp and anchored the canoe well off shore. He spent a restless night.

The next afternoon, after breasting the Kleena Kleene River current for about three-quarters of a mile, they came to the Indian village at the head of Knight Inlet. This village had as yet been untouched by the coming of the white man and his age of metal. The long houses thirty to forty feet wide and fifty to sixty feet long were made entirely without nails, the walls being large planks laid horizontally between pairs of upright poles bound together with ropes of cedar bark or cedar limbs. At the ends of the houses the planks were upright rather than horizontal, and bound together in the same manner.

The arrival of a white man, a rare animal indeed in that part of the world, was the cause of great commotion and Jacobsen found himself surrounded by a ring of men and women truly savage looking. He relates:

I must say the Indians here of this willage was the roughest lot I had jeot put my Eies on — all the men wore just a blanket and some had a short Schirt and of cource a blanket over their shoulders. I supose Tom the Indian I had with me had told the Indians in the willage obout me pulling a Pistol on him, but I doubt he mentionet obout he himself making an atack on me.

The Indians all loket hostoile and it certainly did not look any

227

thing to good for me. The Indians Exspecially looket firch on account of the way they all had their faces paintet black and red — the women the same way — the womans used a single cotton dress motherhubard — and I saw an old womans with just an old blanket on and an Cedarbark apron in the front, this aprons were made of yelow Cedarbark and mountain goads woll.

I at last made arangement and got in to one Indian house where I could sleep. It was a big house, and in all there was between 8 an 10 Diferent famly liwing in this house each of the Famleys had small houses build Inside the main house just rom for 2 to sleept there and m for their blanket boxes and personnal belongings, the owner of the house always sleept at the wery back of the house facing the open fire place. I was given a place to sleep nexst to his rom on the main Flor — near a big box of Olachon grees, the smell was prety power full but I did not main this soo much as it was raining very heavy and I was caritanly glad to be in a house and under shelter.

It seems as soon as I got in to the house all the young popell com in to have a look at me — and all wanted to know whot I wantet to com to the willage for. I had in the mean time paid of the 2 Indians as I rother take my chances to get back some other way than goo back with them again. I would not trust them.

It was another old Indian woman that precipitated trouble for Jacobsen, for the second time, in this village. Coming up channel, Jacobsen had seen some goats up on the mountainside, and since he needed several for the German museums, he made arrangements with an Indian of about 40 or 50 years to go up with him the next morning. Despite heavy winds and rain they went on the hunt, and although they saw three goats they could not get within range as the wind carried the scent of the hunters to their would-be prey. They got back to the village about 9 o'clock in the evening, soaked to the skin.

I got out my Blankets and my trunk took out dry closs and had it all ready to chance near the Big grees box — an old, a wery old Indian woman had her bed on one side of the box and I had my bed on the other side, the old lady was sitting with her back against the Box smoking her evening pipe. On top of the grees box — wich was open and partly filet with grees and on the very top of this was a board acros the box with a sak of Flouer laing. I had difficulty getting my weth clos of and for to ballance my self whie I pullet of my stockings. I put my hand on the Flouer sak — and

228

unfortunately for me it over ballancet and down it went with a splas in to the big grees box, wich was over 3 feet deep — it sems that nearly all the grees jumpet out of the Box and splaset over the old Ladys head that was just leaning against the box.

You can Imagen there was trouble right of. I did not know whot the old lady said but I am sure she gave me hail collumbia — I calld the owener of the house and told him I would give the old lady $5.00 in silver wich I handet to him he then handet it to her, however she was not soo sure about the mony she put it between her teet and bit it, she wanted me to give her 5 Hudson Bay trading blankets, that was more in her line. The blankets where uset as money — $1.00 each ½ blanket all white with a black mark point and a halve, however the owner of the house took the 5.00 silver dollar and gave her 5 of his owen blankets she was then ot once pasified and eaven smilt to me. She then went down to the river and had a regular wash — I certainly fealt relivet the trouble was setlet.

Early the nexst morning when I woke up the old Lady was allready up sitting by the fire, doing her mornings toillet which sisitet of carefully checking her apron for stray anny molls (gray backs) when ever she found one she put it in her mout, it just made me sick to her it crak or goo of like a firecracker between her teeth, I feel certain I was in for it as I slept only a few feet from her and I certainly latter on descovered those things can trawel to my sorrow.

Jacobsen started to work immediately, going from house to house buying the Indian curios. He came unexpectedly on a white man with fair blue eyes and light hair. He looked like a German to Jacobsen, but he did not reply to Jacobsen's questions in that language, nor to one in Norwegian. The stranger spoke in English but Jacobsen replied he could not understand English but could speak Chinook. When a common language had been established, Jacobsen asked the man his name but he refused to give it, nor would he give any other information. He seemed greatly concerned that other white men might be coming up the inlet, and though Jacobsen assured him that he did not think others were coming, the man started up along the river bank. Jacobsen stayed in the village for three days but he saw no more of him, then or ever.

"Who is that white man?" Jacobsen asked his Indian host.

"A King George man," the Indian returned.

"Where did he come from?"

"From away back in the mountains. He came a long way down the river."

"I may say," Jacobsen relates, "I have often later on in years meet white men leike this living with the Indians and in fact addopting the Indian ways altogether, most of thie kaind of men would take an Indian Vife and it is most wonderful the worst carocter the better the Indians would leike them in many cases the Indians have been very proud to keep a whiteman."

On the third day Jacobsen was in the village one of the principal chiefs staged a big potlatch for which he had collected some forty boxes of eulachon grease and a corresponding pile of blankets. Jacobsen admired the workmanship of the boxes containing the eulachon grease. They were of red cedar and grooved to make the joints tight, and the sides and bottom were bound with cedar roots.

A box of this nature was used as a drum and could be heard for miles.

The Master of Ceremonies or rather the man that led the singing gave orders to get ready 2 long boards where laid on the ground with cross pieces under each board — each man had 2 pieces of wod in each hand obout 2 feet long — the Chapel master cald out the words of the song, he had a long carved stik with all sorts of Figurs on, wheales crows bears etc — it was realy interesting to see him calling out each line if the song wich was repeted by the 10 or 12 singers they at the same time keeping exalent tyime with the sticks hitting the boards, but the way the chappel master when he callet out the lines, some times he stood on his heales when the song was to go to a lower note — but when the tune came up he stood on his toes, and the way he was pointing swinging around and bending forward to the publick was very good — when they where to sing heigh he would tell them soo or low as the cas would be durring all of his directing the musik he would halve dance most of the time, all had to sing young and all the children and womans who have really good woises.

The man that was to give the greas away, then made a spech, wich of couce I could not understand. The exseitement got higer and higer as the greas and blankets were given away, there was all sorts of food, Flouer made in to cake like and boilet in Olachon grees, lots of berries — on the beris lot of oill Olachon grees was poret all over the berries and eaten with woden spones —

In the later part of the performeances 2 men went at each

230

other with these dreadful sharp paddles. I do not know what the Row was over as no chinok was spoken, at any rate borth of this men were taken away by some women, no doubt their Wives — soo this trouble was endet.

It was in any way wery interesting taking in the whole afair. There was a lot of Dansing borst by men and women — the women stood on one spot hopping up and down shaking their hands and finger tips. The mens danses was similar but strictly time was keept to the singers and the drum.

When I cam to my house Indians had cut all the buttons out of my coot and over coot and one young boy was just in the ackt of treing to open my Trunk.

Jacobsen decided that he would leave the next morning, and after having one man promise and then back out, he started the next morning with a crew of two men who could not speak Chinook. The tide was out, and the river broken into several channels. His crew chose one which had a big spruce tree across it, and in order to get around they tried to squeeze between the root and the bank, literally under an overhanging portion. Unfortunately their passage disturbed the earth and about a half ton of soft clay fell onto the canoe and split it open. Fortunately the water was shallow just below this point and they got ashore on a sand bar. Among the curios that Jacobsen had bought were some twisted cedar boughs that the Indians used in repairing their canoes. He had a drill also in his collection that the Indians used. It was made from the leg bone of a deer, a piece about six inches long with a split in the end and a wooden handle. To make the hole the man held the drill between his hands and twirled it as fast as he could.

So they unloaded the canoe, emptied it of the clay and the two Indians set to work to effect repairs, Jacobsen watching closely, helping where he could.

The 2 Indian set to work and drillet holes and put in sewerall stitches, juson the same principle as a Docktor putting in stitches, each stitch was about i jot apart, where the Cedar branch rope did not make it teight enough we put in woden pegs — and it took us not very long until the canoe was just as good as ever.

I think I may just as wel mention while I am at it, to exsplain how the Cannoes are made and where this litle bon drill do exaelent work. I had often marvelet and wonderet how the Indians could get the Canno soo exact the same thickness all over by hollowing it out with an ax — when the Indian first falls the Cedar tree which all Cannoes are made of shapes the bottom part of the Cannoe first points the bow and stern, and shape it as goo as he posibel can — after the fine adsing is done on it he goes to work with his six inch bone drill, and if he want the side of the cannoe or the whole Cannoe to be say 2 inches thik he slips a piece of round wod on to the end of the drill just leaving 2 inches of the bone point of the drill bare he then goes to work and drills about 1 foot apart all over the canoe to the Thikness of 2 inches when the drill is nearly 2 inches deep I have seen Indians dip the end of the drill in roten Salmon Roes and charcol mixst wich made a strong paint — this holes are drillet all over the Cannoe — the bottom of the canoe os generall from ½ to 1 inch thiker — after all the holes are drillet he then goes to work turns the Cannoe on oeven Keeall and commence to hollow it out — in olden times it was burnt out but now it is cut out with an ordinary ax to the thickness of say 3 or 4 inches. After this the Indians use their small adses esspecially made by themself for this purpose, the Indians then careful goes to work cut nice long string of chips with his adse, he goes so deep he strikes the small holes drillet by the bone drill, it is easey to see the holes as it shows the stain in the wod of the Salmon Roe oil and charcoll mixsed soo you can see how easely they can get the eoven thickness all over the Cannoe.

After the Cannoe is hollowed out, the Indians builds up a big wood pile criss cros on each side of the canoe — ready to build a big fire when ready, on this cris cros wod pile he carries about 500 to 600 bbls of round rox about the seise of a mans fist, then he sets fire to the wod piles and let it burns to the stones get red hot — in the meantime all the little drill holes on the cannoe has been carefully plugget up soo it cant leak he then carries 4 to 6 Bukkets of watter according to the seize of the Cannoe — empties this in the Cannoe — and then cowers the whole cannoe with Cedar Bark mats or blankets — when the stones are reall Red hot he taks a woden tong easily made of split Cedar take stone by stone and put them in to the Cannoe the watter in the Cannoe ofter a litle commences to boil, like a ketel of wotter on a stowe, after all stones have been put in the Connoe the whole Connoe is carefully coweret with mats and blankets to let no steam out ofter it has steamed long enough to make the hull of the Connoe so hot that you cant put your hand on it, blankets and mats are then remowet in a hurry and a lot of small split Cedar sticks are taken put crossways from each side Inside the Connoe, and in this way they can spread the Connoe from say 4 feet in the first place before it was steamed to 6 feet or 6 ft 6 — and eaven more. It takes an exsperts Eie to judge how much pressure to put on each of this tini little stiks. There is at least about 100 uset of them to spread the Connoe — eaven if the hull of the Connoe before it was spread out would be straight, When spread it got as we say in Saillor ways a fine spring to it. Bow and stern parts get hyer, midle part lower.

Jacobsen liked the two men that he had with him this time, though he could speak no word of their language nor could they speak Chinook. On his way up the inlet he had noticed a bay with a little house in it, and when, about dark, they came upon the spot, he made his crew understand they were to camp there. They had no matches and everything was watersoaked so they supped on cold dried salmon and water-soaked hard tack. The Indians prepared to sleep under a tree, and when Jacobsen took a blanket, soaking wet, and motioned for them to accompany him to sleep in the little house, they demurred, tried to make him change his mind. It was pitch black by now, and when he approached the small house he could find neither door nor window in it. But a board had been knocked off one of the walls and through this hole he went.

He stumbled over some boxes, which he surmised were full of dry salmon, and finding a place on the floor spent a peaceful but miserable night because of the wet blanket.

When daylight came, he noted with astonishment the leg bone of a skeleton sticking through the end of the boxes which had partly rotted away. He had slept in an Indian grave house!

Until the adoption of Christian burial practices the Indians did not bury their dead, rather putting them in boxes and placing them in small houses or suspending them in trees where they stayed until the ropes rotted and the box and contents came tumbling to the ground. Jacobsen said he had seen as many as twenty-four coffins in one tree.

When an Indian died, his corpse was placed in a sitting position, with knees drawn up under his chin, with a rope tied around him to keep him that way. Then he was placed in a coffin which did not measure more than four feet long and two and a half feet each of the other ways. Often an Indian drum would be used for the coffin. Jacobsen tells of the coffin that he was inspecting:

Among the things in this coffin was a Cedar bark blanket, a woden Dans Rattel, mask, woden Dans mask and a whitemans ax — near the box was an old Hudson Bay guin flint lock soo this man must have been burried some time ago, the body was as dry as a piece of dryd codfish, as there was a guin with the coffin no doubt it was a man.

When I got out of the house the Indians was already up, but as we had lost all our matches in the river, the Indians had found my Indian matches wich consist of a piece of wod about 2 inches wide and about a fott long with a piece of wod about ¼ inch thik and 18 inches long in the flat piece of wod small holes are drillet on each side and the long piece 18 inches long wich is sharpenet at one end are inserted in the small holes made. A dry piece of woly Cedarbark cruset and rubet to it looks like carded woll, this is held long side of the small incsertions made in the board and one now commences to turn that 18 inch round piece of wod between the flat of his hand with all the strengt and speed he can command, and I do not think it took the Indians over 20 minits until we had a fire, great care must be taken when the shawings made from the round stick falls in among the Cedar bark wich at last catches fire. This is the time care must be taken with gently blowing on the Cedar bark until it flames up. I can assure you the Coffe we made with dry salmon and watter soaket Pellot bread tested good to us — however if a man's stomack gets filit up he feal soo much better afterwards.

Jacobsen found himself in a new dimension, too. Because he had spent a night with the dead, his two Indian companions looked upon him as a witch doctor with supernatural powers, and everything he commanded was done with great alacrity.

"When a man is green in the Country," Jacobsen said, "he do all sorts of things."

He got back to Alert Bay, left his collection of artifacts with Mr. Spencer and continued his journeying up the coast. In the course of time he visited the villages in the Bella Coola area where he met with the unusual language with its many consonants and saw villages that were among the most highly artistic on the coast.

He liked the area so well that he made several visits before he finally pursued his object of a trip up the entire coast — he did that the following year by going as far as Tongass, Alaska.

The other part of his mission, that of taking a group of natives back to Germany, brought him again to Bella Coola, this time in a sloop, in 1885. A group of Indians from Fort Rupert had promised to go with him, but when he went to collect them for the actual trip, they all refused to go.

"A missionary had got ahold of them," Jacobsen snorted an explanation to White Sam, in Bella Coola, with whom he spent some of his time, finding White Sam both instructive and interpretative, "and he told them if they went to Europe they would be made slaves and end their lives chained to a galley bench. It's five hundred years since there has been a galley slave!"

"You are fortunate," White Sam smiled at him, "there is no missionary here right now."

Jacobsen had in previous visits established very friendly relations with the Indians, and now he went among them attempting to persuade a group of them to go back with him to Germany. The reputation his brother had established, Jacobsen's friendly relations, and the story that had drifted north from Knight Inlet that he was a white shaman stood him in good stead and eventually Chief Tom, who had been converted to Christianity and burned all his heathen accoutrements said:

"It's too hard to be a Christian when the missionary go away," he grinned. "I convert back again to Indian religion and go with you. I will dance and tell white people about us."

The Indians received $20 a month and Chief Tom an extra $250 for the trip as interpreter.

Chief Tom had gained a second name. He was now Tom Henry.

Despite his conversion to Christianity, he still had the influence of a chief and when he added his force to Jacobsen's efforts eight others volunteered. They were all men. No women could be persuaded to go, nor would they let any of the children go.

"That's because white men have taken enough of our women," one of the volunteers said.

"This time we go, and maybe have some women of the white men," another laughed. "Then we have children for you." The troupe laughed.

Jacobsen and his troupe of actor-artist-aborigines went to Victoria on the sloop, transferred to a steamer which took them to San Francisco. Then they boarded a train — the first the Indians had ever seen — and went across the continent to New York, thence by another steamer to Germany, where they arrived three weeks after leaving Bella Coola.

They stayed for thirteen months in Germany, putting on shows and lecturing about their homeland and their way of living. One audience with three thousand children in it scattered like leaves before a gale when several of the Indians completely disguised with dance mask and blankets hopped down from the stage and lumbered awkwardly, after the manner of large birds, towards the children. The dancers, on harmless mischief bent, were escorted, chuckling under their blankets, to the stage and the children brought back to their seats.

"German women followed us around," Billy Jones, one of the Indians said, years later in Bella Coola. "They wanted to marry us but the big German tyee says we could not stay in Germany. So we came back without our German girls."

One wag asked him, during World War II if Adolph Hitler was his son.

"Maybe," was all old Billy Jones would offer.

But Indian dancer, Alec Davis, rather than consorting with many women, associated with only one, and from her he learned to speak the German language, gaining an amazing fluency in it that he had for the rest of his life.

"It is much easier than the Bella Coola language," he said. "I could speak it in three months and after that everything was easy."

And a millionaire German woman wanted Chief Tom Henry to marry her, but the chief said no. He had a wife back in Bella Coola and he was going back to her.

Thirteen months after their departure Jacobsen delivered them all back safely to Bella Coola.

Then Jacobsen went on his way, collecting curios for German museums, that, he said, had more Indian artifacts than the British Columbia coast!

For awhile he took a job as manager of a store at Clayoquot, where he not only built up the business but also managed the affairs of a four-vessel sealing fleet.

It was during his stay at this post that he embarked in a shell of a boat (with Harlem C. Brewster who was later to become Premier of British Columbia) on a raging sea to rescue the crew of the burning sailing ship the *Hera.* He received medals from the Royal Canadian Humane Society and from the President of the United States for "conspicuous heroism."

In his frequent visits to Victoria he tried to convince the

government officials that the Bella Coola Valley was a good place to establish a settlement. He was laughed at. "Would anyone live in that far north isolation? Never!"

But Jacobsen felt sure of his convictions, and going north spent the summer of 1892, with two Indians as assistants, making estimates and maps of the amount of tillable land in the Bella Coola Valley. The following year, because of his reports — and insistence — the British Columbia government officially surveyed the valley for settlement.

At the same time he wrote articles for Norwegian language newspapers and magazines in Canada and the United States, about the British Columbia Coast, and one of these articles fell into the hands of a Lutheran clergyman in Polk County, Minnesota. This particular article told that a Norwegian could indeed, amid the huge trees and towering mountains and the living seas and streams of Bella Coola, forget that he was not in his homeland.

Again Jacobsen returned to the Bella Coola Valley, bringing with him two men from Victoria, Captain Thor Thorsen and family from Seattle, and a very small grant of money for the purpose of putting a road part ways up the valley. Captain Thorsen took up government land on the eastern edge of the Indian reserve, and built his home on the banks of Smootl River, which in the course of time surrendered to the name of Thorsen Creek. Jacobsen, Thorsen and the two men from Victoria worked hard all summer cutting timber out of the way, building bridges, moving rocks and spending the complete grant of five hundred dollars.

The year of the return of Jacobsen and his Indians to Bella Coola, 1886, saw the beginning, for the second time, of a permanent white population. The missionary Edward Nicholas and his wife Kezia established themselves; John Clayton, who bought out the interests of the Hudson's Bay Company in Bella Coola, moved into the company's vacated quarters. Travellers landing at Bella Coola for the journey to the interior were more numerous. And, with the coming of a full time trader to Bella Coola, it was easier for some of the ranchers moving into the Chilcotin country to make the trip to Bella Coola for supplies than to take the longer one to Ashcroft, which necessitated swimming the horses and ferrying in a small boat across the turbulent Fraser River.

A scant quarter or half mile from the Thorsen home on Smootl River were the two bachelor homes of Gus Pearson and Tom Draney.

Gus Pearson was reputed to be one of the best net men along the whole of the coast. Every summer he worked faithfully; every fall after the canneries closed down he went to Victoria, had a brief wild round of parties with the boys, and then spent the rest of the winter in a hand-to-mouth existence. Tom Draney was an Irish Canadian who had worked his way westward with the railway, and then had gone up coast to become cannery manager on the Skeena River. He became Gus Pearson's friend.

"Let's leave the bars of Victoria to look after themselves. Let's spend the winter in Bella Coola and come out in the spring with some money," he told Gus.

So they went to Bella Coola, took a canoe as far they could up one of the almost hidden tributaries of the Smootl River, and building cabins for themselves spent the winter. They did manage to come out in the spring with money. And both of them returned many times to Bella Coola in succeeding years.

Then in 1890 came two families, the George Gibson family and the Bretts with installations for making charcoal for cannery retorts. Beyond them another quarter of a mile lived another bachelor, big, curly haired Jim Robertson, whose sister Maggie was Mrs. Bob Graham of Tatla Lake.

In 1890 also, John Clayton brought a bride to his trading post, and in the course of two years two sons had been added to the list of "whites". By 1894, then, there were sixteen white residents in the Bella Coola community.

And this did not include White Sam, who was not considered, even in his own mind, to be a white man. In the summer of 1894 White Sam took violently ill, from what cause it was not known. He would have died if his wife Mary had not nursed him sometimes with tenderness, and sometimes with violence, a violence bred from fear, for Mary had the blood of fighting chiefs in her veins, and when she was afraid she acted. This time she prepared a broth by boiling a length of a birch limb in water, then forcing quarts of the liquid down the now weakened White Sam.

When the fever continued Mary called in the native medicine men, and they performed violent physical gyrations, pressing their cupped hands deep into the unfortunate White Sam's abdomen as if to scoop therefrom the evil that was causing the illness; then holding their cupped hands aloft, and blowing across them, they dispersed the offending illness.

One of the treatments caused White Sam to lose his fever, for after being more dead than alive for almost a week, he started to look about him. Mary marvelled first at the wide-eyed, ingenuous gaze with which he studied things, then realized to her horror that he had entirely lost his memory, that he was seeing everything now for the first time. When she spoke to him, he did not answer. And when she put food in his hand he did not carry it to his mouth, rather stared at the small piece of boiled fish without recognition.

Slowly the significance of her responsibility came upon Mary. Her husband had become as a baby, and she must treat him as such, train him as such. Train him? Make him a white man? Or an Indian? Teach him the beliefs of the Indians or have him go to the white man's god-man? Or give it all up, let him die, and go live with another man?

This last thought was rejected at once. This man who had changed into a child had saved her from slavery, was the father of her children, had worked with her and supported her. This man was part of her, and she part of him. To him she would be faithful.

Teach him the beliefs of the Indians or have him go the way of the white man's god-man? This was not so easy to answer. White Sam had said that white men had brought confusion with them when they started to teach the Indian about the white man's god. They didn't need another god. But the white man's god-man said to throw out all their old gods, all their old beliefs away and take only his god. The white man's god-man told stories about how great his god was, but the god-man got sick, and you could hurt him and his god didn't seem to care. Mary couldn't decide.

White man or Indian? Indians had been suffering a great deal, their numbers diminishing. Many had killed themselves with white man's drink. Women had gone down to Victoria and New Westminster and Seattle and had ended up dead in the bay. A few had been fortunate enough to find a white man who would marry them but many, most of them, had become slaves, or worse, beaten, scorned, killed. There were lots of white men in their big towns, but Billy Jones and the other men who had been on the train and across the big ocean said that in Germany white men were more numerous than the trees in the Bella Coola Valley. Indian or white man? Maybe make him friendly to both, maybe make him so he could look two ways.

Train him? Yes. Without it he would die.

She picked up a piece of boiled salmon, put it in her mouth, chewed it. Then taking another bit, she put it in his mouth, and watched as his mouth moved awkwardly. Some of the salmon fell out, but she saw with delight that he swallowed some, and looked at her for more.

"I'll teach him Indian first," she thought. "That's what he'll hear most of and I can teach it best."

Her monumental task was augmented by the fact that for months she also had to find a living for the entire family. But it was summer, and food was abundant and neighbors supplied fish. And while White Sam never did regain his recollection in full, the memory that is stored in trained muscles had not been lost, and he recovered his faculties with rapidity. He learned again the Bella Coola tongue, then Chinook, and finally a few words of English.

But when he wondered why he was called White Sam, he would not believe some of his friends who told him he was a white man adopted by the tribe, for somewhere the idea had been implanted in his mind that he was the son of the great Chief Potles with whom he had warred against the Kwakiutls.

The Coming
of the Norwegians

Bella Coola, October 30th, 1894.

When the steamer was within a mile of the river-mouth she slowed down and dropped her anchor. Her weight swung her around as the hawser held, and with the current from the river holding her against the slight breeze from the west, she stood motionless by her perpendicular anchor-rope, like a patient horse on tether.

To some aboard the ship it was a routine landing, for the craft the *Princess Louise* was a veteran of coastal travel. Built in 1869 in New York at a cost of $200,000 she was originally the *Olympia* and planned for service between Victoria and Puget Sound, but competition was so fierce that she was laid up. (Steamers for a short time not only gave free transportation but also contributed free meals.) Then in 1878 the Hudson's Bay Company bought her for $75,000 from her bankrupt owners, renamed her the *Princess Louise,* and put her to work as a public carrier serving the many logging camps and canneries on the coast. In the summer of 1894 she had been laid up for several months.

Then in October of 1894 she was chartered by the Canadian Pacific Railway Company to take a group of settlers to Bella Coola.

Captain John Irving was the skipper in charge.

Besides the crew there were 84 men, women and children on board and as the crew made preparation to discharge the cargo the passengers gazed around them with awe, wonderment and fear. Out of the sea the mountains rose to lose themselves in clouds. East of them, the river discharged itself from a dense forest of dark green spruce and yellow cottonwood. There was no wharf, no sign of human habitation, no indication that humans had ever trod this shore. It was a land of mystery, its feet in dark forest, its head brooding beyond the clouds.

Some of the crew had been detailed to lower the lifeboats which were to be used to make a landing. As two of the boats slapped gently onto the water the sailors watched for a moment, then one called out:

"They're filling, sir!"

Captain Irving stepped to the rail, saw the grey water of the inlet welling into the lifeboats. They had not been used for many months and had dried to the point where seams were wide open. They would have filled in minutes.

"Haul them up," he commanded, and stepping onto the wheel house pulled the whistle.

The hoarse, repeated call screamed and vibrated across the water arousing the sea gulls, and then, after a few waiting moments it seemed the brooding spirits of the wilderness had truly been awakened for out of the river mouth and from the shadows of the forest appeared a flotilla of canoes which, as they first broke away from the forest cover, seemed only logs being paddled through the water. But as they approached closer (and very rapidly, it seemed to some of the passengers) it could be observed that the canoes were dugouts and that the people in them were swarthy. There were men, women and children and they called to each other in gutteral shouts.

"Here are your new neighbors coming to greet you," one of the crew called, "or eat you!"

"Yeesuz, Yeesuz, Yeesuz," one of the bearded passengers exclaimed with ascending emphasis, as he saw the flotilla of savages surround the ship.

"What did you say, uncle?" a little child near him asked.

"I vas — I vas only praying," the man answered, for he, like most of his fellow passengers were of church-going groups and it was not good to take the name of their Lord in vain.

"What do we do now?" asked another of the passengers.

"Maybe they are going to put us ashore with the canoes," another replied.

"Oh, God forbid," a woman replied. "My poor children!"

She was interrupted by several of the passengers cheering and pointing at two more canoes that were being rapidly propelled through the water. These canoes were being handled by Indians but the cause for cheering was a tall slender girl of about twelve standing fearlessly in the bow, her arms held out and her fine blonde hair streaming out behind her in the breeze. She was only lightly clad, seemingly oblivious to temperature, and to many Scandinavians she appeared, among her dark consorts, as a veritable angel.

She was calling to them, animated and excited. And in Norwegian!

"Welcome, Welcome to Bella Coola."

"She is Bertha Thorsen," a broad-chested, bearded passenger who carried a look of leadership about him answered the queries. "Her family lives in Bella Coola. They will also be our new neighbors."

The other canoe had drawn up and in it, the people aboard ship saw, was a bearded white man.

"Mr. John Clayton?" Captain Irving called.

"The same," answered the bearded man in the canoe. "I would like to welcome you to Bella Coola."

"Thank you, sir," the captain replied, "I won't be staying in Bella Coola but I have over eighty people aboard who no doubt appreciate your welcome."

Captain Irving placed his hand on the shoulder of the big, bearded passenger who had told about Bertha Thorsen.

"I will introduce Reverend Christian Saugstad," he said. "He is the leader of the group. Right now they require getting ashore. Could you get your dark-skinned friends to help?"

Arrangements were rapidly made and, with Clayton calling the captain of each canoe by name, the native craft pulled alongside the opening on the lower deck. Goods were handed down and into the first canoe, heavily laden, only one of the passengers went. He was a nimble young man, Torkel Aslakson by name, and as the canoe moved away from the ship one of the crew called out — "And this is the last we see of Torkey."

"Torkey" waved to his companions aboard the ship and thumbed his nose at the crew member.

Canoe load after canoe load left the ship, each with passengers, and under the dexterous handling of the native crew, went up the river a mile or so and landed on the north side opposite the Indian village and above it, on a field that had been leased and cultivated (with potatoes) by Fillip Jacobsen and Captain Thorsen.

By nightfall the last canoe-load had been landed, and the *Princess Louise* had departed down channel, intent on getting back as quickly as possible to Victoria. In the Thorsen potato patch tents had been erected, fires started, food prepared, beds laid out, and by ten o'clock all were in bed, and most asleep, except for the several who did not like the thought of the village of dusky savages just across the river. These lay down in their clothes, with their rifles under their hand. When they heard the sounds of a noisy, shouting party in the village, they worried the more, not knowing that it was a dance welcoming the white men.

And these few were not the less concerned when, next morning, a large group of the Indians appeared in camp. They seemed to be demanding payment for their services of the day before but the new whites, not knowing either the Indian tongue or the Chinook dialect, could not understand to whom money was owed or how much. Trouble was averted when someone happily thought of John Clayton, who came at the messenger's call and explained matters. The fees charged by the Indians were paid out of the community fund and interracial tension subsided.

It built up again in the next week or so when exceptionally heavy rains caused flood conditions and some of the Indians interpreted this as a message from their gods that they were dissatisfied with the coming of the white people. But the murmurings of the discontented ones were quieted when others pointed out that there had been floods before, when there were no white people coming to Bella Coola. And they were further conciliated when they were hired by these white people to take them up the river to their new homesites.

The landing thus successfully accomplished culminated efforts started many months previously thousands of miles away by people who had never heard of Bella Coola nor had anything but the faintest idea of the Coast Range which now towered over them, both threateningly and protectively. In the early 1890's a severe economic depression had struck the civilised parts of the United States and Canada and, while this had excluded most of the B.C. Coast which had not yet become enough a part of the world of white men to indulge in periodic cycles of feast and famine — unless for some reason the salmon failed to appear — it did not exclude the Scandinavian American states of North and South Dakota and Minnesota. After a winter of unusual severity when the price of eggs dropped to six cents a dozen the congregation of a Lutheran Church, made up in greater part by recently arrived Norwegian immigrants, sent their pastor Rev. Christian Saugstad, accompanied by Mr. A. Stortroen, westward to investigate sites for a new settlement. Saugstad was no youngster. He was fifty-seven on June 13, 1894 when he was on this mission of investigation. Nor was he a newcomer to America for he had emigrated to America in 1858 when he was 21 years of age. Graduating from Augsburg Seminary in Paxton, Illinois, at the age of 34, he spent the next several decades leading and pioneering in a life that was by no means an easy one. He was well suited to be delegated to look for a more suitable homesite for a group of farming people.

The writings of B. F. Jacobsen had come to his attention, and among the several places he investigated was the Bella Coola Valley. Coming from the then newly established cannery settlement of Namu on the fish-packer *The Swan,* skippered by Robert Draney, he and Mr. Stortroen received a favorable introduction to Bella Coola.

"I have a nephew, Tom Draney," said Robert Draney who was building the Namu Cannery, "who winters in Bella Coola. Likes the place. Says the winters are mild and there are no taverns."

In Bella Coola they were entertained by Captain Thor Thorsen and his wife and two girls, Bertha and Helga, who corroborated what Captain Robert Draney had told them. When they were taken up and down the Bella Coola River in Indian spoon canoes, it seemed the streams were black with salmon. They went to Victoria and visited the government. Col. James Baker, Minister of Immigration, told them the valley would be reserved for them for settlement if they wished; that if a colony of at least thirty families was established, a wagon road would be built, and each settler granted a hundred and sixty acres of land free as a homestead.

The two delegates went back to Minnesota and Saugstad gave his report to a crowded congregation in the church at Neby.

"In this Bella Coola Valley," he almost quoted Jacobsen, "you have many features of your beloved homeland of Norway. You approach it up a long fiord on both sides of which the mountains rise almost perpendicularly to heights of six or seven thousand feet. Everywhere streams leap down the mountainsides and glaciers gleam in the sun.

"When you get into the valley proper you walk through forests of tall stately fir and spruce. Game is abundant and the streams are never still from the splashing of fish."

His report was received with the greatest enthusiasm and the next meeting was held at a schoolhouse west of Crookston, Minnesota.

Here a colony, to function as a autonomous unit under the laws of British Columbia, was formed. A constitution was adopted, officers elected, money collected and membership recorded.

The constitution, although it was drawn up by people who were churchmen, contained only one clause that might have been dictated in any way by a secular body. There were indeed not many clauses.

The minute book of the colony reads as below, starting on page one:

1. The name of this association shall be: Bella Coola Colony, British Columbia.

2. The purpose of this colony shall be to induce moral, industrious and loyal Norwegian farmers, mechanics and business men to come to Bella Coola and make their homes there under the laws of British Columbia.

3. To take charge of the colonization the colonists elect one president, one vice president, one secretary and two other members who shall constitute the managing committee of the colony. The president and secretary shall also constitute the negotiating committee between the government and the colony.

4. To become a member of this colony, a petition must be made to the managing committee, with which must be furnished satisfactory evidence of good moral character, working ability and possession of necessary means to cover travelling expenses and provisions for one year. The petitioners have also to submit themselves to the rules and regulations of the colony by signing the same.

5. Every member of this colony must abstain from import, manufacture, export or in any other way whatever the use of intoxicating drinks excepting for sacramental, medical, mechanical and chemical uses.

6. Transgressions of these rules, when proved before the managing committee of the colony, shall be punished by banishment from the territory of the colony, and the colonist's real estate, if any, shall be forfeited to the government.

By-Laws.

1. All officers of this colony shall be elected by a majority of the legal voters, and hold their offices for one year until their successors are elected and qualified.

2. The duties of the officers of this colony shall be the same as the duties of the officers of other similar organizations.

3. An annual meeting of the Colony shall be held on the first

Tuesday after the first Monday in the month of June every year.

4. At such annual meeting there shall be entitled to vote every member of the Colony who as such is the holder of and the person mentioned in a free grant agreement from the Minister of Immigration for the Province of British Columbia.

5. These by-laws may only be altered or amended at the annual meeting and the by-laws and any alterations shall be submitted to and approved by the Minister of Immigration before coming into force.

Events moved along rapidly. On September 11, a meeting was held in the school house of Polk County, Minnesota, in which a managing committee of the colony was elected. This committee was made up of President C. Saugstad, Vice President Peder Boken, Members: Iver Fougner, Peder Thorsen, Secretary H. B. Christensen.

The president and secretary were empowered to deal with the railways for fares and accommodation for the colonists.

It was also duly moved, seconded and carried that the expenses of the colonists be equally divided among the colonists and that the membership fee be five hundred dollars.

Engelbret Fosbak was elected treasurer.

It was moved and carried that the colonists leave Crookston for Bella Coola October 17, 1894.

Then followed a month or more of preparation to leave forever the new homes that most of the colonists had created for themselves in America — a month in which many of them were told they were crazy to go to such a new land, so far away — a month or so in which more would have been said if the people who were determined to go had taken time to listen.

Negotiations with agents of the railway companies resulted in an agreement with the Canadian Pacific Railway, who allotted the colonists two large sleeping cars and gave them reduced rates on fares.

At seven o'clock in the morning of October 17 all the colonists were at the railway station when the train chugged in. Last words of encouragement were spoken; the colonists boarded the train, and left, many of them never to return.

Westbound across the flat prairies, and through the mountains, the trip brought scenic variety, and one evening while the train made an extensive stop, the Governor-General of Canada, Lord Aberdeen, and his Lady, with guests, boarded the cars of the colonists and bade them welcome to Canada.

"And I would like to personally urge upon you the necessity to hold fast to the fine religious principles which have brought you together," said Lord Aberdeen. "The Christian religion is the foundation for all success in life. Your efforts and your colony of Bella Coola will be a success with the help of God."

After Rev. Saugstad had duly thanked Lord Aberdeen for his visit and his good wishes, the vice-regal party returned to their private car.

On October 20, at one o'clock in the afternoon, the train arrived in Vancouver and the colonists embarked immediately on a steamer for Victoria where they registered at the Dominion Hotel.

They spent the greater part of the week in Victoria, buying tents, stoves and tools. The party was grouped usually five or six to a tent. One large tent for community purposes was purchased.

On October 26 they were summoned to the office of the Minister of Immigration, the Honorable James Baker, who reviewed the conditions under which they were going to Bella Coola, namely free land for the settlers, and when thirty families had established their homes there, a wagon road would be built through the land occupied by the colony. Moreover, all government land in the area would be reserved for people of Norwegian descent who might wish to join the colony.

Each colonist was handed a printed copy of the indenture bearing the information presented and, in comparison with the simple agreement entered upon by the colonists to express the constitution of their colony, the wording of this indenture was a mystery and a marvel of complexity, as for example:

"Now therefore this indenture witnesseth that in consideration of the performance by the Grantee of the covenants and the stipulations to be observed and performed by and on the part of the said Grantee, the said Grantor, acting herein on behalf of the Lieutenant Governor in Council, as aforesaid, and as far as the Crown hath power to grant the same, but not further or otherwise, doth hereby covenant and agree upon the termination of five years from the date hereof, that the said Grantee shall receive a Crown Grant of all and singular that certain piece or parcel of land situate, lying and being in the District of . . . . . . in the Province of British Columbia, and being composed of . . . . . . lot number . . . . . . in the said district, containing by admeasurement ...... acres of land, be the same more or less, and which may be more particularly described as follows ... "

The indenture could not be signed as the blanks in the legal description of the land could not be filled in since it had not been determined exactly what piece of land would fall to each colonist; but signed or not, to each colonist it was a promise, and each put his copy along with his axe, his rifle and other valuable accoutrements of pioneering.

When he was through with his presentation, the Honorable Minister of Immigration for the Province of British Columbia said:

"We wish to express our appreciation to you for coming west to help us develop this great province, and I speak personally and for our government when I say as you do in Norwegian, "ha saa mange tusen tuk.""

Though he may not have said it exactly as the Norwegian colonist would, his words were understood and the colonists left Mr. Baker's presence with a feeling that they had made a deal.

The next morning, October 27, almost all the colonists were aboard the chartered side-wheeler, *Princess Louise,* and last minute preparations for departure were being made, when up the gang-plank stumbled Ole Olson. It was obvious that he was very drunk. As he stepped from the gangplank to the deck of the *Louise* he shouted:

"Let's go! Hurray for Bellach Hoola!"

Among those attracted by the noise of Ole's arrival aboard was Christian Saugstad.

"Ole Olson," he said, "you're to go below immediately and lie down until you become sober."

"You're right, Boss Man," Ole roared. "Drunk as a skunk. But not sleepy. Too much to do. More to drink. I'm going to go dry in Bella Coola, so let's drink now."

He approached a group of settlers, hauled a bottle from his pocket and held it out. "Have a drink. You fellows look sick. This is for medicinal purposes."

One of the men attempted to take the bottle from Ole and a scuffle ensued in which Ole was overpowered and held, alternately shouting, laughing and attempting to get away. His captors looked to Saugstad.

"Hold him," he told the men, "and someone get the Captain."

The minutes of the ensuing meeting were brief.

"On Board Steamer Princess Louise in the Harbor at Victoria, B.C. on October 27th, 1894. A meeting of the managing Committee of the Colony was held. Moved and unanimously carried that Ole Olsen be expelled from the Colony on account of drunkenness and disorderly conduct. Also decided his fee to the colony be returned. Meeting adjourned.

H. B. Christensen
Secretary."

Ole was conducted ashore, his goods and chattels with him, and his fee of five hundred dollars thrust in his pocket.

"Poor Ole," a sympathetic colonist said, "he never got to the Promised Land."

Other matters of importance were settled with like expediency. Of another meeting that was held aboard the steamer some two hundred miles up-coast, after a storm on Queen Charlotte Sound had rolled them around but had not dampened their enthusiasm, the following minutes were recorded: (although Bella Coola was still a day's journey away, the meeting was date-lined that place.)

Bella Coola, B.C. October 29th, 1894. Steamer Princess Louise.

A meeting of the Bella Coola Colony was held on October 29th, 1894 A.D., for the purpose of establishing a manner to pursue in taking up land in the Bella Coola Valley. Decided that lots be drawn for the land. Motion made by Peder Thorson seconded by Engelbret Fosback adopted. Motion — four men club together and draw lot. One draw for the four of them 1 section and the other three settle amongst themselves. Meeting adjourned.

H. B. Christensen, Sec'y.

And so groups of four formed temporary alliances, from which one drew the section number from a hat. Then four papers, each marked with a quarter of the section, were drawn from the hat and each man received — to put with the indenture and his axe and rifle — a slip of paper bearing the numbers of his land. Not that its loss would have meant much, for the numbers did not tell him whether the land was a river bed of boulders, a swamp or rich bench-land covered with fine, swaying fir trees.

The next day the ship dropped anchor and a party now consisting of eighty-four men, women and children awaited disembarkation. In Victoria, five new members from Seattle had joined the group and the government had sent along P. J. Leech, a government surveyor, to assist in land location, build bridges and lay out roads. This group was destined to form the basis of one of the few successful settlements on the northern B.C. coast.

Their troubles did not cease when they encamped by the Bella Coola River and mistook the natives' welcome dance for a war-dance.

Almost immediately heavy fall rain started. 1894 records one of the worst flood years along the coast, the lower Fraser Valley receiving waters of heavy flood proportions. The colonists saw the river rise at a terrific rate and flow past their camp bearing large trees complete with branches and roots.

"We don't have to go up the valley to see our land," said one. "The river is bringing it down to us."

Despite the rains, some did venture up the valley. While they could undoubtedly manoeuvre a ship through the stormy seas of the North Atlantic or drive a team of oxen as straight as the flight of an arrow, they were no match for the caprice of swollen mountain streams. Witness the writings of Tollef Wiken who, after his return to Norway, resumed his more Scandinavian name of Torleiv Viken, and wrote his memoirs some forty years later.

On November 4, Carl Elg, Carl Kristoffersen, Peder K. Pedersen, Kriken and I went about twelve miles up the valley to view the land. We followed a trail for approximately ten miles but after it became very difficult to proceed since the forest was thick with large trees and impenetrable terrain. Old tree trunks had occasionally tumbled over each other and shut out all travel. The large trees standing were very tall with thick branches which shut out the sun and light making it necessary to use compass and blinkers to find passage among the trees. When we had proceeded for a while it began to rain and we got wet. Towards evening we arrived at a small rise in the ground where we erected tents and camped for the night. It was somewhat chilly since the previous day there had been a little snow, and we were soaking wet. We gathered wood and decided to sit up through the night, light a fire and tell stories. Whereupon Carl Elg shot a partridge. We cooked this on the fire and ate it for supper. The night passed and when we had breakfasted and were to proceed, a large grizzly galloped out of the woods toward us. We had only shotguns and it was impossible to engage such a champion, but when he was only a few steps away he turned and again vanished in the woods.

We crossed through the forest to the river. Here Carl Elg and

Carl Kristoffersen began to build a raft with which to float down river since they were tired of tramping the long way home. They finished the raft and began the journey downstream. Peder Pedersen, Kroken and I continued our return on foot. At 8 o'clock on the morning of November 5th we reached our tent along the sea. But the two sailors, whom we had expected to arrive ahead of us, had not yet arrived. We were afraid they were lost accidently in the river. The water was running rapidly and with a few timber or log jams it presented a dangerous sailing. Two hours later they arrived. They reported they had lost the raft but had been lucky enough to get out of the water, and by crossing through the forest they had found the trail toward the sea, so they escaped spending the night in the forest following their cold bath.

The following day four other colonists reported a similar experience on the river with a log raft from up the valley. This was Peder Bakken, Jakob Johansen, Andraes Svisdal and Iver Westmo. They also had lost their raft in a log jam in the river. Peder Bakken fell in the water but caught a branch of a fallen tree and held on until the others hauled him out. They lost two guns, axes and their overcoats which vanished in the river.

Others of the colonists waited until the flood waters had subsided. And a few others, stating that they had expected nothing like this from the reports given them, never did get farther up the valley and, when next a ship appeared in harbor (about six weeks later), took passage and left. Those who thus made such a short term of their settlement were Tom Olson (with his wife and six children), Sven Marven, Ole Solum, T. O. Sannes, and Peter Pedersen.

Realizing the imminence of winter, the colonists who stayed made temporary partnerships of five or six men, and these groups each built a cabin in which to live while other cabins for individuals were built And a communal camp was set up in a newly made clearing some ten miles up the valley. This communal camp was the large tent they had purchased in Victoria.

The first winter had memorable weather. Starting with the flood in the fall, there followed an east wind in which the cold air poured like liquid down mainland valleys of the Coast Range to the warmer ocean. The result was that the frigid draughts reached a velocity of 50 or 60 miles per hour and dropped the temperature to a numbing 10 degrees below zero. This weather gave way to blizzards that dumped several feet of snow on the ground, and in the reaches of the river – gleefully, it seemed – drifted the snow into huge barrier.

Before the cold weather came, the Indians with their spoon canoes were the freight haulers for the colonists.

Arrangements were facilitated through John Clayton and to him the Indians expressed their bewilderment. White men they had divided roughly into two groups, the King George men and the Boston men. Jacobsen they knew to be a little different but this had not caused them any concern since he had spoken to them first in Chinook which they understood; then secondly, he had learned their language. Now came the colonists, many of whom did not speak English easily, neither did they speak Chinook nor Bella Coola.

"Real white men?" they asked Clayton.

"Yes, white men," he replied, "Norwegian like Jacobsen."

"Norweechan, Norweechan," the Indians repeated after him.

When the river partly froze and then closed over with ice completely, the spoon canoes of the Indians could not carry the goods of the colonists, so that it became necessary to pack all supplies on the backs of the men of the group.

The Clayton store was the 'Rome' to which all trails led, and weary colonists were always served as big a meal as they could eat whenever they visited the store or its owners.

Through the winter the colonists held several meetings in the home of E. Nordschow and, at one of them, started a precedent that has not been broken for almost three generations.

The unhappy ones who had turned back at the very entrance to the valley had taken a ship which landed them at Victoria. Once there, they had a story for all who would listen.

"It is stupidity to think of trying to make a home in that valley. The forests are so dense they are black and there are no natural meadows to graze cattle and horses. The rest will see the folly of their ways, you can bet. We are but the first to leave."

It would not have been effective if one of the dissenters had not written back to one of the colonists in Bella Coola with the message that the government was doubtful the colony would persist.

At a meeting of March 2, 1895 the following minutes were recorded:

> The regular monthly meeting of the Colony was opened by the president, March 2nd, 1895 A.D. at the usual time. Secretary

being tardy, I. Fougner was elected secretary pro tem. Moved and seconded that a resolution be sent to the government to urge the speedy construction of the wagon road, said resolution to be draughted by the managing committee of the colony. After some discussion the motion was voted on and carried. Moved and seconded that a member of the Colony be sent to Victoria to present the adopted resolution to the government. Motion carried.

Moved and seconded that the delegate sail with the first steamer if possible. Carried. Moved and seconded that the president of the Colony, C. Saugstad, be elected as delegate. Carried. Moved and carried that the colonists make declaration of assurance to the government of its intention to settle in the Bella Coola Valley permanently."

(On January 5th, two months previously, in a similar meeting Rev. Saugstad and H. B. Christensen were asked to make arrangements with railways, etc., to bring the families of the colonists to Bella Coola in May.)

The letter was drafted immediately. It read:

Bella Coola, B.C.

To Hon. James Baker,
Minister of Immigration,
VICTORIA, B. C.

Sir, —

The Colonists are grieved to learn that the government entertains doubt as to the Colonists' intention to remain permanently in the Bella Coola valley. As this may tend to retard the carrying out of the vital question of the Colony viz. the construction of a wagon road, we in public meeting assembled on the second day of March 1895 declare that it is our intention to do all in our power to make Bella Coola our future home. In proof of the sincerity of this declaration over thirty houses have been built or nearly so, and a considerable number of acres of land cleared. We petition and pray that the government carry out their part of the contract as stated in the agreement.

C. Saugstad Pres't
H. B. Christensen Secy.

So Saugstad went to Victoria, and the government appropriated $10,000 for roads and bridges in the valley. Many of the colonists went to work on the road and with pick and shovel, crowbar and peevie earned the $1 a day paid as wages.

Groceries were bought on a communal basis, accounts being scrutinized by a committee made up of I. Fougner and C. Carlson.

In the first part of May the colonists started awaiting the coming of the steamer and, after pitching a large tent in John Clayton's field and waiting for several days, they were rewarded on May 6 at 5.30 in the morning by the arrival of the steamer *Danube* carrying the wives and families of the settlers, along with several new recruits. Among the newcomers was one Barney Brynildsen.

It had been a rough passage and many wan faces showed a haggard joy at coming ashore. The women stayed at the Clayton camp until the next day and then started the twelve-mile hike up the valley. The trip took two days, the night being spent in the cabin of Rasmus Levelton some seven miles from Clayton's. This cabin, about 16 by 20 feet, helped create the legend that in a Norwegian's house there is always room for one more guest. The Levelton cabin that night sheltered nearly forty people and, possibly because some of the guests were very small children, there could indeed have been found room for one more.

Some new descriptive terms were also added to Bella Coola phraseology; anyone who came in 1894 was one of the "originals" or old-timers, and those who came later were "new-comers."

With the families reunited time rolled on quickly. Numerous bachelors, too, enjoyed the presence of many young people. Some people left but more arrived. With the coming and going of steamers and after the arrival on November 4 of forty-nine more colonists, the Norwegian colonists numbered about 220.

During the summer the road had been extended twenty miles up the valley. At the main settlement, about twelve miles from the sea, which was called Bella Coola Hagen B. Christensen built a store and the small collection of buildings he erected was a borg, and suddenly Bella Coola became Hagensborg (Hagen's Borg). But before this happened, an appreciable number of settlers found their land lower down the valley between Schnootly Creek and Smootl River and, to distinguish this territory from Bella Coola proper (Hagensborg), they called it Lower Bella Coola. In the course of time, when a village appeared by the sea and was called Bella Coola, no end of confusion was visited upon the uninitiated who ascended the valley to come to a community designated as "lower".

Just before the colony was a year old, the first marriage took place, between Kristian Karlson and Ovidia Baarli.

And then, on October 30, came the first annual celebration – at Hagensborg. Trader John Clayton came up over the newly constructed road with a wagon load of meats and other edibles as well as a pack horse carrying three hundred additional pounds of meat.

Speeches reviewed the year: a post office had been established; the wagon road was 20 miles up the valley; a church congregation had been established, called Augsburg; a choir, with Rev. Saugstad as director, was started; homes and gardens were well established.

Plans developing at that time resulted, in a few weeks, in a school in the large communal tent. A large fir block served as the teacher's desk and logs as seats for the pupils. Iver Fougner was the teacher. On Sundays Rev. Christian Saugstad used the same facilities to lead his congregation in devotions.

In January of 1896 foundations for a larger school building were laid at Hagensborg, and the building finished in April. Again Mr. Fougner officiated for five days a week and the Rev. Christian Saugstad on Sundays.

In November early snow followed by warm rain brought about flood conditions. A span of the 600-foot bridge across the Nusatsum River was washed out.

In February of 1897 Rev. Christian Saugstad went to Victoria to buy horses and machinery for the colonists and returned home with a severe kidney infection. He died on March 17th, one day after his return – the first of the Colonists to die.

Above his homestead, rising 10,000 feet from a base altitude of about 100 feet, Mount Saugstad rises as his memorial. It is the highest peak visible from the lower forty miles of the Bella Coola valley.

Almost immediately after his arrival in Bella Coola, Barney Brynildsen showed an interest in retail trade rather than in farming. For several years he partnered with Hagen B. Christensen in a store at Hagensborg. A second store was set up not far distant by Hagen's cousin, Adolph Christenson. It was the beginning of competitive retailing that was to outlast the life of one and almost the life of the other.

Down at the sea the established storekeeper, John Clayton, felt little effect from the increase in community merchants. An adventurous Englishman, he had walked into Bella Coola overland from Barkerville and from his first position as assistant to the

Hudson's Bay trader had risen to be as much a rajah as any prince of the East. Not only was he more powerful than any Bella Coola chief for, having bought out in turn the interests of the Hudson's Bay Company at Bella Bella and then at Bella Coola, he virtually ruled both districts. Had the occasion arisen, he could have enlisted the services of the entire population of the two districts. When the Indian Reserve had been allotted in 1882 (by Commissioner O'Reilly) and surveyed in 1888 and 1889 Clayton, as assignee of the Hudson's Bay Company's rights, retained the land south of the Bella Coola River to the foot of the mountain, and from the tidal flats almost to the Tatsquam River.

A small parcel — only an acre or so — of flat land snuggled under the mountain at the southeast corner of the Clayton property, next to the Indian Reserve, and this land Barney Brynildsen acquired, along with sixteen or seventeen acres of mountain.

In the autumn of 1896 a dock was built on the south side of the bay but at first it was useful only as a place to moor a ship or to store goods for it had no access. In anticipation of the road, however, Brynildsen had moved from Hagensborg and built a store within ear-shot of the falls on Tatsquam Creek and a quarter of a mile from the Clayton store.

When the government came to build a road to the dock it was found that the terrain on the mountainside was too rough to permit anything but a very steep and rugged trail. Clayton would not allow trespass for a road on his flat land. In time the so-called road to the dock became known as the "Cannery Trail". Goods for each of the two stores, Clayton's and Brynildsen's, came up the river by Indian canoe, with the advantage to Clayton since his store was immediately alongside the river and his goods did not have to be carted for a quarter of a mile on wheels.

At this site the Brynildsen store stayed for almost eight years.

In an endeavor to get wheels from the colony to the sea the provincial government secured a right-of-way along the foot of the mountain on the north side of the river, built a bridge across the Bella Coola River at Four Mile and another across the Necleets-connay River coming in from the north. The colonists made a road connecting the two bridges and thence to the dock which was built now on the north side of the bay, and wheels were called into full service.

In 1904 the government surveyed a townsite on the Necleetsconnay River, just below the canyon, and sold lots. Among those who bought were Barney Brynildsen and to this new site he moved his store. To this site also came the second store from Hagensborg, that of Adolph Christensen.

This new settlement was called Bella Coola and, in the course of time, it was to become "Old Town". But before that it was to know growth and hope, disaster and failure.

In this village on the sunny side of the valley were established a bakery and a bank, followed by stores and a newspaper, the *Courier.* A sawmill was built on the outskirts of the village, and the people of the Bella Coola valley formed a hospital association which built a hospital. For a decade and more everything was keyed to growth.

To the north side of the river also went the Indian village. When the missionary Nicholas built the first church in Bella Coola he chose a site north of the river and built a little church complete with a window of stained glass. When a larger building was built a few years later, those who believe in poetic justice and the reaping of what one sows will be pleased to know that the old church, a much warmer and more practical building than the smoke-house he shared with W. H. Pierce, was given as a residence to Bella Coola's first Indian Christian, Chief Tom Henry, who now became known as Church Tom. Near him lived a partner of his adventure to Germany, Billy Jones. When the federal government established an Indian Agency in Bella Coola and appointed Iver Fougner (the Colony's first school-teacher) as agent, the office was established on the north side of the river close to the white settlement, and in time almost the entire Indian population moved there.

To this village came, by way of weary miles of pack trail, long strings of pack horses carrying, on their return journey, supplies to interior ranches and communities as far east as Tatla Lake and Redstone, for the nearest source of supplies to the east was Ashcroft, beyond the turbulent and unfriendly Fraser River.

From this village poured northward and eastward in 1912 to 1914 groups of land-hungry settlers bound for the Ootsa Lake and other even more distant regions made attractive by government literature aimed at getting people on the land. So strong was the flow of people that in 1912 a bridge was built across the river at the site of historic Boat Encampment, removing the necessity of canoe crossings and, although the district has since seen no canoes except for the occasional adventurer or the more frequent steelhead fisherman, the bridge and the area is still known as Canoe Crossing.

The trails left by these land-hungry pioneers were cut so deep that sixty years later they are still discernible in the forests and meadows.

Through the village at Bella Coola came other settlers who found their homes among the towering fir trees near the site of Mackenzie's friendly village on Kayilsk (or Burnt Bridge) Creek. These were Seventh Day Adventists, who have their sabbath on Saturday, the seventh day, instead of on Sunday. They called their district Firvale.

One frontiersman-trapper describing the valley to a visitor was reported as saying:

"Up to Canoe Crossing Sunday is on Sunday. From Canoe Crossing to Burnt Bridge Sunday is on Saturday and beyond Burnt Bridge there isn't any Sunday."

South of the river nearer the waterfront things were happening, too.

The reserve that the government had put on crown land in favor of Norwegian settlers disappeared in the stated five years and settlers of other races mixed with the Scandinavians. Among these were the Grant family, emigrants from Scotland to River's Inlet via Iowa, in 1888 for S. Le C. Grant, in 1889 for his wife and 2 year-old daughter Eve.

At the turn of the century the growing fisheries were of vital interest. Brunswick Cannery was built in 1896 and Green Cannery (which was to prove a total business failure) in 1897, as well as the most long-lived of them all, Wadham's. The year 1896 was one of the most abundant, with fish literally jumping into the boats of the fishermen. The fisheries' boundary, beyond which fishermen cannot operate, was up the Wannock River instead of being in salt water. That year one of the canneries put up 40,000 cases. The next year, 1897, was one of the poorest years and the pack for the same cannery was only 3,000 cases.

And B. Fillip Jacobsen came back, married Helga Thorsen and settled down, as much as one of his energetic character could, to a life of farming, prospecting, timber cruising and curio collecting.

Down in the Indian village the native people were adopting European and North American names, influenced by the missionaries and traders. The Biblical names of Joshua, Judas and Nebuchadnezzar automatically reveal their source, while John Clayton is credited with giving the name of King to the ruling family of chiefs.

Names also were anglicised, and out of Skuna came the name Schooner. And others, for reasons more or less obvious, received such names as Snow or Saunders, Whitewash, or Alexander or Johnson. Men were also named in accordance with the locale from which they came, and on the books of records which were shortly to appear were such names as Kimsquit Alex or Talio Jimmy. Also names that were entirely obvious became the legal names — Lame Charlie or Skookum Mary.

In 1900 the schoolhouse was built at Lower Bella Coola, which should by this time have been called Upper Bella Coola.

Also in 1900, John Clayton and Tom Draney formed a partnership and built a fish cannery at Bella Coola. It was the beginning of scores of years of harvesting the silvery wealth of fish noted by Saugstad, and it was only natural that the Norwegian colonist — who was not a colonist now since the colony had outlived itself and had become a settlement — should look at this development with interest and nostalgic recollections of seafaring days only recently passed. The fish book, which recorded the deliveries of fish, registered in 1901 the names of the fishermen as follows: J. Hoidstin (Widsten), O. Arneson, P. Lauritsen, O. Kellog, S. Gromsdal, P. K. Pederson, T. Engelbretson, J. Nygaard, Simon, Bobby.

The last two were Indians who had not yet acquired a double name.

The contract between Clayton and Draney is a classic of simplicity:

An agreement made this fourteenth day of March 1900 between John Clayton of Bella Coola in the Province of British Columbia, canneryman, and Thomas Draney of Bella Coola aforesaid, canneryman:

1. The said parties agree to enter into partnership as cannerymen under the Bella Coola Canning Company for — years from the date hereof, or until the partnership is determined by either party giving to the other a three months' notice in writing ending with a current year of the partnership;

2. The partnership business is to be carried on at Bella Coola wharf in the province aforesaid;

3. The partnership capital is to consist of the sum of $10,000.00 of which the said John Clayton shall contribute $8,000.00 and the said Thomas Draney shall contribute

$2,000.00, and of the property, credits and stock in trade of the firm for the time being;

4. The said Thomas Draney shall act as manager of the said cannery business for which services he shall receive as salary the sum of $600.00 per annum and ten per cent of the net annual profits;

5. The said John Clayton shall attend to the financial affairs of the said business;

6. The profits of the said business with the exception of the ten percent of the annual profit as provided in paragraph four hereof shall be divided between the said partners in the following proportions, namely, four-fifths to the said John Clayton and one-fifth to the said Thomas Draney and the payments and the liabilities are to be borne by them in the like proportions;

7. Neither partner shall give credit after warning from his co-partner; nor shall, without his written consent borrow money, or compound debts, or become surety or bail;

8. Any engagement or liability entered into by either party in contravention of the above clause is to be at his exclusive risk, and the firm is to be indemnified out of his separate property.

Accounts shall be kept in books of all partnership transactions and such books together with all other documents connected with partnership business shall be kept at the place of business at Bella Coola, and accessible to each partner;

9. At the termination of each salmon canning season, or as conveniently as can be arranged thereafter, an account shall be taken of the partnership property, stock, credits and liabilities and the sum found to be due to each partner shall be carried to each separate account.

In witness whereof the parties hereto have hereunto set their hands the day and the year first above mentioned.

"John Clayton"
"Thomas Draney"

Witness:

"Samuel Schultz"
Victoria B.C.

The partnership lasted for several years then for the strangest of reasons dissolved. British Columbia Packers Association (later to be called British Columbia Packers Limited) bought the cannery and operated it until it burned in 1930, then replaced it with a new cannery which operated until 1935 after which it operated as a net-camp, all the while giving work and a fish-market to people of two races. And the reason for the dissolution of the partnership after two years of successful canning was that the sight of fish made manager Draney acutely physically ill. As the season advanced the docking of a loaded fish-packer nauseated him and forced him to the edge of the dock where he could be sick, very sick. During 1901 the cannery put up 4,849 cases and during 1902, 4,158 cases.

This was an at-home cannery for the Bella Coola fishermen who had previously gone fishing in Rivers Inlet. There they had fished four men to a skiff — called the Columbia River skiff — and, of the four men, two were net men who operated the net and received sixty dollars a month, while the other two were boat-pullers (oarsmen) and received forty dollars a month. All four also received free food and, since cooking facilities on board skiffs were extremely limited, the crew went ashore and cooked their meals on the beach.

In Rivers Inlet the only salmon caught at first were sockeye, the luxury fish, although the fish books of the Bella Coola Canning Company indicate that Spring salmon were being bought also. The fish book recorded that on July 8, 1901 a Monday, 26 fishermen delivered 1317 sockeye and 85 Spring salmon.

Shortly after this period John Clayton, with his interests in Bella Bella calling him out there frequently, bought the only steamboat owned in Bella Coola. It was forty feet long and called the *Bella Bella,* most of its space was taken up with boiler and fire-box, and it burned wood for fuel. A deck load of wood lasted four hours so that at many places along the channels cord-wood, cut and stacked by Indians, awaited the coming of the craft. The navigator was a Bella Coola Indian, Captain Myers, named, curiously, after the captain of a large steamship the *Sardonus* that plied the coast for several years.

In 1906 the colony hall was built by community effort and in 1906 first plans were laid for a local telephone system. This was formed in 1907, received its charter in 1908 and was given right-of-way through to Clinton approximately two hundred miles distant. Here it was to meet with the government telegraph service. Eventually government telegraph service did reach Bella Coola (1916) but the grounded lines (one metallic line, using the ground as a return) of the Bella Coola Telephone Company reached only thirty miles up-valley. It did provide a humble service and its charges were moderate. Phone holders bought their own machines and paid line rental, which was established in 1908 by-laws at $10.00 per year, while the exchange operator, "Central", was to receive $50.00 for the year.

Tom Allan, who married Christian Saugstad's daughter Gea, listed with the pioneers of 1894, built a sawmill on Klonik Creek in 1898, followed shortly by another on Snootli Creek. These mills supplied the timbers and lumber for the dock on the north side of the bay as well as for the village growing there.

About this time it was announced that a pulp and paper mill was to be built, for which the government gave great tracts of timber in the valley. The mill was erected but at Ocean Falls, sixty miles westward, where a new town was built on a mountainside to accommodate the workers.

In 1911 the Pacific and Hudson's Bay Railway received a charter to build a transcontinental line from Hudson's Bay to Kimsquit. Shortly thereafter the proposed western terminus was changed from Kimsquit to Bella Coola.

The top man in this promotion was W. D. Graham Verschoyle who, in 1912, suggested a merger between the Pacific and Hudson's Bay Railway and the Pacific Great Eastern Railway, making Bella Coola a terminus of the P.G.E. It would turn this railway northwestward at Clinton and open up the tremendous Chilcotin plateau for development. The suggestion received little attention, for the boss of the P.G.E. was the Premier of B.C., Richard McBride, a political opponent of Verschoyle.

At this time Verschoyle listed his Bella Coola assets as close to three million dollars and included in them five miles of waterfront, 1500 acres of land and an application in good order to purchase 3360 acres of Indian reserve.

He claimed 3000 lots had been surveyed ready for sale. Travellers along the cannery trail overlooking the tidal-flats could indeed see neat rows of survey pegs, some above high tide, some below, marking off the streets, blocks and lots of the proposed town. Not an inch of space was wasted and lots had a frontage of only thirty feet. Three thousand dollars was the average asking price per lot and there was strong assurance by the vendors that the value could double or treble within months.

If the proposed purchase of 3360 acres of Indian reserve in Bella Coola had been realized the Indians would have had no place in which to kindle home fires, for the original reserve was only 3363 acres from which several rights-of-way for roads had been granted.

Of course, by the time all this was taking place the P. and H. B. Railway had decided on Bella Coola as its proposed terminal and had forsaken Kimsquit.

One amazing aspect of the Pacific and Hudson's Bay Railway was that, over several years, it was the fourth railway to be proposed with a Bella Coola terminal. In 1911 a Canadian group applied for a charter to build the Southern Central Pacific from Alberta through Pine Pass to Bella Coola; the same year a French syndicate proposed building the Pacific and Peace Railway from Dunvegan, Alberta, through the same pass to the same terminal. And in 1911 yet another group this time more Canadians, prominent Victorians and Vancouverites sought permission to build the Mid-Provincial and Nechako Railway from Bella Coola to Peace River Crossing in Alberta, again via Pine Pass.

And in 1913 still another railroad was proposed, this one to terminate at the mouth of the Dean River sixty miles north, where the P. and H. B. Railway had originally planned to terminate. This last railway, to be called the All Red Line Railroad, was supposed to run from the boundary of Quebec and Labrador.

Had all these railways been built there would have been a screen of steel from the Bella Coola area through Pine Pass to the prairies, and Albertans would have been afforded a fine opportunity to make a mass migration to Bella Coola.

In the fall of 1913 F. M. Britton, rights-of-way agent for the Pacific and Hudson's Bay Railway, was in Bella Coola buying land for right-of-way and for development purposes and met with every co-operation. The Bella Coola Indians at a meeting of the band agreed to sell a right-of-way for the railroad at five hundred dollars an acre.

1913 saw developments in other fields also, which helped contribute to an upsurge of activity. One of these was the completion of the government telegraph line to Bella Coola. The first message went over it on February 15 after several years of building. A second was the establishment of a branch of the Bank of British North America, which opened its doors on the 10th of April. Also appearing for the first time on September 14, 1912, and swinging into free-wheeling journalism by 1913, was the *Bella Coola Courier,* a weekly paper, (subscription $1.00 per year). "It seems that Bella Coola is now at the dawn of the long-hoped-for development and one of the signs is the increase in price of real estate," is an excerpt from the very first issue, and the beginning of an exhortation to people who owned land not to charge the high prices which would hold up development.

About this time also the Salloompt Mill was built at the mouth of the tributary (Salloompt) valley. The five partners were John (Honest John) Lokken, Torger Olsen, Oliver Kellog, Andrew Nesvold and Karl Skjepstad. They harnessed a mountain stream for power, hauled logs in with oxen, and when the huge trunks were too big for their saws they split them with blasting powder.

In 1917 B. F. Jacobsen built a salmon cannery at the mouth of Nieumiamus Creek about a mile and a half from the B.C. Packers cannery. It was bought by R. V. Winch and Co. Ltd., who in turn sold it to Draney Fisheries Ltd. It finally became the property of the Canadian Fishing Company Ltd. and called Tallheo Cannery. Its flag colors are red and white while those of the B.C. Packers are green and white.

In the spring of 1914 railroad fever hit Bella Coola. Survey crews under engineers J. M. Rolston (later Colonel Rolston), Leroy S. Cokeley, W. Meyerstein, R. Lowe and J. H. Gaine, marked out rights-of-way, took grades, spent money, courted girls and told the civic fathers that, because Bella Coola was 200 miles closer to the Peace River District than any other port of the B.C. Coast and several hundred miles closer to oriental ports than Vancouver, it would soon surpass Vancouver in importance. And because Bella Coola already thought that Vancouver was drawing unto herself all the fruits of the development of the province and because Bella Coola wanted Bella Coola to develop, it all sounded good.

Little was it suspected that in several theatres of activity the stage was set for events which would rob Bella Coola of its importance as well as its dreams.

On April 5 the final spike in the building of the Grand Trunk Pacific Railway was driven near Fraser Lake, and on April 8 the first through-train reached Prince Rupert.

Immediately Prince Rupert became the northern seaport of the British Columbia coast. No longer was it necessary for land seekers, prospectors or trappers bound for the vast interior, to make Bella Coola their port of entry and then go by slow and expensive pack train. Because Bella Coola was so busy with its own developments it did not realize that a bar of steel had been placed across its back door, and only another railway would effectively remove this.

The outbreak of World War 1 in August of that year brought more immediate results, for railway activity ceased. Crews volunteered; residents of the Bella Coola valley volunteered, and there was no one left to carry on the work. Many men who had meant to make the Bella Coola valley their permanent home never returned.

Of those who had volunteered from the long established families on the Bella Coola valley Fred Grant, son of Mr. and Mrs. S. Le C. Grant, joined the Air Force, became second lieutenant and, on August 14, 1917, flew into oblivion. His brother Eddie joined the artillery, and was killed in action. Thorvold Jacobsen, son of B. F. Jacobsen, who lost a leg by cannonfire on Paaschendaele Ridge, returned to Bella Coola. And John Nygaard rose to the rank of second lieutenant.

The outbreak of World War 1 was followed by a general depression which Bella Coola did not feel as much as did the urban centres, but it did feel the impact of a series of floods, one of which in 1917 took out the Four Mile bridge.

Soldiers came home to a boomless Bella Coola and took up life anew.

In the very early twenties the fishing was not rewarding.

Then in 1924 a series of three floods, the first in August contrary to all the laws of nature, tore up the town. The Bella Coola River flooded, and the Necleetsconnay River brought down huge batteries of trees and rocks which it hurled against the bridges, buildings and roads.

Premier T. D. Pattullo came personally to look the situation over.

"We'll move the town to higher ground south of the river," he said. "There is no more use trying to rebuild this."

Back on the scene again appeared B.C.L.S. Leroy S. Cokeley who surveyed into townsite lots property purchased from the widow of the late John Clayton. The work, commenced in 1925, was finished in 1926 and the government exchanged lots on the new townsite for lots in the old town, and people began tearing down their buildings and moving them across the river, rebuilding them on the new sites.

The exchange was not a happy one. It was the trade of a developed lot for one with trees and stumps, gullies and rocks. It was the trade of what was a sunny lot on the sunny side of the valley for a lot that for much of the winter was in the cold shadow of the mountains.

The move was completed by 1929, shortly after which the traffic bridge, which had stayed so long that it was rotten and dangerous, was blown out. People who wanted to visit in the Indian village or to haunt scenes of livelier times in "Old Town" had to walk a swinging bridge.

Among those who rebuilt were the Brynildsens whose store, only a few yards from the site of their original store of thirty years previous, was exactly a block away from the Christensen store. Both buildings had the same architecture, and the corner on which Brynildsens' store was built was known as Brynildsen Corner, and the one a block up the street as Christensen Corner.

NAMES OF THE COLONISTS

(These were recorded in the beautiful artistic handwriting of Hagen Christensen, and remained intact except for several changes as noted by the particular name of the member.)

1. Anderson, Aron
2. Arneson, Liver
3. Aslakson, Torkel
4. Atvie, Ole
5. Baken, Peder
6. Bangen, Ole
7. Braff, Emil
8. Bangen, Anton
9. Berg, Peder
10. Christenson, Carl
11. Christenson, Martin
12. Christenson, Adolph
13. Christenson, H. B.
14. Charlson, Chr.
15. Elg, Carl
16. Engelbretson, Ole
17. Evenson, Peder
18. Flaat, Sveinung
19. Fougner, Iver
20. Fosbak, Ole
21. Fosbak, Engelbret

22. Gaarden, Ole
23. Gaarden, Esten
24. Gromstul, Sigurd
25. Gunderson, Thor
26. Holt, J. R.
27. Hammer, Albert
   (The youngest colonist to receive a grant of land. At the time of registry he was eighteen years of age.)
28. Hammer, Mathius
29. Hanson, Olai
   (and added in another handwriting George, Geneila)
30. Hanson, H. O.
31. Hanson, Sigrid
32. Hvidsten, John
   (This name was struck out by a different hand and listed as Widsten John. Some Norwegians did have a language difficulty, particularly with translations from V's and W's.)
33. Hanson, L. W.

34. Jorgenson, John
35. Johnson, Jakob
36. Jacobson, Sophia
37. Kjelhoug, Oliver
    (This name also was struck out by another hand and the Anglicised name Kellog inserted.)
38. Lunaas, Halvor J.
39. Lima, Reias
40. Levelten, Rasmus
41. Marven, Sven
42. Myri, P. N.
43. Nygaard, Jakob
44. Nordschow, Erick
45. Oveson, Andrew
46. Olson, Ole
47. Olson, Thom
48. Olson, Ole T.
49. Olson, Gunder
50. Olson, Valborg
51. Olson, Gertie
52. Odegaard, Hans
53. Olson, Nils
54. Olson, Torger
55. Pederson, Peder K.
56. Pederson, Osmand
57. Pederson, Peter A.

58. Ramstad, Eli
59. Sylvester, John
60. Salveson, John
61. Sorenson, Gunder
62. Sannes, Fyge O.
63. Sannes, Gustav T.
64. Saugstad, Ole
65. Schulstad, Ole
    (Wife and three children.)
66. Sjepstad, Carl
67. Saugstad, C.
68. Sandness, Ole J.
69. Salum, Ole
70. Saugstad, Gea
71. Tharaldson, Andrew
72. Thoreson, Peder
73. Thoreson, A. S.
74. Urseth, C. H.
75. Urseth, Simon
76. Vestmoen, Iver
    (This name was struck out by another hand and listed as Westmo, Iver.)
77. Wiken, Tollef R.
78. Westmo, Iver
79. Widsten, John

11 The Pygmies and the Mountain Pass

The decade of the 1930's — the Hungry Thirties — the Dirty Thirties — germinated seeds in the Bella Coola Valley that were to bear fruit over the years.

The economic depression, which in much of the North American continent sent great waves of distress, both financial and personal, over society as a whole and individuals specifically, touched lightly on the Bella Coola population. Insulated by three hundred miles of wilderness in every direction, shocks were softened by time and distance when they reached Bella Coola. The weekly mail, which arrived on the faithful, friendly Union Steamships vessel every Thursday, could be ten days old even the day it arrived.

The local telephone system did not reach out of the valley, and the Dominion Government Telegraph system, which operated a reasonably efficient service as a conveyor of telegrams, had a phone system which was operative only a hundred miles or so. If many receivers were down, as happened in the case of "party" lines, the sound of voices failed in direct proportion with the number of listeners.

Attuned also to the varying fortunes of the fishing fleet, Bella Coola suffered depression or enjoyed prosperity according to the salmon run and almost disregarded what was happening in the outside world. There was always game in the forest, potatoes in the field, and fuel with which to keep warm.

The decade of the thirties also saw the mechanization of the salmon fishing fleet. The fishing vessel had been, at first, a skiff with two or four men, half the number providing motive power by pulling on long oars — "misery sticks" — while the other half of the crew operated the gill-net. Every Sunday afternoon tenders — boats of

269

about fifty feet in length called packers — towed long lines of skiffs out to the fishing areas and dropped them off. There, for five days the skiffs were subject to tides and winds, and on Friday afternoon those who had not struggled back to base fish-camp or cannery were picked up and towed in.

When the round-bottomed sail boat replaced the skiff, the crew was reduced to one man. The sail added to mobility and activity, while the larger hull added comfort. In the sunset, when fishermen were moving to a new setting for the night, it appeared as if golden butterflies were skimming across the shimmering waters of the inlets.

When the idea of putting a gasoline motor in the hull of a small boat was suggested, hands were raised in horror.

"The noise of the exhausts will scare the fish away!"

"It will cost more to operate than you will get out of it!"

"I'm a fisherman, not an engineer!"

But when it was found that the fisherman with a gas boat could get to the favored spots ahead of sail boats, that he could set his net much faster, and could compete with more chance of success in highly competitive areas like the fishing boundaries, prejudices were put aside. Canning companies financed new boats for fishermen; fishermen turned boat-builders and built boats for themselves or their neighbors. Sailboat hulls were given keels, skag-irons, propellers and net guards, and inside the built-up hull a single cylinder engine was placed, and with a new coat of paint over the generously puttied seams and holes, the re-born craft putted proudly out to the fishing grounds.

When fishing boats became bigger, they were heavier to pull, for when the fisherman gathered in his net, he pulled the boat through the water, rather than the net which was as firmly fixed as a sea anchor. Hence, with a motor for power, a winch was installed in such a way that the power of the engine gathered in the net. Following this, a large spool or drum was rigged, so that the net was rolled onto the drum by motor-power, and unwound into the water on the fishing ground.

And with the motor having progressed from the 4 horsepower single cylinder putter to a multicylinder, hundred horsepower heavily muffled power plant, the age of push button fishing had been introduced.

All of which was made possible by increasing prices for fish. In the middle of the decade these were low. Fish were bought by the piece, not by the pound, and three and a half cents for a pink salmon could mean that the fish sold for less than a half cent a pound. Sockeye salmon brought forty-two and a half cents a fish, and in 1938 the canning companies declared the price would be thirty-seven and a half cents per fish. The Indian Agent at Bella Coola, James Gillette, told the canning companies that this was below subsistence level and if the price structure could not be elevated, he would find work for seven hundred and fifty Indian fishermen from the reserves under his jurisdiction. By the time negotiations ceased, the price of sockeye had been raised to forty-two and a half cents per fish. A red spring salmon at the same time brought fifty cents, which in some cases was less than a cent a pound; and at the same time a white spring salmon, distinguishable from its red brother for the most part only by the color of the flesh, brought only 25 cents per fish, while the canine-snouted chum, more commonly and uncommercially called "dogs", brought only five cents per fish, regardless of the fact that they sometimes weighed twenty-five or thirty pounds.

There was room for upward revision of prices, and when it did come, better boats and equipment came also.

The forestry industry previous to the 1930's had been carried on in the Bella Coola valley only sporadically, and then mostly to supply the small sawmills that appeared. The huge stands of fir had been considered too far from Vancouver, the lumber market and the financial centre of the province, to be of any value. Past the middle of the decade, ideas changed enough so that some settlers, in dire need of cash, were able to sell their land. But, while cash was relatively valuable because of its scarcity, prices were not high. Land with 200,000 f.b.m. of timber per acre changed hands for as little as five dollars per acre.

The first logging company from the "outside" to commence operations in the Bella Coola Valley in the thirties was the Viking Timber Company, which operated only months, as long as its credit lasted, then ceased, leaving among other debts, an unpaid labor payroll.

Many of the creditors on this payroll were the sons and grandsons of the pioneers and these men joined to form the Northern Co-operative Timber and Mills Association. This Co-operative took over the dubious assets and the multiple debts of the Viking Timber Company, and its members had an opportunity to work and worry and build. These, all three, they did, living on a meager level that their earnings might go back into building the business. The Co-op built a sawmill and a garage and their business did indeed expand. The members reorganized into the Northcop Logging Company Ltd., and some organized the Hagensborg Mercantile Ltd. and built a store. The group of buildings housing the garage, the Northcop office, the store, and the post office became (again) Hagensborg.

Not all activity in the 1930's was progressive. In 1934 a disastrous flood struck hard in the Hagensborg area, sweeping away the bridge across the Bella Coola River to the Salloompt valley, and in November of 1936 another flood, brought about by early snows followed by a heavy warm rain, swept out the swinging bridge that crossed the river from the white village on the south to the Indian village on the north side of the river. The removal of the bridge also cut off the water supply to the Indian village since the main from the water intake at the Chief's Ledge on the Tatsquam River was suspended under the swinging bridge.

The story of this water line is worth recording. Much talk had been expended on plans for a pipe line from Tatsquam Falls to the Indian village, to go right by the white village. While many of the details had been ironed out, the inevitable red tape, the unwinding of which was delayed since Ottawa and the final decree were a whole continent away and the mails very slow, had not yet been unravelled. The Indian Agent was away on a trip to other villages in the agency, and when he came back, the pipe line had been laid and water was on tap not only in the Indian village but also in many of the homes in the white village! A wily young white merchant, who stood high in the respect of the Indians, talked them into laying the pipe lines, not only across the river, but into the white village as well. He ordered the pipe from Vancouver by telegram, and there was feverish digging of ditches and joining of pipes and when the Indian Agent came home the red tape had to be scrapped.

Now, when the pipe line to the Indian village had been cut, by an act of God, the query went to the Ottawa office of the Indian Department:

"What can we do for a water supply for the Bella Coola Village?"

The answer has been treasured as a classic: "Connect with the Bella Bella water system."

Since the Bella Bella water system was eighty miles of rough mountains and several very deep channels away, the Indian Agent considered the solution impractical, to say the least. The need was urgent because of an epidemic of typhoid fever in the Indian village caused by the residents using water from shallow wells. Came the answer to the question: "We'll move the Indian village back to the south side of the river, just east of the white village."

A forest of spruce and cottonwood was cut down, streets and avenues and residential town lots were surveyed, and again residents were given new lots for old, again an exchange in the tradition of Aladdin of the new for the old. (It required imagination of more than human proportion to look on a raw lot with stumps and boulders and gullies as a shiny new one, to replace the old developed lot with flowers and garden-plot.) There was a driving necessity to get things done and for many months, growing into several years, houses were torn down; the lumber was brought across the river in convenient spells of cold weather when the river froze hard enough to allow horses and wagons or sleighs to be driven across; later in the spring it was transported by rowboat or gas boat.

One house was towed to the river on skids and pulled across successfully with a caterpillar tractor, a trial run.

Then, on a sunny day in May the Emmanuel Church building, minus only the steeple, was seen majestically moving along the road through the forest toward the old bridge site. Motive power was two caterpillar tractors and these moved the church with the assurance of good planning toward the river, and then, without hesitation, into it. From the building came the stirring notes of the hymn "Onward Christian Soldiers" played by the fifteen-piece concert band of the Indian village.

"When we were discussing the piece they should play, someone suggested playing 'Nearer my God to Thee' but it was vetoed," Mr. Gillette stated.

The tractors dipped into the river, followed by the church building. A flotilla of dugouts, which in their time had been used for hauling freight for the Hudson's Bay Company, or for hauling tons of eulachons out of the self-same river, gathered around the building, and sea gulls, amazed at this strange invasion of their territory, wheeled overhead in white clouds. In the middle of the river the fan of one of the tractors picked up water and sprayed it over the driver and passenger, Indian Agent James Gillette, but this lasted for only a half minute before the machine started climbing to shallower water. Fifteen minutes after dipping into the river, the church building was hauled safely out on the south side.

That evening the church sat on its new foundation on a new site, and within a week services were held in it.

Now that the Indian village was again south of the Bella Coola River and close neighbors of the white village, the water pipe line which had brought about this closer union was buried deeper, and when mains were extended and an increasing population made larger demands on the water supply, the Chief's Ledge with its rock-carving telling the uninterpreted stories of a past people was blown away.

The 1930's saw the reawakening of interest in a road connection with the rest of the province. At the beginning of the decade, a road survey was made on the route of the old pack trail along the Hotnarko Creek and over the precipice, and for years the governments used the results of this survey to point out that a road into Bella Coola was not possible or practical.

But the Bella Coola populace refused to accept this verdict. Groups of citizens, banding together under one name or another, petitioned the government for action. The Liberal Club, the Conservative Club, the Citizens' Welfare League, the Business Men's Association all presented their pleas and all met delays that amounted to refusals. Other things that these groups asked for were forthcoming — but a road out of Bella Coola? That was impossible!

During the 1930's the road westward from Williams Lake had crept another two score miles nearer the coast, due to the effort of the pioneering rancher and trucker, Stan Dowling, who, with the aid of winches and pump-jacks, proved that a truck could be driven as far as Anahim Lake. Where wheels could go, that set of tracks was called a road. Dowling established a trucking service from Williams Lake to Anahim Lake and changed the pattern of commerce. For fifty years ranchers from Tatla Lake westward had looked to Bella Coola for their supplies and huge pack trains kept trails open winter and summer. The bridging of the Fraser River at Chimney Creek and the coming of the P.G.E. to Williams Lake in 1919 made that town the supply centre for the Chilcotin country, but for Anahim Lake, with a wilderness as an obstacle for 40 miles to Kleena Kleene, it was better to pack supplies in from Bella Coola. Now, with Dowling hauling supplies over his new road, wheels took over from hooves and all trade east of the crest of the Coast Range went to Williams Lake, 210 miles distant.

During World War II, a group of soldiers were encamped at Anahim Lake with bulldozers, explosives and engineers. The story filtered through the mountains that they had orders to build a road through to Bella Coola. And when this was corroborated by officers who came down the trail and were fishing with hand grenades in the Atnarko River, the population of Bella Coola breathed a sigh of relief and expectancy. But both were premature, for when the road did not materialize — it was to take six weeks to build — another story came that on the eve of the commencement of building orders had come that no road requiring post war maintainance was to be built. Which might have been a true story, for, for years after, the signs of caterpillar tractors were found in the most amazing sections of the woods and mountains.

"Just those army boys," the Indian guides would tell their parties.

And then there was the story that the army, having looked the situation over, decided that if it could not get from the Interior to the coast at Bella Coola, the Japanese, by this time the only potential enemy, could not get from the coast to the Interior.

The mountain walls that surrounded Bella Coola remained a prison wall.

But to some the conquering of that barrier became almost an obsession. Logging companies within Bella Coola valley built many miles of good roads, and were aware of the cost. They knew that no community as small as Bella Coola could afford to build a road through those rugged mountains. Then a small pack horse trip by a couple of logging bosses changed the whole picture.

Norman Saugstad and his wife Shirley, Curtiss Urseth and his wife Louise, holiday bound decided to go on a pack horse trip, instead of going to urban centres or tourist resorts. Since the husbands were two of the top men in the Northcop Logging Company they were going where there were trees, but in such a place where they could not be tempted to cut them down — on the tops of the mountains.

The first night out, their host and hostess were Bert and Peggy Matthews. They talked about the road — or the dreams of a road.

"I wish you would go up the Bunch Grass Trail," Peggy Matthews urged. "I think that is the natural route for a road into the valley."

The next morning, the holidayers put their horses up the Bunch Grass Trail, and gained the plateau country which stretches away to the distant Fraser River country. For a week they crawled along the side of canyons, tumbled over fallen timber, skirted quivering muskegs, daily got drenched with heavy mountain rains, and returned to report a wonderful trip.

"And there is a road route through there," the men reported. "Much of the time you could travel faster with a bulldozer than you can with a pack horse. In a month you could bring a bulldozer road to the rim of the valley. That would leave only about a two-mile gap before the Bella Coola valley road could connect with the rest of the roads of the province."

For a few months the fuse that this story ignited burned slowly. Then all of a sudden there was some action. Peggy Matthews and son Billy went up over the Bunch Grass Trail down to Red Hill Crossing near the end of October to blaze a trail for possible road builders. A week later a party of three white men and an Indian went up the same trail with the intention of looking over the terrain. They camped the first night in a whirling blizzard that shoved the temperature well below zero, and made the three men wear more clothing on their heads than on their shoulders. Next morning there was a foot of snow over everything and the ground was frozen hard. Deciding discretion to be the better part of valor, the party — the horses had smooth summer shoes — slid down the mountain to the Bella Coola valley floor and comparative summer. Their tenting spot of the night before they called "Bald Head Camp."

A week later, a day before a party was to go in and rescue her, Peggy Matthews came out. She had blazed several miles of trail and her son had broken to saddle a half-wild stallion.

The next step was to form a local branch of the Board of Trade with the avowed purpose of bedevilling the provincial government into doing something about building the road.

A representative of the Bella Coola District Board of Trade was sent to Vancouver to the annual convention of the Highways and Tourist Bureau of the Vancouver Board of Trade. He listened to representatives from all over the province complaining about the way snow was removed from their roads, how dust was kicked up in the dry spells, how potholes developed.

"My community hasn't got any of these problems," he told the meeting when he got the floor. "We haven't any road. Would you please," he asked, "send us your potholes and we'll lay them end to end and make a road of them."

The representative was subsequently given the title, "King of the Potholes," and presented with a small bag of cement from which to fabricate a permanent pothole. But no pothole filler was forthcoming from the government.

The winter snows had scarcely left the summits when another pack horse party, including among others Peggy Matthews and husband Bert, and grizzly bear guide Clayton Mack, who went along only on the provision that he be supplied with a horse that would buck every morning. It did, and in one engagement on the steep crags of Bunch Grass Hill trail he was thrown, for which he loved his mount all the more! The party swept with real success in a semi-circle that brought it to Anahim Lake in time to take in the stampede.

The urgings of the Board of Trade reached a higher note in about three weeks when Bert Matthews guided government engineer Scotty Love in a rapid, cowboy inspection of the route, starting at Anahim Lake. Nomenclature being almost absent in this virgin territory, one meadow was given, for identification purposes the name "Love Meadow". It subsequently became an attractive spot for youthful wayfarers.

In a meeting with the Board of Trade Council Love said, "It is indeed an easy matter to put a road through the flat jack-pine country right to the rim of the valley. Coming down the side of the mountain will be expensive. In fact, the last two miles will cost a half million dollars!"

"What's a half million dollars?" the men of the Council asked — and well they might for such figures were certainly beyond their personal experience.

When it seemed evident that the Love trip was to be unproductive, some members of the Board of Trade Council suggested that perhaps the engineer had really stated in his report how close to straight up-and-down the last two miles were. And at a Council meeting road prospects were again reviewed.

"It doesn't look as if we're going to get even a survey this summer," was the conclusion. "Maybe we'll have to build the road ourselves."

Six weeks later the Board of Trade sent a telegram to the Department of Public Works, Province of British Columbia, Victoria, B.C.: "This is to advise that we are going to start immediately building the road from Anahim Lake to Bella Coola."

If this startling message caused any stir in government circles, it was never known in Bella Coola. "We've got a route the government doesn't know anything about, which is necessary. If we were building along a known route, they'd stop us right away. We'll start at

Anahim Lake, take the easy going first and make a good initial impression. If we tackle that steep mountainside first we could be beaten before we start."

So to Anahim Lake went Elijah Gurr, the emissary of the Board of Trade. Gurr — tall, victim of several logging accidents, now with silver-plate bones and silver pins holding them in place — had much experience in building logging roads. He explained his errand and his hopes to the ranchers at Anahim Lake. "This big basin between Anahim Lake and the rim rock of the Bella Coola Valley is forty miles around one side and thirty miles across. I want to go straight across."

Their reply was none too encouraging: "And you'll go straight across hell, too. There's bog-holes in there that'll swallow a bulldozer the same as a trout swallows a fly. And there's swamps there that if you stand on one side and sneeze, the other side a couple of miles away ripples and splashes."

"I still want to go straight across. Is there anyone here knows that country?"

"Thomas Squiness is the man. He hunts wolves through there."

So Gurr hunted up Squiness, the Wolf Hunter. Thomas Squiness was a supple, muscular Indian who ranched in summer and trapped and hunted wolves in the winter so that his children could go to the high school in distant Williams Lake and be better equipped to compete in the world of the white man. Coyote hunting in the Anahim Lake country meant chasing a coyote through the snow until the animal was too exhausted to run farther, then stepping from your horse and clubbing the victim with a piece of wood or a hammer. Squiness expanded this method to hunt the stronger, wilier wolf by guiding a strong horse over fresh wolf tracks and pursuing the animals until he overtook them and could shoot them down with a small rifle. If it took more than one day he slept at dark under a hastily-constructed bivouac, wrapped in a blanket which he carried behind his saddle. There was no place a wolf could go that he could not — and return from, even though blizzards raged or clouds sat down around the tree butts.

Squiness listened to Gurr.

"No," he said, quietly. "I won't show you. I haven't time. Besides, the ranchers around here don't want a road. Too many people will come."

Gurr took the Wolf Hunter figuratively by the throat.

278

"Thomas, a road is coming. If you show us the best way through that basin for a road, you get the best road, and if you don't show us the way, it will be a poorer road." He looked him right in the eye, clamped a hand on his shoulder. "You can make it easier for us all." Squiness finally agreed.

At a brisk gallop, heels tucked up behind the saddle and head down on the horse's mane, Squiness led Gurr through the jack-pines, up and down ridges, through black spruce copses, across swampy meadows and then, at a more leisurely pace, skirting the swamps, angling up and down ridges so that wheels eventually would have a minimum of difficulty, Gurr blazed the trees at strategic points.

"I never saw such a man," Gurr said of Squiness. "I swear he can see through solid rock. He's Radar Joe if there ever was one."

Next, Gurr contacted Bill Graham of Tatla Lake, fifty miles away. The Graham Ranch, established by Bob Graham and his wife sixty years before, stretched from horizon to horizon, and their ranch house was the centre for community activity. Bill and Alec Graham and Betty Linder were the sons and daughter of the "old folks" and were now running the "spread."

They had a bulldozer, a new D6 Caterpillar tractor with an angle blade. Yes, they thought the road building idea a good one. Their father used to pack supplies for the ranch from Bella Coola, and there should be a road through. Yes, they would put their "Cat" on the job. "Even if we haven't the money to pay you right away?" Gurr asked. They agreed to wait.

In the sharp morning sunlight of September 14, 1952, the Graham "Cat" bit into the eastern edge of the wilderness, its destination the Pacific Ocean, its route not yet completely explored. The man at the controls, a tall, soft-spoken rancher who wore a mechanic's cap and a pair of Indian made buckskin moccasins, was Alf Bracewell and his directions were to follow the blazes on the trees and keep going.

"I'm told to go to blazes," Alf grinned.

More specifically, he was to build a road through thirty miles of jack-pine jungle, find his footing along the lip of canyons, some of them three thousand feet deep, then bring his machine from the top of a mile-high mountain to the floor of the Bella Coola valley, thereby piercing the Canadian Coast Range, and giving North America another outlet to the sea.

For this his employers were renting their machine for 100 dollars a day.

Renting the services of the machine, "man and all expenses found", were the Council of the Bella Coola District Board of Trade. They had determination, hope and two hundred and fifty dollars in the bank — enough for two and a half days of operation.

Ahead of the machine went Gurr, blazing the trail, working from daylight to dark to prepare the way for the rampaging bulldozer.

Forty-two days later bulldozer and crew were 32 miles out into the wilderness, with a road behind them. For 42 days the machine had worked 10 hours a day, unceasingly. Now, poised at the rim of a high valley only ten miles from the Bella Coola valley, it lifted its blade and started trundling homeward. It was quitting for the winter, as a heavy snowfall and breakdown would have spelt disaster; trucks would not have been able to reach or to rescue it.

Now that the die was cast, exploration to find the best way down the six thousand foot mountainside was pursued with a vigor comparable only to that of searchers for a gold mine or for a beautiful, lost young heiress. Holidays and weekends were spent on the mountainside from valley floor to high horizon.

And disappointment grew; the mountainside, steep and craggy, offered little hope of an easy road route.

Said Jack Allison, partner in the generations-old Allison Logging Company — after a twelve-hour day with compass and level on the mountainside during which it was discovered that 38 switch-backs would be required to attain 3000 feet of altitude and maintain an eight percent grade — "If you yahoos think you can build a road up there, you're crazier than I think you are."

"Why not come straight down Young Creek? It looks pretty good to me," said Elijah Gurr.

Young Creek, starting in the Rainbow Mountains to the north, cuts down a precipitous narrow valley about a mile east of the Bunch Grass Hill trail.

While the "Cat" up on the plateau was pushing steadily toward the rim of the valley, search for a route down from the height was intensified. Blondie Swanson, Superintendent for Northern Pulpwoods Ltd., moved around the Young Creek sector with the assurance and speed of a mountain goat. One man, trying to follow him, wore out a pair of boots and came out in his socks. Board of Trade Council meetings consisted of studies of maps and aerial photographs. "Here's a control point, and here is another one. We have to climb high to get above that big canyon slicing into the mountain there, but we can do it."

Blondie, the goat-footed logging superintendent, took a government engineer part way up the Young Creek cut.

"Elevation at Red Hill Crossing is 3400 feet, and where Young Creek joins the Bella Coola the elevation is 1000 feet. The distance between the two points is six miles, and if you drop 2400 feet in six miles it's roughly an eight percent grade."

He convinced the government engineer and the Bella Coola District Board of Trade that the road could be brought down Young Creek from "the top" for ten thousand dollars. When the possibility of snow stopped road building "on top", plans were promoted to start from the bottom of the mountain. The first step was to apply to the government for a grant. "We have built 32 miles of road and have ten miles left. Could we please have ten thousand dollars to finish the job?"

Within three days came the answering telegram: "Ten thousand dollars has been deposited to your account for the use for future bills in your road building."

The Board of Trade knew they could use no portion of this money for the payment of a forty-two hundred dollar bulldozing account with the Grahams. They realized that the government was at last giving help even if not actively participating.

What they did not know was that in the office of the Minister of Public Works the new Minister, P. A. Gaglardi, listened to his Deputy Minister, Evan S. Jones. In the interim between the beginning of the Board of Trade road effort and its actual attack on the wilderness barrier, a provincial election had taken place, ousting a coalition government and placing in power the Social Credit government under the leadership of W. A. C. Bennett. P. A. Gaglardi was made minister in charge of roads, and it was he who would make decisions about the Bella Coola road. Deputy Minister Evan Jones, who had been chief civil servant in this department for a considerable number of years, had read the correspondence of the Bella Coola District Board of Trade.

"They say they have found a new, easy route from the plateau to the valley floor and can build a road ten miles for ten thousand dollars."

"And they have already built a road for 32 miles at their own expense? Make arrangements for them to get the ten thousand dollars."

"May I suggest that you reserve fifty thousand dollars for this project? They just can't build a road through a mountain range for ten thousand dollars."

"Make it fifty thousand then," the minister said to his deputy. "If those people are ready to help themselves, we are ready to help them!"

With money to spend, the Board of Trade rapidly bought what it had to, borrowed what it could and established a camp amidst the swaying fir trees at the foot of the mountain close to Young Creek. High above the camp the mountain soared to the heavens, and visitors could see no possible route for any road up its almost perpendicular sides.

This time the attack was made with an ancient bulldozer, an International TD18 that had seen better days. Its operator, George Dalshaug, was as lean as Bracewell and, if anything, quieter. His job was to get his iron steed as far up the mountain as possible and this he did, spending evenings – sometimes long into the nights welding and monkey-wrenching on his machine to ready it for the next day's push of a few hundred feet, or maybe a few hundred yards. And in the many months on the job not one day was lost through non-operation of the bulldozer.

An hour, perhaps, but not a day.

Winter closed in, but fortunately, very little snow fell on the mountainside. In the Bella Coola valley the snowfalls were repeatedly sufficiently heavy to block normal traffic. When this threatened to jeopardize the road building effort Curtiss Urseth, of the Board of Trade Council, bought a truck with four-wheel drive and spent many a midnight plunging into drifts so that supplies might be on hand. Porridge or powder, or whatever was needed, was always there on time.

This time the road builders found that bulldozing a road along a steep mountainside was not the same as a dash through the forest. Now, with control points that had to be arrived at and grades that had to be recognised, obstacles could not be bypassed; they had to be met and cut through. Rock slides, considered hazardous because they might become active if touched by a heavy machine, lay across the proposed road route.

"Do you think the slides are dangerous?" Dalshaug was asked.

"They are in the way; we can either cut through them or quit," he said quietly.

The next day he dug into the edge of a five-hundred-yard slide, worked uphill at a 15-degree slope, cut a narrow track across, repeated it without comment the next day and, still without comment, got above the slide and started back down again, bulldozing a road wide enough for cars or trucks. The slide had not moved.

A powder crew with an air compressor to power the jack-hammers softened the way ahead of the bulldozer but, since the air compressor travelled on wheels, it could reach only as far as the air hoses and the bulldozer had to keep the air compressor constantly near the front of operations. Races between the powder crew and the bulldozer operator occurred "just to push things a bit."

At one point in this great out-of-door play it became necessary for the bulldozer to cross a rib of rock, nearly vertical, that lay in the way. The powder crew was down-mountain and could not be brought up to cut a way through the rock-rib. A sturdy fir drew Dalshaug's attention and solved his problem. Taking the cable from the drum on the rear of his "Cat" he climbed to the tree with it, passed the line above it and thence back to fasten it to the front of the bulldozer. When the line, looped around the fir, was made fast and taut Dalshaug inched his machine across the rock-rib, a sheer drop of almost three thousand feet below and, gaining the slightly less steep terrain on the other side, took off the cable and again started bulldozing the road.

"That dam Dalshaug," one of the powder crew complained, "works with so much of his machine out in space it makes us jittery watching him. We can't look at him when he's working on a new spot."

Once Dalshaug did go too far, and his machine started slithering down the steep incline that ended thousands of feet below. About fifty feet down, a previously unnoticed solid outcrop of rock stopped the bulldozer's slide to destruction. Dalshaug, who had leaped to safety just seconds before, found an anchorage for his cable ("a tail-bolt for his line"), and climbing onto his machine winched the line in and drew the bulldozer back up to the cliff-hanging road and resumed work.

Eventually the powder crew did have the last word with Dalshaug. When the machine was working on the edge of the road, which was also the edge of space, a flat slab struck under the bulldozer in such a manner that when Dalshaug tried to reverse, the rock levered the machine into the air. Attempts to turn proved futile, and there was no alternative; to go ahead would be to drop many thousands of feet.

"There he sat, jill-poked and as helpless as a hog across a log," one of the powder crew related. "There wasn't anything close by to offer a tail-bolt for his line, and with a hundred feet below his blade he didn't have a snowball's chance in a furnace to get himself out."

Dalshaug appealed to the powder crew for help.

Mike Stolar, "Big Mike", was the powder man. He had taken this job because he wanted to get as far as possible from civilization. His doctors had told him to report to hospital but this was "healthier than hospitals." "Hell," he expostulated, "I met a grizzly bear the other day and ran for camp so fast my elbows dragged on the turns. You couldn't do that in a hospital."

Now, studying Dalshaug's problem, he grinned. "We've got to blow the rock," he said. "No other way out of it."

He crawled under the bulldozer with a heavy jack-hammer and carefully drilled a hole in the offending rockslab. Crawling back out, he rolled up his pant leg and cut four or five inches off the bottom of his heavy woollen Stanfield underwear. "What are you doing that for?" Dalshaug asked. "I've got to give it a soft shot or a soft blow," Big Mike replied. "I don't want to hurt your machine."

Carefully pouring about three ounces of powder into the thick segment of underwear he went under the bulldozer and set his shot.

After the muffled explosion Cat man, powder man and powder crew returned from their shelter and looked at the few wisps of smoke rising around the bulldozer. The starting motor barked for a moment, then the throaty roar of the diesel motor drummed the air. Dalshaug stepped aboard and when his machine, unharmed, moved off the now pulverized rocks he smiled back at the grinning powder crew and returned to his work of pushing rock.

Carving a ledge into the side of a rock mountain, the Board of Trade found, was more demanding and expensive than pushing through a jack-pine forest. At the end of forty days of work the road had been cut only about a mile and a half up the steep wall, and the ten thousand dollars that was to connect the road ends was almost gone. An appeal to the government for more financial help was answered, almost without comment, with another grant of ten thousand dollars.

Winter gave way to spring, and still the mountainside fought the men for every foot of territory gained. What looked like easy sections of earth or rubble were found to be solid rock with an overburden of gravel, sand and moss. Progress was measured in feet per day, and the struggle became one of ants moving boulders or of pygmies challenging giants. Men shrank in size and the mountain grew.

Spring was marked by endeavors to collect enough money to pay past bills, and by strenuous efforts to finalize the exact location of the road on the mountainside. The first was accomplished by a loan from council members, and the second by intensive search. A deep lateral canyon necessitated a decision – whether to lift above it with very heavy grade or to make a switchback and lengthen the road. The switchback was decided upon, and on the broad shoulders of Elijah Gurr fell the task of blazing out the exact route – a job that took him many months with the bulldozers growling at his heels. Once he was carried off the mountain by rescuers who supposed he had had a heart attack. "No heart attack, just extreme fatigue," said the doctor at the hospital at Bella Coola. "He will have to take it easy for a week or two."

When spring moved into summer it was decided to ask the Grahams to put their bulldozer on the job again. As soon as the Anahim Lake Stampede was over, Alf Bracewell took the machine out to where he had left off the previous fall and started road building. When ribs of rock appeared across his path, a powder crew and an air compressor were supplied to him. The powder man in charge was Melvin Gurr, Elijah's son and Big Mike's pupil. Henceforth pupil and teacher were to compete to see who could cut the most rock. The air compressor was moved into the wilderness by truck from Williams Lake to Anahim Lake, thence out to the Graham camp by the largest farm tractor in the district. Heavy rains had turned the bulldozed road into a series of mud holes so deep that no loaded truck could get through.

Now, however, progress accelerated. The Graham machine, on a downhill push and with only occasional rock to deal with, chalked up miles per week, while the other machine sometimes counted gain in only hundreds of feet in like time.

Money ran out and another request to the government, this time for a realistic twenty thousand dollars, was granted.

But the supplies brought out with the Graham machinery also ran out and, with a road almost as impassable as the jungle through which it wound from Anahim Lake, a new way of supplying the camp had to be found. Pack horses were called into use, and a train of horses under the care of an Algatcho Indian, Jamiss Jack, wound up over Bunch Grass Hill trail and dropped to Red Hill Crossing to supply the mechanized road builders with the sinews of construction - dynamite, diesel fuel and food.

The exact road route had not yet been marked out and, with a pincer action taking place, the wilderness area on the side of the mountain was searched and re-searched for the best route. Blind alleys had to be blocked off and every foot of advancement had to be in the right direction. The mountain, six thousand feet in altitude, had a slope nine miles from crest to foot and six miles from road-end to road-end, so that over fifty square miles of crag and canyon had to be investigated. Gurr wore out ninety dollars' worth of boots in his search and once, when long overdue at the lower camp, he was found ill and preparing to bivouac for the night under the partial shelter of an overhanging rock.

Eventually, when the two bulldozers were within several miles of each other, a trail for the pack horses was cut between the two roads, and although the trail was steep and narrow, packing time was cut by it to a sixth. And then, when the distance between the two machines had been cut to less than a mile, another innovation was installed.

Ole Nicoli, a bronzed giant with an Indian mother and white father, worked with the road crews, a Goliath of all jobs. He said to Gurr, "I think I can pack stuff across to the other camp cheaper than you do it with horses." Gurr looked at the man; the speech he'd made was the longest heard from him since starting with the road crew last September. "You mean, if we send the horses home, you can carry powder, oil, beans over there?" Ole nodded. Said Gurr, "We'll give it a try."

So next morning, a five-gallon can of oil in each hand and a pack on his back, Ole Nicoli, who sometimes went by his father's name of Robinson, clambered up over the horse trail and took his load to the Graham camp in the time it took merely to put the pack on three horses. The horses and their owner were paid off and Ole Nicoli became the first man in the history of North American road building to keep a construction crew – with a bulldozer, air compressor and jack-hammers – supplied with all the necessities of building a road.

Again money problems arose and were solved with another grant of ten thousand dollars from the provincial government coffers. The amount advanced had now reached fifty thousand dollars, and since the budget for road building had suffered a province wide cut the Bella Coola District Board of Trade considered they were very fortunate.

The ten thousand dollars was spent. And there still remained a barrier of almost three thousand feet between the two machines. Another telephone call to the Department of Public Works was taken by Evan Jones, the Deputy Minister. "Could we please have some more money? This time we would settle for five thousand dollars."

"You have only twenty-eight hundred feet to go? Are you sure you can get through for five thousand dollars?"

"Today," said the Board of Trade spokesman, "we are sure of nothing. Every bank of gravel we attack turns out to be solid rock."

Two days later the reply came. "Sorry. No more money until next fiscal year. Have positively scraped the bottom of the barrel."

It was a difficult position. The next fiscal year was nearly seven months and a whole winter away. The two road ends, a measured 2800 feet apart, for practical purposes might as well have been the original many miles apart. To stop now would mean loss of impetus, and the merciless tongues of opponents of the project would make another start a matter of doubt.

On the mountainside the crew with Dalshaug had shut their machinery down for the night. In the sudden quiet you could hear across the wilderness gap the Graham "Cat" ambling the few hundred yards back to camp. A man laughed, then swore, then laughed again, and the sounds were as plain as the scars and wrinkles illuminated by the setting sun on the mountainside across the narrow valley.

Elijah Gurr called Dalshaug and crew to him and told them of the financial situation.

"Now, that's the story, fellows. If you stay working, we will promise to try to get your wages. But that is only a promise. We haven't got the money."

"Another hundred cases of powder will put this road through," Mike Stolar said. "You get us the powder and we'll get you your road."

Machine owners, operators, cook, laborers all stayed with the job. Groceries were delivered, as was fuel oil and a thousand dollars worth of powder, all bought on credit and faith.

Now the contest against the mountain became a personal one, Wages or hours were of no concern. If clouds shrouded the mountainside, the enveloping blanket completely muffled lesser sounds from the other crew except for the reports of exploding powder. From early morning to late evening the mountain shook under the charges laid by the powder men as Stolar and his pupil raced against each other and time.

"Give each shot a little more powder. Rip the hide off this dam mountain so those Cat men can sleep their machines closer together."

Fifty miles to the westward, in the tiny village of Bella Coola, two blackboards appeared. The first day they bore the date and the legend "930 feet apart." A day later the distance had been changed to 790 feet, showing an advance of 140 feet. Each morning Board of Trade Councillor Mike Christensen, son of the pioneer merchant Adolph Christensen, posted the messages he received from the road camp. Each day, regardless of sun, cloud or slashing rain, the signs showed progress. Then the message: "Tomorrow the Cats meet."

The next day a hundred people met at the road camp at the foot of the mountain. Above them the high rock towered more than a mile, with the road good enough only for trucks or jeeps; those who came in passenger cars were transferred to suitable vehicles and carried up the mountain.

A quarter of a mile from the bulldozers the vehicles were stopped.

"They have to put off one more shot," the visitors were told. "They're loading it now."

In a few minutes the visitors saw the powder men take shelter behind a big rock. Then a cloud of dust and smoke spurted from the mountainside, the terrain shook and mighty thunder roared from crag to crag. In a few minutes the visitors were called up.

The two bulldozers were some fifty yards from one another, their motors gently purring as they waited for the spectators to get into position to watch the wedding of the two roads, the uniting of East and West. The operators at the controls, Gurr threw his hat in the air and shouted, "Finish it!"

The bulldozers moved toward each other thrusting rubble over the edge, backed away, got another load, advanced, backed up. A huge tree complete with roots and limbs was caught between them, tossed back and forth like a giant's bouquet until finally it slipped over the edge and dropped out of sight.

Finally, jointly, the two blades pushed the last yard of rubble over the edge; then, backing up for a few yards, the machines advanced and touched their blades together. Dalshaug and Bracewell stepped out onto the blades, reached across and shook hands.

A mighty shout arose. The road had been completed!

Everyone there knew that now Bella Coola had road connection with the rest of the world.

Only the planners knew that the road they had just seen joined rose to an altitude of 5200 feet, dropped to 3400 feet to cross Young Creek, then rose to 4200 feet to drop again to 1000 feet at the road camp.

Nor did many know that the only survey instruments Gurr had used to mark out this mountain-conquering road were an old Aneroid barometer, borrowed; and an Abnee Level, about as big as a cigar, worth seventeen dollars, also borrowed.

When the dust had settled, with some of it washed down throats with liquor straight from the bottle, and the shouting and hand-shaking had waned, Stolar seized his hat and nailed it to a tree. Then he took off his boots and nailed them below his hat.

"Here's another road finished," he shouted as he turned to the crowd. "now you can drive to Chicago, San Francisco, New York, any place you like!"

Traffic was established that afternoon when a jeep station wagon driven by John Markham of Centralia, Washington asked for right-of-way through the crowd and wound carefully down the mountain, the first wheeled vehicle to enter the Bella Coola valley entirely under its own power. And that afternoon several truck loads of Bella Coola people drove out over the new road in a fiercely victorious mood and, horns blowing, arrived at Ike Sings store at Anahim Lake, the first motor cavalcade ever to emerge from the Bella Coola valley.

The celebration held for this motorcade was to grow into a legend. Stories and bottles flew about and, among other things that happened, a bottle of linseed oil passed from hand to hand and was almost half consumed before it was discovered that the contents were not the usual undiluted fire-water of the frontier country!

Others of the group who had watched the wedding of the roads returned to the farms and forests, and to the village of the Bella Coola valley and resumed their tasks.

In a few days the Vancouver daily papers announced in headlines an inch high: BELLA COOLA BUILDS ITS OWN ROAD INTO B.C., and telegrams of congratulation came from all over the province.

In a few weeks Board of Trade Secretary Wally Stiles told the council that the last 2800 feet of mountain road had cost $8,740.

"And worth, every dam cent of it," quipped one of the council members.

"We have about thirty-five dollars in the bank," Stiles informed them.

"No use starting to pay our bills with that. That's only about twelve feet of road."

"Yes. If we paid, the problem would be - which twelve feet of road would we pay for?"

"Worth every dam cent of it," again quipped the council member, "and every inch of it built on credit!"

"Just for a while, that is," a companion offered. "We started the road, and paid the bills. And we'll pay the bills for the finishing of it if we have to."

By this time it was estimated that twenty thousand dollars worth of planning, management and supervision had been done free of charge by the Board of Trade, augmenting the sum of $4,000 collected from the public. Yes, if necessary, they would pay the final $8,700.

The snows collected on the peaks, crept down to cover the mile-high scar left by the road-makers, then swept down and mantled everything with white, even the tide-flats, when a letter came from the Deputy Minister of Highways. "Would you be so kind as to send us detailed bills re the last 2800 feet of your road."

The bills were duly submitted, and in the last mail before Christmas – the Christmas mail – came the information that the money had been deposited in the bank and they could proceed to pay the bills.

The road, cutting through the Coast Range, that had been built with $4000 of citizens' money and $58,000 of government money was forty-eight miles in length, and cost less than $1,300 a mile. The Minister of Highways, the Honorable P. A. Gaglardi, was to call the project "magnificent in its conception and astounding in its completion."

"By thunder, I'm sure glad we finished it," a Board of Trade member spoke for his companions. "Gaglardi stuck his neck out for us. It would have been political ammunition for his enemies' guns if we had left the two ends unconnected. And if Evan Jones hadn't been pitching for us, too, we would never have been able to build the road. Now we're part of the World!"

Canoe Crossing Bridge. This bridge was washed out in a flood in the late 1960s and replaced by a modern one further down river. Photo – Cliff Kopas.

Left: Bella Coola fishing fleet at a time when the boats still had wooden hulls.

Below: Lobelco Hall, Lower Bella Coola (which is higher than, upstream from, Bella Coola) was built in 1928 and remains the centre of community social life.

Right: Tweedsmuir
Park, Bella Coola.
Photo – Cliff
Kopas.

Below:
Tweedsmuir Lodge
in the 1930s, Bella
Coola. Photo –
Cliff Kopas.

Above: Bella Coola Hospital built in 1927. It was replaced by a modern one in 1980. Photo – Cliff Kopas.

Left: A "stink box" for curing the small fish in the preparation of eulachon grease, a dietary staple.

Eulachon Fishing.

One room schools in the Bella Coola Valley in the 1940s. Left, the Hagensborg School and below the Mackenzie School, in the Bella Coola townsite.

Above: The Cardena, one of the Union Steam Ship vessels docked at Bella Coola. Photo – Cliff Kopas.

Right: Pack train in Glacier valley, 1930s. Photo – Cliff Kopas.

Above: Bella Coola Fishing Fleet, 1935. Motorized company packers towed a fleet of small sailboats down North Bentinck Arm to the fishing grounds. Strong summer westerlies allowed the fishermen to sail home loaded with fish. Only a small canvas deck tent protected the men from wind, rain and flies.

Left: The Augsborg Lutheran Church, completed in 1904, is now used weekly by the United Church of Canada congregation.

These remarkable switchbacks were carved out of the mountainside by local residents in 1953, connecting the valley to the provincial highway system. Freed from reliance on intermittent water transport, the route has aptly been called the "Freedom Road".

Two views of the Bella Coola town in the early 20th century.
The lower photo shows the 1927 hospital on the site of the
19th century Hudson's Bay Company grounds.

Right: This photo shows the techniques and equipment that were used in logging in the 1950s.

Below: Single-log loads of this type were common in the 1950s.

Above: The original Kopas Store, 1938. The main business then was photography and photo supplies.

Below: Cliff and Mae Kopas present a copy of *Bella Coola* to His Excellency the Right Honourable Roland Michener, Governor General of Canada, and Her Excellency Norah Michener in 1972.

Mae and Cliff Kopas, 1972, with a copy of the first printing of *Bella Coola*.

Index

The Author

Cliff Kopas was born and raised in southern Alberta from where, as a teenager, he undertook packhorse trips into the nearby Rocky Mountains. Then, in 1933, he and his first wife, Ruth, travelled by horseback along Alexander Mackenzie's route to the Pacific Ocean at Bella Coola. There, Cliff worked as a writer and photographer while supplementing his income as a fish guardian and bookkeeper.

In 1937, together with his second wife, Mae, he opened a general store which continues in business to this day. Cliff and Mae were active in the community and prominent in the completion of the "Freedom Road" portion of the famous Chilcotin Highway. In addition to *Bella Coola* (originally published in 1970), he wrote *Packhorses to the Pacific* (1976) and *No Path But My Own* (completed by his son Leslie in 1996).

Photo – Mary Whitely